CW00926837

Author photo by Paul Neads

Gerry Potter is a poet, playwright, director, actor, and both creator and destroyer of the infamous gingham diva, Chloe Poems. A favourite son of Manchester and his home town Liverpool, he is an Everyman Youth Theatre alumnus and National Museums Liverpool lists him amongst the city's leading LGBTQ+ icons. His published works are included in both the poetry and philosophy collections at Harvard University and the portrait documentary *My Name is Gerry Potter* [Dir. Alejandro Negueruela/Prod. Mike Carney] premiered at Homotopia in 2015.

Gerry has a reputation for putting his Scouse voice on the line, and is strong on poetry and strong on the causes of poetryism.

By the author

Universal Rentboy +•
Adult Entertainment +■
I'm Kamp: Thoughts of Chairperson Poems +•
Chloe Poems's Li'l Book o' Manchester +◆
Planet Young
Planet Middle Age
The Men Pomes
Fifty
The Chronicles of Folly Butler
The Story Chair
Accidental Splendour of the Splash
Manchester Isn't the Greatest City in the World

+ As *Chloe Poems*

Published by •The Bad Press, ■Route
◆ First published by Mucusart, re-issued by Flapjack Press

GERRY POTTER

MANCHESTER ISN'T THE GREATEST CITY IN THE WORLD

The Rise and Rise of
The Bourgeois Zeitgeist

Flapjack Press
www.flapjackpress.co.uk

Exploring the synergy between performance and the page

Published in 2018 by Flapjack Press
Salford, Gtr Manchester
www.flapjackpress.co.uk

ISBN 978-1-9996707-4-0

Cover design by Paul Neads
www.paulneads.co.uk
Adapted from an idea by
Maria Barrett & Gerry Potter

Printed by Imprint Digital
Upton Pyne, Exeter, Devon
imprintdigital.com

Definitely no Inspirationalism and absolutely no Positivia!

Monday 8th September 2018, on the News...
The Bureau of Investigative Journalism has recorded 449
deaths due to homelessness in Britain – *in one year*.
How many mentally and physically ill, how many
right now facing homelessness, how many dead
before/since last recorded, how many more will die?
Reason, if reason was ever needed, why no place in
our greed 'n' perilous land can call itself
the greatest city in the world.

And also on the News... a clip of Theresa May at the
previous week's Tory Party Conference, standing in front
of a big blue backdrop, emboldened with white lettering
proclaiming OPPORTUNITY!

This book is dedicated to every one of the above
and all who continue suffer under Conservative Austerity.

Contents

Foreword

Manchester, Gerry and I

A pause – long enough for Gerry to polish off Liquid Gold in his
Rave New World – and across a cement void I am languidly
ushered into late 1980s Manchester; my birth providing Mum
with a distraction from mourning the well-groomed matinée
idol Cary Grant and thus halving the hefty Kleenex bills. Grant
having been dead for a few months, the melodramatic MGM
mourning was turning Mum into the commuter belt's very own
Queen Victoria in slingbacks.

The Manchester of my childhood wasn't Rodeo Drive of the
North. It was a malnourished place; a lattice of digestive biscuit
beiges, a ravishing Gothic cemetery frozen somewhere between
The Peterloo Massacre and that spinster hoax of fashion that
was the shell-suit. One of the poorest suburbs in Manchester,
flagrant violence was considered polite if kept to a non-carpeted
area, school was perpetually battling through the Lice Age,
scruples were as desired in a family unit as Type-2 Diabetes and
the word 'fucking' was advisory that a noun was on its way. An
M40 postcode provided one with little other than, what I feel, is
a great survival skill – namely the ability to pop the kettle on
and prepare toast mere seconds after receiving bad news. Still,
disarming altruism often blossoms in areas where denizens are
told to be little more than missed opportunities on the bingo
card of life and red-brick gossiping neighbours will ration out
the contents of their bread bin or throw a packet of duty-free
cigarettes to those in need. Some things are as constant as the
North Star and working-class suburbs remain the same; albeit
with more avocado hand cream.

Having the opposite of Seasonal Affective Disorder, the dour
shotgun grey of the city I knew suited my frosty countenance
and by the age of 11 [having renounced all sporting activity] I
retired to a maroon duvet, camply vowing to only flounce back

outside when I'd digested every celluloid moment of Irene Handl, Esma Cannon and Bette Davis. A friendship with Gerry really was inevitable.

After living in London for two years I returned to Manchester in 2010, fresh skyline as high as Pat Phoenix's beehive, not a pac-a-mac in sight and still under the impression Tesco shopping trollies were a type of working-class canal swan... which, of course, they are. Gerry and I met in the dressing room of a gig at an over-amplified pub near Piccadilly Station. The dressing room/green room/designated smoking area was a kitchen which had never seen a 5-star hygiene rating. We exchanged a mildly-friendly nod – which would be the butchest moment of our eventual friendship – and were introduced by a queen in a Play-Doh wig with a chin like a cheese grater; "This is Gerry – you'll like him. He also refuses to humanise The Royals. This is Caleb – you'll like him. He sounds like Edith Sitwell wandered onto *Coronation Street*."

You've got to love queens.

Gerry and I got on very well, but the Manchester bars would have to wait. During this time, outworn, he was suffering from sobriety [due to medication and detailed in his collection *Fifty*] and I'd discovered that dating was an adequate substitute for being lead drinker of a band, as it keeps one both extremely busy and tapeworm thin. It was to be two years before Aldi Tanner and Una Stubbles would become the class-a-ist ladies in town and paint the cobbles puce.

In Paddy's Goose pub, December 2012; a building held together entirely by cackles, mascara and tales of trade, Gerry and I were part of a gregarious gaggle of gays. Each purse-lipped queen clambered to topple the last on the conversational plinth. Fog horn voices, camp lisps, regal stances, impoverished charity shop drag, eyes exchanging hands under the table, hair lacquer that could bring down a Boeing 747 and enough vicious one-liners to end peace in Heaven. A boozy paradise of friends where occasionally Gerry and I weren't even the loudest. There was Pearl [eulogised later in this book] who possessed a Her-o-Shema boom of a voice, was obsessed with Diana Ross, ABBA, Eurovision and known for Golden-Era Hollywood impressions – more often than not set in Aldi and always covered with a Lancastrian accent thicker than week old gravy. His love of Manchester was such that his every utterance could have been scripted by Tony Warren, highlighted perfectly by the first thing he ever said to me, "Nice to meet you, luv. I've had a bastard weekend. I was concussed by a rebounding shed door when I was hoovering the gas meter." It was this December 2012 that Gerry and I power-minced out for an impossibly neon night which, no word of a lie, we fell in from six months later. We were out six out of seven nights every week, taking only one night off to negotiate a sandwich and some chips. A reputation was quickly stitched together about town – not all of it favourable and there is still a steady list of people prepared to blind us with cocktail sticks. To this day neither of us know how we afforded such a raucous lifestyle or how we have a septum between us, but we do know that we'd make the worst lab rats in the world. Our lives enbitchened, we were Slags Reunited and a hysterical friendship sturdier than The Berlin Wall had begun, with Pearl christening us the 'Harold and Maude of the disco floors'. I'd like to share a few stories from those months as it was [and I think Gerry would agree] the last days of a Manchester we'd known, a Manchester whose face wasn't yet entirely contorted with confusion, whose Embassy No. 1 laughter wasn't yet finger-hushed by debt and where the homeless sheltering under benches weren't yet being ushered on to make room for a statue of a worker bee, erected by those richer than Croesus. The following are a mere sprinkling – there is a certainly a book of half-rememberings to write about the intellectual, witty, off-its-heels hedonistic times my sister Gerry and I gloriously share.

January 2013

Gerry and I were in The Thompsons' Arms, packed on a weekday, hunched like camp vultures over a single bottle of poppers. Already half-cut on £6.95 bottles of white wine, we were howling uncontrollably when the bar staff greeted us with, "Oh Christ, *you* two again", which naturally leads to us to try reclaim the muddled memories already owned by last night.

I knew the day had started with me waking up next to a chap best described as mutton-dressed-as-dog. Quietly escaping the bed, I made my way to leave and was halfway down the stairs before realising it was my house. Studied layering of hangover-upon-hangover, Gerry and I met at Paddy's Goose for 3pm.

"My only memory prior to The Thompsons' Arms is us both being so tipsy we were genuinely convinced that Hep B and Hep C were members of The Spice Girls."

"Yes!" screeched Gerry as the universe hurled back a memory. "We were telling some queens that Fanny Craddock was the van Gogh of cookery and the Valkyrie of anarcho-socialism."

"Jessica H. Christ..."

"I remember being in some club where an unattractive twink you fancied was dancing at me and not you – then you called me a cow and stormed out."

"So," my curiosity stoked, "what did we do wrong at The Thompsons' then?"

"No idea. Some things are best left with the night. However, I do remember we nicknamed two vicious queens Jack 'n' Vera and a glass being hurled at us whilst shouting 'share the infamy'. Just another night causing murder on the dancefloors, babe."

March 2013

With poems under his garter-belt such as 'I, Slag' [in *Accidental Splendour of the Splash*] and 'Clap Magnet' [in this book] the following can act as a sort-of sister piece for some of Gerry's proud odes to slagdom – think of it as *Bar Wars:*

The Femme-Pire Strikes Back.

In a men-only bar which resembles a methadone drop-in centre for bears, a tall Irish chap starts chatting me up. Startled into silence by such a rare occurrence, Gerry takes it as an opportunity to go and cruise in the toilets. The Irish chap quickly looses interest and balance is restored, so I dance and await Madam's return from his toilet love. Ten minutes pass, then fifteen. At the twenty-minute mark, two men from the behind the bar rush into the loo with undisguised panic. Moments later they're carrying out an avalanche in Ralph Lauren of a man who looks rather unwell. Then Gerry appears, shaky legged and ashen faced:

"Are you okay, love?"

"No, gerrl."

"What's wrong?"

"Well... I was in the cubicle with some fella. He was having a go and he... well... he had a stroke."

[Holding in so much laughter I'm fearing a hernia] "My word! This just happened?"

"No, gerrl. It happened about fifteen minutes ago, but he was too fat to move from the door... I had to do an SOS with loo roll over the door."

"I've heard of a dick-of-death, but that's ridiculous."

April 2013

Gerry and I were going to give our anarchic, camp, jolly old nights out a rest for a couple o' weeks, to attempt green tea and trips to museums instead – then Thatcher died.

We were out on *Thatcher Death Day* expecting Manchester to be alive with the fervour of a city that had helped shape the notion of socialism. It wasn't. This was the first night we'd experienced where Manchester's Gay Village wasn't particularly busy and certainly not zhooshy. It may surprise, but we're not one for drama and hyperbole on a boozy night out, but it often found us.

We were The Militant Martinettes, in full socialist-socialite bloom, traversing bars and clubs partying for comrades lost. Not appreciated in many – usually because of private conversations to which people look great insult. Damn our arched velvet megaphone projection!

In faithful ol' Paddy's Goose we needed a break from the disturbing level of jingoism the media was flinging at us, all over a vicious tyrant in brogues. A fortnight in Pyongyang would have done it. All was fine until a staggering spluttering mess in his fifties approached, shouting:

"You can't say such vile things about Margaret Thatcher – she was somebody's mother!" [To children, we must note, who didn't bother to visit her and left the burden to June Whitfield.]

"Yes," I replied "– and the Argentinian boys aboard The Belgrano were somebody's sons, but she expected all of Blighty to celebrate their deaths… What's your point?"

Silence.

As the defeated made his way back to his John Smith's pint, Gerry, in that silvery way that he has, said, "It's happening. The Bourgeois Zeitgeist is strangling Manchester."

Over the course of the next four years Gerry continued to write, document and publicly denounce that which was dehumanising the working class – what he has termed 'The Bourgeois Zeitgeist'. The souls are falling out of the bars and clubs, replaced by cocktails in jam jars and cheap mince being passed off as a £12 burger. The poor becoming a living Lowry landscape, queuing at foodbanks stocking badger meat and cubes of lard. Fighting revolutionary spirits rejected from The Arts and anything deemed controversial [thus not deemed pant-splittingly drug-free happiness] is Kryptonite to those with the cheque books who talk in self-hate therapy tongues. Art with a budget is now designed to be accessible for everyone which, I think, is a dreadful idea. What could be duller than Art purposefully designed for everybody to enjoy? The greatest Art of any generation is supposed to make the generation previous relieved that death is closer for them.

The treatise in this book deconstructs the Machiavellian temper of The Bourgeois Zeitgeist and slaps onto the autopsy table its patron's smiler-with-knife approach. These zombies maim and destroy with tiny, supportive phrases like 'think positive', delivered like some rosy-cheeked 85 year old member of the WI – all the while demonising the working-class and the homeless. Muffling anger with quinoa and romancing nothing but personal finances and mortgages [see the play *The Manc Vampire* later herein]. So, it's not really Manchester, or indeed Mancunians, getting it in the neck in this totem because it isn't contained to one city. Manchester is where Gerry resides and if he lived in Preston you'd be holding a similar book, albeit with a title few would scowl at. I consider reams of the writing, certainly the prose, to be a lament for a city poisoned by the distraction tactics The Bourgeois Zeitgeist who can use sadness as a weapon to veil.

Pearl's death knocked sadness into those who knew him, but a veil of concentrated sadness fell entirely over the city he loved six months later when, in May 2017, twenty-two people were murdered at the Manchester Arena and twenty-two families plunged into grief. Sirens replaced birdsong, but the sun-bright beauty of the residents was just as loud; cab drivers instinctively offered free rides to the wide-eyed and panicked outside the arena and hundreds went to social media offering up their spare rooms and couches to those in need of somewhere to stay for the night. Though the sky was not entirely without vultures. the overwhelming solidarity of Manchester made me want to wrap my pasty arms around the place itself. Gerry writes eloquently about the aftermath of this horrific incident and how The Bourgeois Zeitgeist took its lack of social care even further and did so with the propaganda of the worker bee.

If there's any justice, this book will create such a storm that the implicated will drag Gerry into some darkened woods and take aim whilst he's proudly yelling in an octave-defying screech: "Bourgeois cupcake-munching bastards! Take me to *Planet Dead*!"

Laughingly,
Caleb Everett

Ms Punk Meets A Certain Arts Body
or
When Zeitgeists Collide!

Scene: *Hulme, Manchester. In the pre-Punk explosion of 1976, an incredibly excited Ms Punk decides she'll time travel to 2018 and ask A Certain Arts Body if it will fund a series of creatively wild parties; parties based on freeing art, on the instinctively primal understanding the party itself is a 'happening', even if the only thing happening is the party. In A Certain Arts Body's city centre office, a certain arts official is awaiting her decades-jumping arrival...*

Pascal: *[Via office intercom]* Mr Artsbody, there's a Ms Punk just arrived, appears to have stepped from what can only be described as a pulsing seventies BBC special effect, all very *Blake's 7*. Says she's an appointment to see you. I can't quite find her name anywhere, but Crispin Sharpe rang, profusely apologising – seriously, he couldn't stop – says he's running a bit late, so just wondering if you're willing to squeeze in a little one?

Mr Artsbody: Thank you, Pascal. I've a funny feeling this is one of those predestined writing moments favoured by Gerry Potter, you know how he loves to re-orchestrate time and event. Bloody writers ay, control freaky Time Lords the lot of them. If that is the case, then I've been expecting her, and even if hadn't, well quelle surprise, am now. So, of course I can squeeze in a little one.

Pascal: You can go in now, Ms Punk.

Ms Punk: Cheers luv! *[Enters]* Ah hello, hiya, erm, I'm Ms Punk and you are?

Mr Artsbody: I'm Mr Artsbody and it's a pleasure to meet you Ms Punk, please take a seat.

Ms Punk: Thanks very much, here? *[Sits]*

Mr Artsbody: Wonderful. Tea including green/herbal/fruit infusions, coffee with decaffeinated option of course, and/or water? We have Arvian.

Ms Punk: Could murder a can of cider.

Mr Artsbody: Just tea including green/herbal/fruit infusions, coffee with decaffeinated option of course, and/or water, which by the way is Arvian. We did have some organic gluten free apple drink, but I'm afraid I greedy-guzzled the last of that.

Ms Punk: Never mind cocker, I'm fine; I'll go down The Sally after this. Fancy a dab of whizz?

Mr Artsbody: No, thank you, just put one out, but lovely of you to ask.

Ms Punk: Y'know, just a little pick-me-up. Time travellin' can wear y'out. Knackers the crap outta me. *[Dabs whizz]*

Mr Artsbody: Quite, but I think I'm picked up enough as it is.

Ms Punk: All ace mate, each to their own.

Mr Artsbody: And just what is it you think we can do for you?

Ms Punk: Well, er, I've heard you dish free bread out for artists to make art happen?

Mr Artsbody: Free bread?

Ms Punk: Er, sorry mate, money.

Mr Artsbody: To a certain extent, yes, but as you've probably guessed it's a little more complicated than simply that. It's true to say though, we're certainly into the agency of practice.

Ms Punk: Agency of practice?

Mr Artsbody: Funding art and artists.

Ms Punk: Oh, for a moment there thought you said agency of practice.

Mr Artsbody: I did, that's what that means.

Ms Punk: Couldn't you just say funding art 'n' artists?

Mr Artsbody: Just did.

Ms Punk: Brilliant, so, er, you're really into fresh ideas 'n' all tha'?

Mr Artsbody: We must be completely set free to do whatever we will, Ms Punk. Ideas and the libertarian freedoms of said ideas are the seeds of all art, and I hope we here at A Certain Arts Body are the creative compost allowing germination, pollination and, of course, its blooming.

Ms Punk: Fuckin' great mate!

Mr Artsbody: *[Points to a sign]* Sorry to tell you Ms Punk, but this is actually a no swearing zone.

Ms Punk: What!

Mr Artsbody: Yes, just in case there are any youngsters bobbing about, we think it best people – if they can, of course Tourette's and accompanying ticks are tolerated – politely refrain from cussing. It's A Certain Arts Body rule; as a public arts body we don't want to offend anybody, now do we?

Ms Punk: But this is Manchester isn't it, surely kids swear all the time? They certainly do in 1976.

Mr Artsbody: Times change Ms Punk, and perhaps these times are slightly more accommodating of certain people's needs than say, other times. No offence.

Ms Punk: *[Obviously offended]* Er, none taken.

Mr Artsbody: Wonderful. So, you've, how we say in the business, an idea?

Ms Punk: Better than tha'!

Mr Artsbody: An idea better than an idea? How confidently colourful.

Ms Punk: More a visceral gut understandin' of a not-quite-formed idea.

Mr Artsbody: Ah, a piece of immersive theatre no doubt?

Ms Punk: Immersive theatre?

Mr Artsbody: Oh yes, we absolutely adore immersive theatre, can't get enough, fund it all the time. Now, don't tell me, let me half-haphazard a rather educated guess. You've found a site-specific place to conjure an urban dystopian stupor. Perhaps a car park, bus station, or even council estate, and using every theatrical trick in the book you'll find a way to eventually revolutionary reanimate the long-beleaguered socially-embittered battered and broken. Back-lit bullet-holed flags scrawl-daubed in blood-red Swastikas furiously billow as wailing choruses of discordant Asgardian trumpets herald the oncoming strobing apocalypse. Giant industrial bins are set wildly a-fire and then by metal, or indeed wood, violently hammered upon by masculine ragged dancers, posturing a ballsy challenging often sensually rip-denim'd end of days... a bit like STOMP meets Mad Max. Perhaps a doddering bloodied bewildered bespectacled bank manager flailing apologetically about this unimaginable carnage, four deliriously drunk beehived menstrual-leaking tatty ballerinas, even a local band and/or stand up comic, can tumble in and out of these seemingly unstoppable surreal as damn it nightmare-scapes. Oh, oh, oh, and in the explosively-crazed nowhere of this anarchic world-ending maelstrom, just when we think we can't take anymore, you then gently sit everybody down and give them their dinner. Perhaps soup, a local stew – always good for box office to reference the locale's cuisine – or those delightfully petit crustless triangular sandwiches... I love them, yum yum, haven't had those at a show for ages. Such wonderfully dynamic productions, such awe-inspiring spectacle and great theatre to attend if you're ever feeling a little peckish. On occasion, and if you're luck's really in, the odd but very welcome glass of wine, perhaps served in a ram's horn or whatever site-specific receptacle, what a super-treat. We at A Certain Arts Body are really into the anachronistic diverse energies made palpably inherent by the ultra-malleable dimensions caustically spitting/ splitting in the dangerous revolutionary uncertainties of immersive theatre. We love how it reaches non-specifically out and without plot or any linear lead whatsoever retells the audience's stories, whatever those stories may be, back to the audience themselves. Who needs narrative, eh! Personally, if I'm being terribly honest, I love the half-lit smoke, dry ice if you will, reminds me of Ultravox's wonderfully atmospheric 'Vienna' video, occasionally Toyah's 'Thunder in the Mountains'... love Toyah, just can't get enough of the eighties.

Ms Punk: Sounds wild.

Mr Artsbody: Oh, yes, 'Wild Boys', Duran Duran.

Ms Punk: What, Ultra-Toyah Duran who?

Mr Artsbody: Oh of course, 1976. What I mean is, they always are. Wild, that is.

Ms Punk: Always?

Mr Artsbody: Yes, we've just allocated funding for our fifteenth one this year and it's sure to be yet another all-out smash. In fact, a little dickie-bird tells me they're going to feed Cadbury's Smash, you know, that dried potato stuff, to the audience.

Ms Punk: The one with the tacky laughing aliens?

Mr Artsbody: On the nose Ms Punk, on the nose. You'd feel very at home with it actually. It's called *The Bleak Mid-Winter of Our Malcontents*, obviously Shakespeare-inspired, what isn't these days, all set in the crumbling dystopian seventies. The really exciting thing is I think everybody's going to be given NHS crutches, so we all become our own versions of Richard the Third, oh I do hope so, such a vividly thrilling, teetering on the almost barbaric idea, don't you think? Two hundred decadently insane Richard the Thirds right royally tucking into Cadbury's Smash whilst the whole world crumbles/tumbles about them, imagine that, *[sings]* "for mash get Smash"… genius! Then, after the now ubiquitous back-projected flaming apocalypse accompanying your plate of Smash, you get a pint of Pale Ale or Double Diamond, non-alcoholic option if preferred, and matching ashtray, no smoking allowed, of course. It'll be an all-out sensation, people really do go bat-poo crazy for this kind of socio-anarchic super-relevant nostalgia shtick.

Ms Punk: But y'fifteenth one – a bit repetitive, don't y'think that's a bit much?

Mr Artsbody: Absolutely not Ms Punk, repetition sells; they rake it in, real money-spinners.

Ms Punk: They certainly sound pretty similar to me.

Mr Artsbody: Oh, they are. To be honest, I can't tell one from the other, but the audience loves them, particularly popular with festivals, they're absolutely huge at Latitude. It really is avante garde dramatic spectacle gone accessibly mad, blam splat POW! Indecipherable-flashy apocalyptically connects. That really is the great thing with immersive theatre. On its many distorting surfaces I suppose there may be scratches of truth, but you don't have to be bothered uncovering them if you don't want to. That's very probably why they so often do food and drink, even if you've just eaten, as intervals are seldom provided, helps break up the anarcho-dystopian monotony of it all. So, what's your idea Ms Punk? If you don't mind me saying, you look a little theatrical, so is it theatre, perhaps a one person show?

Ms Punk: Well, it's more—

Mr Artsbody: Oh, we go crazy for one person shows, identity politics all the way, more individual the story the better. Can be about anything you want, addiction, prostitution, perhaps being Queer-bashed, disability, PTSD, abuse ritual or otherwise, but the big rule – and there's only one – is it has to be family friendly for rural touring purposes.

Ms Punk: But what if you don't want to do a family friendly show about abuse, particularly if the abuse is within the family?

Mr Artsbody: Very difficult to fund non-family friendly these days Ms Punk, particularly for rural touring, got to be very careful. It is, after all, 'the sticks', isn't it? What we really look for are individual stories of tremendous hardship, particularly in your youth. We want grit, turmoil, gutter understandings of isolation; addiction's fabulous for that, dyslexia's really hot right now, perhaps parentally abandoned, communally ostracised, pummelled, beaten to any number of metaphorical pulps by the ongoing hardships of just-unreachable survival. So unrelentingly brutal these experiences, suicide seems an almost definite option – again, no profanities, they don't swear in the countryside. Then, ending with a nice springy optimistic inspirational *whoosh*, sending the audience home happily smiling. Content after all your struggles, you've finally found personal fulfilment, empowerment and agency of place.

Ms Punk: But what if you haven't?

Mr Artsbody: Haven't what?

Ms Punk: Found what you just said, personal fulfilment, empowerment 'n' agency of place.

Mr Artsbody: Oh, you will, we've workshops for that.

Ms Punk: Workshops?

Mr Artsbody: Yes, oh we've workshops in absolutely everything, particularly in Positivia and Inspirationalism; they're really big right now, *really* big! It's all very simple: we send you away for six weekends, somewhere leafy, Victorian, perhaps by the sea. Before you know it, we're gently force-feeding you endless sessions of mindfulness and lightly balsamic drizzled quinoa… and lo and be bold, you're an inspirational workshop leader in no time, perhaps even becoming TED Talk material. All of these experiences coming in terribly handy for workshops after the shows.

Ms Punk: What if the piece is so traumatic for you, you don't feel like doing workshops in Positivia 'n' Inspirationalism, whatever they are, after the shows?

Mr Artsbody: Again, Ms Punk that would be very difficult to fund. We really do find you can take an audience emotionally anywhere, so long as there's a happy upbeat ending: an old fashioned big finish, drama equivalent of jazz hands. That way everybody's happy. Don't want the audiences sobbing into their Bratwursts or cheeky half-priced cocktails now do we – even half-price those things are bloody expensive. Oops, terribly sorry about that Ms Punk, I did a no-no and said 'bloody'. Best watch it or I'll have to give myself the chop for swearing. Certainly a little slap on the wrists for Mr Artsbody, smack smack, there there, all better now.

Ms Punk: Swear away mate, it's just language.

Mr Artsbody: No, no, no, must keep to the guidelines, lest we descend, tumble even, into pointless-directionless-uncontrollable anarchy… and we don't want that now do we?

Ms Punk: Well, yeah, actually.

Mr Artsbody: Sorry?

Ms Punk: The releasin' power of anarchy's at the very root of what I'm looking for fundin' for.

Mr Artsbody: An immersive theatre kind of anarchy?

Ms Punk: No, proper anarchy, pop cultural social upheaval anarchy. The real deal, mate.

Mr Artsbody: How potently quaint.

Ms Punk: Not at all, quaint's the last thing it'll be.

Mr Artsbody: Well, what is 'it' exactly?

Ms Punk: Y'see, that's it Mr Artsbody, it'll be any number of things to any number of peoples. Where I'm from there's an energy, a vibe buzzin' around the clubs, we feel something really big's about to happen.

Mr Artsbody: You sure that isn't the amphetamine talking?

Ms Punk: Absolutely not! In 1976 stuff's starting to get a bit difficult, unemployment's kickin' off again, that sorta thing. Thing is, there's a real vibrant counter-culture out there and I'm part of it, independent, bohemian, dark, light, that truly 'other' vibe. Bigger thing is, there's somethin' rumblin' on the horizon, can feel it shakin' me bones, boilin' me blood, we all can. We're gettin' bits of music coming to us from a couple of London bands we think's really gonna rip it up, they'll be playin' 'ere soon. I'm talkin' brutally honest zeitgeist stuff 'ere mate, the stuff shapin' 'n' informin' lives, times, creativity. That vibe where if you wanna do it, you just immediately go out 'n' do it, make it y'own 'n' special. I see it as genius-grubby, about where y'from, who you are, could be, 'n' what all that unapologetically actually means.

Mr Artsbody: Sorry… what does all that unapologetically actually mean?

Ms Punk: Well, for starters, it'll be of the streets, look like the streets, sound like the streets, be clever like the streets and fight like the streets. Sayin' tha' though, won't matter where you're from, wha' class 'n' tha', whoever y'are, y'can just be part of it. There's gonna be a lot of anger round it all too, a pure informed/uninformed kinda rage, proper oppositional, raw, partyin' 'n' out there, but it'll be that collective celebratory anger unifyin' 'n' bringin' peoples together. I think it's also gonna be profoundly iconoclastic, challengin' the rule makers, all in authority actually, certainly the monarchy and take great pleasure in debunkin' them. It's also, as a vibe, gonna be so generous, lettin' people be themselves, bringin' all those city centre tribes together with music, clothes 'n' dancin'. Oh man, it's definitely gonna be 'zine crazy 'n' brill for first-time writers, illustrators. For me though, I think it's gonna be viscerally/intellectually powerful for women, no longer on the sidelines, but right in the mucky scrum of it all. Not being pretty pretty for men, but real for ourselves, makin' our own clothes, formin' our own bands, bein' as vivid as the blokes, even more so. I truly believe there's gonna be some great bands created 'n' fronted by women, breakin' through, smashin' taboos, unafraid unapologetic warrior boards rippin' it up 'n' tearin' it down. There's a fearlessness in humanity seldom seein' the light of day. What's comin' mate is gonna shine a big bold spotlight on that fearlessness, settin' it free, givin' it absolute, what was it you said before... 'agency of place'.

Mr Artsbody: Oh, we love that word here, we can't stop saying it... agency, agency, agency, agency, agency, agency. *[Pause]*

Ms Punk: You OK?

Mr Artsbody: Yes, of course, I can sometimes get a little carried away. Well, that all sounds pretty wonderful Ms Punk, exciting, edgy, certainly energised... if a little unfocused.

Ms Punk: Unfocused?

Mr Artsbody: There's rather a lot going on isn't there?

Ms Punk: Yeah, that's the point. We think everything's gonna go on 'n' go off.

Mr Artsbody: Interesting. I'm wondering if I can politely offer you an 'A Certain Arts Body Opportunity Package' to help you perhaps, first of all define/dilute it a smidge, and second whittle it down a bit, shave of the edges, if you will. I'd suggest taking a little longer looking at the bullet points of the idea, go for the hits as it were, giving us some snappy upbeat snippets and who knows, in six months or so, get together for a communal sharing.

Ms Punk: Sharing?

Mr Artsbody: Yes, or as we sometimes piquantly call it, 'a scratch'. A small piece of it, about forty-five minutes, maybe less, and then open it up to a specially invited audience of industry experts for valuable developmental feedback. Take on board best bits of said feedback, polish it up a little and perhaps in a couple of years' time and after a few more essential material-building/editing and shares/scratches, tentatively go for a whole show.

Ms Punk: I'm talkin' about art 'ere, not scabies.

Mr Artsbody: So am I, Ms Punk.

Ms Punk: That's not what it's about. Can't be that deliberately cautious, it's not an already-thought-through idea then augmented 'n' reshaped by opinion, not about the compliance of committee, it's far more underground-visceral than that. I see it as red-hot molten lava roar-pourin' through a subterranean seam, furiously tryin' to find a crack to burst 'n' explode from. Whole thing about plannin' is the very opposite of what it is, any sense of controllin' will diminish it, it's gonna be like a bang, a splash.

Mr Artsbody: A splash?

Ms Punk: Yeah, like when you throw a rock into a lake, the most spectacular moment is the splash and all its anarchic accidental splendour, there for a second, all over the place, wild but undoubtedly gorgeous. It's why people throw rocks into water: they instinctively need to see that naturally unstructured beauty, cos like the best Jazz it's never the same splash twice. I seriously believe that's what it's gonna be, raucous empowerin' accident, openin' us up to the guttural intellectualism power, beauty, artistry 'n' tenderness of rage.

Mr Artsbody: What about the ripples?

Ms Punk: Ripples?

Mr Artsbody: You didn't socio-compassionately eulogise about the ripples.

Ms Punk: Surely ripples speak for themselves, Mr Artsbody.

Mr Artsbody: Well, Ms Punk, that all sounds very creatively volatile, but can't stress this enough, we really like sharings and mindfulness here.

Ms Punk: It's not a sharing or mindful thing, it's more a moment of monumental explosion and I think the fall-out of that moment will be impactfully sensational.

Mr Artsbody: Wonderful. So, tell me, where do you think you and this idea will be in five years' time?

Ms Punk: What?

Mr Artsbody: We've courses in business and accountancy, affording you, 'the artist', career-defining opportunities to build up a five year business plan, enabling – giving you 'agency' – to devise clear linear fiscal strategies. In many ways becoming your own manager, accountant and workshop leader.

Ms Punk: This agency gig, it's all on your terms isn't it?

Mr Artsbody: Of course not, it's all about the artist.

Ms Punk: Then what about the art?

Mr Artsbody: What do you mean?

Ms Punk: The art. Where's the art in all these plans, numbers and workshops?

Mr Artsbody: What I'm saying Ms Punk, is your idea's passionately lovely, I clearly see you're searingly into it and that's super-great, but if I may say, it's a bit foggy, can't quite visualise its legs. We believe to super-seriously follow your dream you need to think with a little more business acumen. Five year business plans are marvellously useful tools to map out both your artistic and, of course, fiscal journeys.

Ms Punk: Follow my dream?

Mr Artsbody: Yes, we passionately believe it incredibly important for every artist to set identifiable business goals, enabling them to map out and positively manifest their dream, whatever that dream may be. But I will say here Ms Punk, a little nod in your shell-like, if that dream happens to be immersive theatre you'll be quids in, we've bags of money for that. Bags!

Ms Punk: *[Pause]* Have you followed your dream?

Mr Artsbody: Sorry?

Ms Punk: What I just said.

Mr Artsbody: I'm afraid I don't know what you mean.

Ms Punk: A very simple question Mr Artsbody, have you followed your dream?

Mr Artsbody: Well, depends what we mean by dream.

Ms Punk: What I mean by dream is... what was your dream?

Mr Artsbody: I really don't think that applicable right now Ms Punk, do you?

Ms Punk: Actually, I do. I genuinely would love to know what your dream was.

Mr Artsbody: Would you really?

Ms Punk: Yes.

Mr Artsbody: Nobody's ever asked me that before.

Ms Punk: Well, I am now.

Mr Artsbody: Feel a bit silly actually, but, yes, seeing as you've asked, I'll say it. I did once more than toy with the absurd notion of becoming an actor.

Ms Punk: Why absurd?

Mr Artsbody: Because I just said so.

Ms Punk: So, being an actor was your dream?

Mr Artsbody: Oh, most definitely Ms Punk, I really wanted to tread those boards.

Ms Punk: So, you didn't follow your dream and you've a job advising following dreams? As qualifications go that's, well, interesting.

Mr Artsbody: By life's necessity dreams change! Surely by definition dreams or whatever you like to call them are the most malleable of intangible moments/thoughts; personally, I like to think of dreams as sleep's version of immersive theatre. I may not be the new Olivier or indeed Langford, Ms Punk, but I can get three holidays a year out of this job and a brand new kitchen every four. Let me tell you, me crossing an Indonesian rope-bridge earned twenty-two likes, three loves, a laugh emoji and not a single negative comment, *not one*, on Facebook. I'm not stupid, I soon made it my profile pic, which made me seriously think of opening an Instagram account, or how the young ones say, Insta, so don't talk to me of dreams.

Ms Punk: But the person who didn't follow their dream can talk to me of dreams? Bit of a dream job if you ask me.

Mr Artsbody: Yes, it is! *[Pause]*

Ms Punk: Right, so I'll get to the nitty-gritty, shall I?

Mr Artsbody: Please do.

Ms Punk: To help stoke up the fire of the oncomin' vibe, so to speak, I was wonderin' if I could get hold of a couple of grand to throw some parties, really mad off their nut creative do's. Nothing too artistically specific, keep it wide open, people can bring to it whatever they want. Just bonkers moments of crazy togetherness, bondin' unifyin' madness, fireworks, that sorta thing, gettin' us all organically involved 'n' ready to fly into whatever directions the 'moment' may take us.

Mr Artsbody: All sounds pretty 'immersive' to me.

Ms Punk: If y'like.

Mr Artsbody: And a health and safety nightmare.

Ms Punk: A wha'?

Mr Artsbody: Time really is pressing on and I've an up and coming young urban poet to see very shortly, so I'll just pass you these. *[Gives Ms Punk a huge pile of forms]*

Ms Punk: What's this?

Mr Artsbody: The relevant forms, Ms Punk.

Ms Punk: There's fuckin' loads!

Mr Artsbody: Now, now, Ms Punk, no swearing, there is a sign.

Ms Punk: Sorry Mr Artsbody, but my 'ead doesn't work this way, forms 'n' me just don't get on.

Mr Artsbody: I can't help that can I, Ms Punk, we need costings, we believe fiscal understandings of your project are paramount to the success of said project and your personal development.

Ms Punk: My agency.

Mr Artsbody: Exactly! We also need to know just who your target audience is/are, is there enough diversity and a few other very essential things… the forms will spell them out.

Ms Punk: I don't want anythin' spelt out, I just want some dosh.

Mr Artsbody: Now, I know all this may seem initially daunting, but we can offer you the essential opportunity of attending some of our 'A Certain Arts Body Form-Filling Workshops'. We've some super-thrilling networking opportunities coming up soon, too; you'd love them, wonderful environs in which to meet like-minded artists and makers.

Ms Punk: That'd take too much time, this shit's gonna blow soon, real soon, for art's sake we need the bread now!

Mr Artsbody: Bread simply can't happen, not even for the more important things like immersive theatre.

Ms Punk: Haven't you got something like an immediate slush fund so artists are just set improvisationally free to do things?

Mr Artsbody: Absolutely not! We have to keep tabs on all aspects of whatever the production, both artistically/financially. So, for example, we'll need receipts.

Ms Punk: Receipts?

Mr Artsbody: We absolutely insist on them! Receipts are the heartbeat of our – of any – acutely ordered organisation! Simple, Ms Punk, no receipts, no show!

Ms Punk: But what about the moment, the impact, the splash?

Mr Artsbody: Unless it's an immersive theatre spectacular, we don't really do moment, impact or splash.

Ms Punk: But that glitzy showbiz stuff takes fuckin' ages, I'm talking now, right now, the zeitgeist man!

Mr Artsbody: To be incredibly honest with you, we don't really do 'zeitgeists' either. It's all a bit old fashioned 'counter-culture' that malarkey, isn't it? We're very clear on what we do here and don't think we could be clearer if we tried... we like planning, sharing and receipts.

Ms Punk: Manners, finance 'n' control, more like.

Mr Artsbody: Thank you.

Ms Punk: But if everything's all too planned, where's the mystery, the energy, the power of not knowin'?

Mr Artsbody: Because of our, and may I stress here, extremely successful five year business opportunity packages, we've largely eradicated that; nobody really does 'not knowing' anymore. Times have changed Ms Punk, and I think for the better.

Ms Punk: I don't!

Mr Artsbody: Well, I can see that... you look like you're about to explode.

Ms Punk: Y'know what, Mr Arts-fuckin'-body – Stepford Arts-fuckin'-body, more like – I am! That's exactly what I'm gonna do. I'm gonna go back to 1976 and explode all over it, even if I have to do it on the dole.

Mr Artsbody: Dole?

Ms Punk: Yeah, the fuckin' dole, 'n' thank fuck for it! It's not a lotta money, but if y'clever with it y'can just about get by. The dole, Mr Artsbody, means y'don't have to work to do what you do, the dole means we don't have to be pointed politely to the direction of itchy scratchy sharings, it means we can just do what we want, why we want, when we want. It's why there's an 'old fashioned' counter-culture where I'm from. Loads of artists use it to chill out a bit and make art and for whatever's coming next punk – yeah, that's it, *Punk*, I'll name it after me, it's gonna be called Punk. The dole, Mr Artsbody, will be the seventh string of a guitar tearin' this country in two.

Mr Artsbody: You get more immersive sounding by the second, Ms Punk.

Ms Punk: This isn't gonna be just theatre Mr Artsbody, it's everything; music, art, poetry, clubbin', fashion, the whole fuckin' shebang 'n' anybody wanting to can jump on board. No cunt's gonna ask anyone for a five year business plan, we're just gonna be it, 'n' y'know what Mr Artsbody, I wholeheartedly believe it'll be remembered and constantly culturally referenced. I bet Punk did menstruatin' tatty ballerinas long before any other fucker; you probably wouldn't have apocalyptic Swastika-daubed immersive theatre if it wasn't for Punk, and wha' the flyin' fuck's Asgardian trumpeting? The music scenes 'ere in Manchester, my Manchester's, not that great right now, but Punk will shove a bomb so far up its arse it'll keep it incendiary for years. Yeah, I know that sounded a bit too scatological for the likes of you, but believe me, shit's really gonna hit the fans. We're gonna be a raggedy Molotov Avante Garde smashin' 'n' smearin' a liquid fire over the whole fuckin' country, over history! The thing is, it'll just happen, 'n' the sharin' of it will be done by cataclysmic osmosis, no polite sittin' down, no advice, no too guided pointin' to individualist landmine opportunity 'n' mind control—

Mr Artsbody: Surely you mean mindfulness?

Ms Punk: I know wha' I mean! It'll just be 'wha' it is' and in that 'wha' it is' it'll be whatever the fuck it wants to be! However long it lasts, and might not be tha' long. Anyway, who gives a tossin' fuck how long it fuckin' lasts! Since when have we needed to measure the time art takes to be art? I believe it's gonna shine forever. Actually, maybe y'right Mr Artsbody, perhaps you can't fund tha', just has to be what it is, because I can't fiscally break it down for ye, can't tell you just how many it may attract, although diverse as fuck, can't tell you how many of the supposed diverse it will have attracted. Anyway, just who's deciding who's diverse 'ere? Tellin' ye now, the gays are gonna love it, the lesbians, the bi's, it's gonna fuckin' rock androgyny! I believe it'll be of international proportions, peoples all over the world findin' 'n' bein' their own culturally mutated versions of it... how's that for fuckin' diversity! But the most important thing, Mr Artsbody, is I can't control it. More than tha' – I don't fuckin' wanna! I want it to be whatever it becomes and yeah, it might be shit sometimes, things are, fact of life, but let it be shit, let it make mistakes, let it get bold, boisterous, loud, out of control 'n' for fuck's sakes dick'ead, let it swear! *[Pause]* Warra y'thinkin', Mr Artsbody?

Mr Artsbody: I'm thinking it's a really good job we don't operate a swear box young lady, or you'd be quids down!

Ms Punk: Fuck this, Mr Artsbody. I'm back off to '76, goin' back to me flat in the Hulme Crescents. We can all feel it comin' there, we're fuckin' buzzin' mate!

Mr Artsbody: Did you say the Crescents?

Ms Punk: Yeah I did, you 'eard of them?

Mr Artsbody: Oh yes, very much, and all I can say it's a good job you can time travel.

Ms Punk: Why?

Mr Artsbody: Well, you wouldn't be getting home if you couldn't.

Ms Punk: Wha' d'ya mean?

Mr Artsbody: The Crescents are long gone.

Ms Punk: How d'you know?

Mr Artsbody: Ms Punk, I've recently bought a three storey town house where they once stood, believe me, they're finished. Little more than half-formed romanticisms murmured by ageing punks in broken pubs, halcyon-remembering the 'good old days'. Who knows, one of them could be you.

Ms Punk: I hope it is Mr Artsbody, because I'd much rather be that than you. I'm gonna go back to '76 'n' really bang it up, because even if I end up murmurin' pissed in pubs I'll be safe in the knowledge, even with all your money, you couldn't touch what we did. Fuck roarin' Mr Artsbody, next time y'in a pub in Hulme, keep y'ears peeled.

Mr Artsbody: Why?

Ms Punk: Because I am Punk, hear me murmur!

Mr Artsbody: Well, I think we're finished here aren't we.

Ms Punk: Definitely, yer up y'own arts mate.

Mr Artsbody: Quite. Super-lovely to meet you Ms Punk, and hope your project goes really really well.

Ms Punk: Thank you, Mr Artsbody. Oh, er, just one more thing.

Mr Artsbody: What's that, Ms Punk?

Ms Punk: Fuck off! *[Exits]*

Mr Artsbody: Well, my oh my, mouth like a sewer, if anybody needed our six week course in mindfulness, Positivia and Inspirationalism, it was certainly Ms Punk! What an angry young woman, all that rage and what for? What on Earth will it achieve? I mean, come on, is there really anything to be that angry about? Mind you, she's from the seventies, you couldn't even get a half-decent coffee in the seventies, never mind a Skinny Fiery Franciscan Frappuccino. Let's face it, in between power cuts and three day weeks, bread strikes, strikes, more strikes, candle-powered light, what could you get? Wasn't like now, a decade famed for well-honed fiscal/career-based opportunity. Opportunity, hmmm, what a wonderfully all-encompassing word, one of the best words ever worded, perhaps the very best. I'm really glad she's gone, put me a tad on edge, unnerved. I really must sit down and dribble a little Rescue Remedy onto the back of my tongue.

Pascal: *[Via office intercom]* Mr Artsbody, Crispin Sharpe's arrived… can't contain himself and I can see why, it's all very, very exciting.

Mr Artsbody: Why's that, Pascal?

Pascal: He's a brilliant idea of creating a one man show, a hip-hop inspired version of *Cathy Come Home*. He's saying he wants to make it all immersive, revolutionary and relevant, no swearing; so sounds perfect for rural touring, and get this...

Mr Artsbody: What?

Pascal: Set in a foodbank. Isn't that brilliant, a fucking foodbank!

Mr Artsbody: Pascal please, the sign!

Pascal: Oh, I'm awfully sorry Mr Artsbody, please forgive me, I'm just too excited, because it gets even better.

Mr Artsbody: How could it possibly?

Pascal: In the middle of the piece, he'll offer every one of the audience a glass of Smart Price cherryade, a tin of prunes with condensed milk and the pièce de résistance... there's only one tin opener!

Mr Artsbody: Wow, one tin opener, now that's super-amazing, at last an idea with good strong proper legs. I can almost feel the soft downy flesh of its dense muscular calves, can't wait for him to scratch it. Send him straight through. *[To himself]* Fuck you, Ms Punk! Fuck you and your fucking amazing fucking anarchic fucking moment. I've something far more fucking concrete, more fucking relevant, more fucking organised than you'll ever fucking have! A one fucking man show, a hip-hop *Cathy Come* fucking *Home*, set in a food-fucking-bank... re-fucking-sult! Oh, and my three storey fucking town-fucking-house has already turned over a very tidy fucking profit, thank you for not fucking asking! Fucking sweat on that, you fucked-up old fashioned fucking inglorious going nowhere fuck-up!

Crispin: *[Enters]* Mr Artsbody, cooee, it's me, Crispin, Crispin Sharpe.

Mr Artsbody: Crispin, how super-wonderful to see you, hope you're super-well, do take a seat. And how's good old Sussex this time of year?

Crispin: I'm and it's super-fine, Mr Artsbody.

Mr Artsbody: Tea including green/herbal/fruit infusions, coffee with decaffeinated option of course, and/or water?

Crispin: It's 'Say No to Caffeine Week for Cancer' Mr Artsbody, so water would be mega-ace. Is it Arvian?

Mr Artsbody: Of course it's Arvian; they are the official sponsors of 'Say No to Caffeine Week for Cancer' after all! I just love their campaign catchphrase, a brilliant piece of rebranding, "Free radicals drink more water!" – such wonderfully relevant stuff!

Crispin: Yeah, it's just so super-catchy isn't it?

Mr Artsbody: Yeah, super-so!

Crispin: Awesome!

Mr Artsbody: Seriously though, we can't tell you how genuinely mega-psyched we are about your proposal, an octopus of an idea, if anything ever had limbs. More than mere limbs, it's the trajectory and sheen of a shark fin slicing through water to devour its about-to-be flesh-torn bloodied prey. The melding of the best of sixties televisual kitchen sink into the never-ending theatrical possibilities of today's immersive experience, wow, mega-mega-wow, super-mega-wow! I simply adore the anarcho-communality of it all, our dispirit/desperate audience simply have to come together to use that one tin opener, otherwise they don't get the prunes... truly inspiring stuff! Can't wait to see what colour you'll do your flaming apocalypse in, and Crispin, got to say, foodbank, wow... fu—reaking genius! Oops, I nearly did a sweary then.

Crispin: Oh Mr Artsbody.

Mr Artsbody: I know, I'm literally sat here shaking with abject excitement about the workshop opportunities. There will be workshops, won't there?

Crispin: Oh yes Mr Artsbody, and they're going to be mindfully super-apocalyptic-expialidocious.

Mr Artsbody: Ooh, super-umdiddle-umdiddle-umdiddli!

The Bitter End

MANCHESTER ISN'T THE GREATEST CITY IN THE WORLD

The Rise and Rise of The Bourgeois Zeitgeist

I'm A Manchester Ache

My skin's developed brains and is hell-bound,
every inch blasted by dancing,
it's that Manchester ache announcing
Gerry, the party's over.
It's not without pleasure,
built from joy
and whirling around like a pre-teen dervish.
Ooh, it's an ache though,
that Manchester ache,
made from ancient and wow.

I'm a Manchester ache,
been built-in for years,
I'm its stone, red brick and rainwater,
it 'n' I, we're partnered.
It grooves liquid,
turns me, mercurial,
ankle-winged and soaring.
Thing is baby, when you fly too high
you just gotta come down.

Hard-skinned, erect,
without manners 'n' grace,
bangs your arse to untold oblivion.
It's that Manchester ache,
I'm that Manchester ache,
filled, flawed and hollowed,
sleepy.

Hello morning,
never again
until next time.

The Me Of Thomas Court

Musings on my tower block and flat, where I've lived for over twenty years. These poems are respectfully dedicated to my past/present neighbours in this so often high high-rise: Michelle Green, Louis Bee, Marie Luc and Claude Cunningham. The underground/overground Queer contingent of Thomas Court.

Very messy now, never used to be.
I loved it,
useful to crash when coming down.
Shag-pad, seen so much,
if these walls could talk they'd be
babbling bubble-butt mouthfuls of Porn Hub.

Seen me weep-sad,
very,
ceiling closing in, floor pushing up,
a sixties TV trapped,
spiked!
I am not a free prisoner,
I'm a me man!

The drugs, near misses,
trade not doing kisses.
I've seen this flat revolve,
face chipped 'n' spaced out.
Residing alien,
bent out, proportionless.
Every planet forgotten,
every star danced with,
long since supernova'd.

From curtainless windows,
worlds collide.

The Buddhist Of Thomas Court

For Olga.

Slow ache baby steps,
inch splinters of pain.
Maid of wood,
like you could hear her creaks.
Body-stop,
wrinkle-wince,
seconds time-out forever.

Your Recorder Group and Post-Its,
we knew you were there.
Eighth floor,
knocking-on,
Christmas cards.
Gifts in the lifts,
I took your Tupperware,
still have it,
no lid.

Hardly in winter, more summer,
I'd window-look and wonder.
How faith kept you keeping on,
believing.

Author,
poetry,
travelling an ever so slightly haughty.
A maybe bohemian in an Ealing Comedy.
Bastard sister of Charles Hawtrey.
If a novelist I'd write you,
just another poet, guessing.

Big flower dress,
childlike silhouette,
you are sticks.
Floppy yellow hat and crutch'd.

Every time at the crossing,
bang,
I recall your hit and run.

Olga,
I don't faith,
but part of me seriously hopes you're flying.

The Witches Of Thomas Court

For Tina 'n' Trish.

Cackling like staggering is glamorous,
so is buckling under,
handbag-splatter of all you are,
keys, fuckin' keys, ciggies,
loose change, thunder-thighed 'n' lighters.

Seventies rock bitchin',
two hot tomalleys sniffin' in the kitchen,
loose limbs eat chips
and in the howl of kin, wigs.
The trade's drunk;
trade's always rotten drunk 'n' waiting.
Witches' spread-eagled banter,
legs a-limbo,
dating.
Spring, summer, winter, fall
girls for all reasons.

Trish cawed me woman, transmutation awry,
she flies when telling, twinkle-crows.
Tina silents, a sixth-storey tall.
Pie-eyed tinkled-belle, looks after all.

They are rock-chick coven bonded,
bubbling hubbles of double-dating trouble.

Trish spirited away,
cat-walking sky's oblivion,
Heaven's crone.
She's missed,
Tina still broom brooms 'n' witches alone.

The Fox Of Thomas Court

Skinny teen,
dark robber,
taught 'n' loose.
Skin ochre,
tripping through mud and conkers.
There's not a flight of fantasy
she hasn't glided in on.

Story sliver,
hen-partier,
bird-roasted spit-lover.
Soft kisses of silent paw,
she's the hungry,
the hunter,
the red breath shiver;
shimmering around bins and bushes.

Head turn, bright-eyed,
danger round cornered.
She visits not preys,
skimming magic's better nature.

On really wild nights I am her,
she lets me be,
they're the best wild.
Slyboots and Hollyhock,
night city-centred,
calling.

The Gangs Of Thomas Court

These tower blocks
are dominoes on gambled horizons,
too many games played and lost.
Knock,
school of hard!
In the tiddlywink of eye
lives lived in their shadows,
gone.
Jenga-built,
toppling
under four decades of mass unemployment.

Is it any wonder these pieces riot,
drug-boozed and fighting.

A Foggy Day In Manchester Town

I'm in its darkness,
a half-nude romantic,
sepia-lit with exotic intention.
Red brick horizons really suit,
really work,
echoes a canal-sided erotica.
Bleaks cascading,
tumble-flesh,
silver-fish,
shadow industries of intimate fantasy.

Fog cinema stories,
mysterious, thrilling,
excites my inner vampire,
my simmering werewolf,
gives my drunk-stumbling Frankenstein guy
a lumber for its money.

Manchester's masculine, a handsome dude,
in chilling swirl, dangerous.
There's reasons legends creak here,
shriek here,
demons emerge,
people go missing,
cloaks swish operatically.
One push and a howl-hack cackle
from Jackie the Dipper.

Three death wishes,
candles blown out
and whispering around the wick,
billowed footsteps stutter.

M'Face

*For Peter Kelly, my boyfriend for eighteen months in the rare auld Mancunian
Rave times.*

Nose on nose,
one big eye,
no you,
no I,
M'Face,
heart-thumpin', speed bumpin',
keep on jumpin',
pulse race.
Shape grace,
in the red light,
deep night,
ass tight,
hold right,
place.
Nose on nose,
one big eye,
no you,
no I,
M'Face.

The share of it unique,
troughs, peaks,
laser light sleek.
From glow smoke,
tighty-whities clung to hung physique.
Statuesque,
Greek,
heart-breaking silhouette,
out my league.

Chase,
bit of a case,
bass.
Nose on nose,
one big eye,
no you,
no I,
M'Face.

That New Year's Eve when Canal Street went skyward.
On Flesh's trancefloor in amongst the fluid 'n' awkward.
The fractal piercing melodies of cave walls eroded.
Acid fucking bum-cumming of soul-bodies exploded.

The glare of it opaque,
the rare of it awake,
snare of it, break,
in step,
pecs, buns, biceps,
hot disco bunnies, drug schlepped.
Best things in life are free,
best thing we took was E,
flying inland,
sometimes out at sea.
Laced,
fast-paced,
disc-raced,
nose on nose,
one big eye,
no you,
no I,
M'Face.

Dike, Part Two...

For Dike Omeje, 1972-2007. To represent our poetry scene, I first wrote about Dike in Chloe Poems's Li'l Book of Manchester. *Thinking about poetic representation again and for this book, I could only really come up with Dike. If anybody deserved two poems...*

Often in song,
Princed,
touch silk,
purple,
audible soft 'n' love breath.

The stance,
secure, welcoming,
powered and guarding.
Something in the lifting of eyes,
wideness and wisdom, pierce.
Eyes have it,
mortal-mirror, shine,
words trickle-flow.
They're caressing.

Half-smile beams trust,
letting the audience in.
Half-smiles confidently whispering *listen*.

There's a space with your name on,
behind the mic,
invisible, tangible and flirting.

Gill

For one of my very favourite past Manchester and continual life memories.

So I plod to the hospital,
it's strange,
disinfected,
not Gill 'n' I at all,
like everything 'n' nothing's happened.
Eurovision Song Contest TVs.

Our amazing nights out,
Mancunian blurrings,
and once again ladies 'n' gentleman,
ends, beginnings.

Fab Café boogying,
disappearing lines,
that low-fi-sci-fi, too high bisexual vibe.
Sky-scrapin' sauce-pots,
we're clocking the same fellas,
throwin' shapes,
spinnin' plates electronica.
We secret twirl,
brassy bitches Tijuana,
sassy Bassey, Bacharach Burt 'n' Shirley.

Baccara exotica,
not sorry we're ladies,
doin' doin' again
what we've always done done again
with hysterical love.

Gill's got sixties cat,
pop duo,

high-jinxin' pussy-purr,
fingers maskin' sexy eyes,
mixin' it,
vixen it,
got her entice on,
she's gonna getcha getcha getcha!

There's nothing like it,
owning the fuckin' night,
gin genies out the bottle 'n' smokin'.
We've been weekending for centuries now,
time-flyin'
and thigh-highin'.
We know drunks matter,
have stories,
Oliver Reed.
They've always mattered
and it's because of them we're dancing.
Ask Treeza, she knew.

In the hospital,
room's all light angles and white sheen.
Something's happened.
Eurovision Song Contest TVs.
Gill thinks she's got the winner.

Freakin' Gorge Mornings With Gayna

For Gayna Williams, another of my favourite Manchester moments and dancers.

On the hip with heightened twirl,
smile wide in groovin' face,
we spin without the within,
bass,
right,
glidin' around an uplift flight.
Freakin'
new waves breakin',
dawn's promise just keeps on givin'.
We're not arsed,
breathe it in 'n' kill chillin',
there's a trippin' kinda jiggin' to be done.

Two bodies,
soul one and far too much goin' on.
We're working out eternities,
why they feel so good,
how they roll.

Lava-lamp'd in hot-pants,
hot-tramps hot-tranced,
we're every moment of seventies and day one.
Funk's knowin' when dancin' should be done,
where it's begun,
fusion.
True flow,
shebeen, shebang,
goin' on a-go-go,
no shade, roller-blades.
I'm bald,
but pretty damn sure she's psychicin' me up a 'fro.

Freakin' gorge mornings with Gayna,
flips lights fantastic,
memories bend prismatic,
movin', groovin' a never-static magic.
Gorge!

Tiger Tiger

Written for a good old Rave pal of mine for his fiftieth at the New York New York, without doubt the best gay club in town. Tiger initially asked me to get Chloe out of retirement for this gig. I ever so politely refused, but suggested I write him a special something. I came up with this and performed it for him at his party, one of my favourite Mancunian gigs ever. A real zhuzh to write and read this in front of one of my favourite Manchester legends, family and friends.

Manny years ago, in club full of strangers and strange gays,
Manchester night, burning bright,
I met Tiger
'n' thought to meself *phwoar, warra foxy l'il mister*
'n' after just two minutes chattin' I then thought *forget it Gerry,
this gorge zhuzhy queen's gonna be y'sister.*

With his ponytail whippin'
'n' everybody trippin',
music blarin' full-whack,
I instinctively knew this gorge zhuzhy queen
would always have my back.

Whatever the Rumba,
whatever the rub,
Strangeways, Flesh, Paradise, Cruise, Danceteria,
always felt safer with Tiger in the club.
Because he's seen what I've seen,
been where I've been,
safer because she was all man 'n' pure Manc warrior queen.

I got how he moves,
got how he bends,
the connection of his family 'n' friends.
Got the cracklin' joy of his dirty laugh,
got how he always cut through crap,

got he understood the profundity of night,
got he wasn't a scaredy-shite.
Got his vivacity, hail 'n' hearty,
got he was life 'n' soul of the party.
Some of those souls sadly gone,
but he still holds them there,
cathedrals of love sing inside her.
Get how he hears it,
get he sings along,
get he knows many of us share that same song.
He is Tiger, hear her roar.
I get the ferocity,
the supreme sisterhood of his rock 'n' roll generosity,
and Tiger I say this with thanks 'n' ease
cos I've had far more than my fair share of freebies.

It was in the magic of The Number One
where Tiger 'n' his gang so vividly shone,
verve 'n' colour of that Mancunian time
etched in my heart, a House Music shrine.
The energy, the character, lights 'n' dancin'
meant Manchester was the only city to prance in.
Like a museum needs someone to curate it,
gay scenes need fantastic queens to embrace it.
Fearless, feisty, carefree 'n' true,
queens who know the 'Right 'n' Exact' things to do,
queens who didn't forgo or forsake it,
queens with the balls to go out 'n' create it.
'Where Love Lives' queens who've never been so high,
queens bold enough to touch the sky.
Because cities aren't just roads 'n' steeples,
cities are the raw of its peoples,
people who rise above grit 'n' gloom,
from the Bowie 'n' Numan of their bedroom.

People who scratch 'n' sniff their patch,
people with cunning plans to hatch,
people who know they're on a mission,
people with the force of nuclear fission,
people knowing an underground sound,
people gettin' dancin's profound.
people with wild abandon in their hearts,
people in the gutter, starin' out the stars.
Wild like Tiger, no one could tame her,
and right now I just wanna say *Gaynor*.
People showin' me a better way
'n' how to be a much better gay,
people who knew the right 'n' exact thing to do,
cos let's face it, today's lot 'aven' gorra clue.

So at fifty,
Tiger Tiger's still burnin' bright
in my memories 'n' of course tonight.
Seriously luv, no one can best yer,
so Rave On Tigerchester!

The Morrissey Factor

Or 'Manchester Has Born'd A Martyr'.

Cobbles have turned upside down,
Elsie's a deeper shade of blouson rouge,
Rita's hushed, Youtha's gone,
around the fountain's really been ring-fenced.
Is it about keeping them out,
whatever/whoever them and out is?

English/Irish starts with immigration,
bleeding hearts starved on famine boats.
Is it the where we belong,
the who we are,
the why we've been and are going to?

Hatefuls hollow an un-bona drag,
an empty pill to swallow.
Dallesandro can only silent,
what's left to say when there's too much said?
Heaven knows what's difference,
what's miserable now.
So here's to you Tommy Robinson,
Jesus forgives more than you will know,
apparently.

Before Sheila took a final
she painted a back-street multicultural,
a Manchester of questionable sea,
of how now is soon faraway.
Charming that man,
then.

Will last of the gang shut that unstable door?
We're met in murder
when we choose to forget.

Chiselled From Loathing

Chip away
at all yourselves 'n' others,
splinter-spit trajectory,
field the tragedy,
work the room's comedy.

In demolished history,
what went before gone,
pointy shadows bat-wing bedtimes.
Fucked-up thing with never-ending
is never-ending never ends,
regurgitating nightmares are pitch.
You're a slurry of quips,
intention ready,
lips pouting 'n' positioned.
There's hiss bubbling,
you witch,
a hostile force of aim hits.
You got him,
he's hurt
and cackling gives you away.

You think you're this glamorous rock,
diamond-hard, shining, multi-faceted,
a dodecahedron of poise.
Not a seamless lump of coal, anthracite and wronged,
jagged, sharp and chiselled from loathing.

For Falling's Sake...

For Mark E. Smith.

Name says it,
The Fall,
what's in it and all about.
What, who!
Couldn't be about compromising,
falling isn't,
name wouldn't/couldn't allow.
That's what's in it.
The singing chap channelling fall,
wouldn't/couldn't allow.
Stunning city sin singing.
Knowing!
That dirty old angel
made us a canal of his pissed.

'What' is compromise!
Crumpled face, sweet bag sticky,
mud snarl,
primal drinking, dib-dab done.
Fight shadows,
Saint Pugnacious of the Immaculate Round,
boxing,
clever,
sickly.

Arse ballet by bandits, arse banditing ballet.
Pride cums.
We are dubious mélange.

Drink!
Pavement party,
natives of collapse.

Witty little shit,
played and sung,
flowing,
flung,
throwing it,
wrung,
mangled machismo sound, crumbling.
Rock 'n' roll mumbling!

Until pavement, falling is flying,
hit the ground,
the North,
drunk,
fell singing,
Punk,
joke,
sung falling,
flew.

Poetry!
Bloke!

Ego

Ballooning 'n' vivacious-coloured,
in rapturous enveloping, watch as it overcomes
what might and what might not be true.
More faces than a two-headed masquerade,
every mask slipped, has its eye-slits covered.
After all, gauze softens blows,
cushions corners,
stops you stubbing yer big toe,
gives contacts a blurry break.

Polite, it whispers compliment
because it wants compliment shouted.
All ears for bloody-minded sound.
It's all you want it to be,
for what it wants,
needs,
demands.
Ribboned and thinking outside the boxed,
tied-up in nots,
makes-believe it loves you.

Doesn't need blood,
not that kind of vampire,
but its monster burns in your Hell-hole.

You Really Were So... So!

Attending Quentin Crisp's Manchester funeral with only eight other people [my two performance artist friends David Hoyle 'n' Michael Mayhew being amongst them] was a truly bizarre and searingly, humanly, mystical experience – in itself, it's very happening presence, a real/fantastical piece of performance art. I went as performance tart Chloe Poems, thought it needed lipstick, gingham and a Louise Brooks bob. Being with what was left of his lovely family, sifting through old photos of him and his very early life in the Ealing Comedy-like Chorlton Victorian house where he died will live with me forever... I'm remembering it now like black 'n' white photographs. Drinking QC sherry if you please and eating silver knife-sliced, china-saucer'd Battenberg, it felt like subtle-coloured sepia icing on a sad, eccentrically strange, other-worldly gay cake... curiously modern as it was antimacassar'd Edwardian. A bit 'through the looking-glass' if the looking-glass was a handbag'd compact, monogrammed, magnified 'n' tiny. As mercurial Mancunian experiences go... it sure was a doosey.

A bubble day,
tenses decades, folding a clash,
time travelling's easy
when we own history.

The tales tall and feathered,
trailing through.
Marlene,
the romances of war,
all the nice boys love a backroom.

Surety of shadows,
lamplight hitting your bones,
poise is purpose.
The pout-brown folds of a ten bob note,
blackout,
whatever a blow job costs,
whatever a wank.

Miss Viaduct's arched, eyebrow'd.
Black Cat Soho sipping
builder's tea,
holding court,
couture-countered 'n' lipsticking.

Piquant sharp,
pinnacled,
find your own pedestal,
posing, classical,
arms flowing are musically nasal.
Mr Cupid's day off,
today Miss Cleopatra,
and the robed great dark of Mr Anthony.
You were every one of my carefree silhouettes,
the dance of still, forever reaching.

Don't let's ask,
moon 'n' stars are there for taking.
Light the paper blue, touch and stand.
America knows,
it's always known,
monochrome teaching and walking the,
talking the,
talkies.

I'm gingham frock-coated,
you're encased in large wooden drag,
the funeral parking next to us
startles.
For a boggle-eyed moment
forget they're grieving.

Half-catch David seeing the same things,
sky-blurred eternities coalescing.

Someone's passed and passing something,
baton, rouged in hand.
We'll mince with it,
leave running for others.
We're thorough fairies,
gossamer louche, compassioned 'n' powdered.

I've the space of it,
under-grounded heroine,
moth-flit-flap of candle flame,
in between flying see it.
What we all are,
were,
will,
the flaring uniqueness.
I am an effeminate homosexual!

The trees,
their shade,
and you corner-eyed,
glamour-wrapped green-tint in every shadow.

Binge Sinking Shevil Twirls

Part Two of The Chronicles of Folly Butler's *'Binge Drinking Evil Girls'.*
This time though, it's about 'straight' girls hen-partying on a Saturday night
out in the Gay Village. Again, with thanks to the marvellous John Aggy.

They're all lip-puff, flesh-ballooned,
mouth-quash and sequinned.
Silicon ballets bruise,
routined shoes set-pieced in tiny diamonds.
Heels, higher, higher, higher.
Trench foot.
Wench, drench-guttered,
deliriumed, drained 'n' draining.

Held together by straplessness,
gurning bras bolster.
Coke dreads give head
in scars 'n' strobes of moonlighters.
Gone are the days alcopops seemed other.
Alcopopalypse wow!

Mother's milk's melted, molten,
plip-plopped, flip-flopped,
exploded.
A gel gal, well-jellied,
jollied-on by yelling pot-bellied Beliebers.
Daydreamed schemers skim full-blown nights.
Wide boys skinny-dip pockets.

Friday, Saturdays, stopped.
Propped up 'n' poppered.
Fights,
stocked up on one liners and binge.

The Reach

You're gonna tell me *nah*,
can see the downturn in your not-looking eye.
All I need to know,
there's no point talking,
winking,
no point preaching.

I've poppers and erupting memory of youth,
E'd-up, lava-camp and class-A contrary.
The shove of joy envelops,
pushes away need,
desire,
the communion of reaching fades.

"Who run the world? Girls!"
Thank Christ for Beyoncé.
Girls!
Thank Christ for Caleb.
Girls!
Poppers do screech!

Last Night's Trade

Even booze-goggled you were fit,
shoulders arm-wide, stoic,
weight of life heavy on your face.
Scabbed nose a dead giveaway.
"I lose more fights than I win these days,
but it's a living!"
Handsome and forthright you say,
"If any cunt tries to cut you up, I'll break their necks!"
Fighting talk to swoon by,
I feel pulp-written and winsome.
Not used to being the heroine,
but for you I'd wear the dress.

For the first time in a long time
I feel protected,
even when you tell me it was manslaughter.
I'm tripping in The Shiver
and all nights should carry this poetry.

Naked and you shame Adonis.
I say beautiful.
Bedsit-shadowed, you weep.

Clap Magnet

A sister piece to Accidental Splendour of the Splash*'s 'I Slag'.*

You name it
had it,
a smorgasbord of hallucinogenic venereal.
Serial slag,
bit of a bag,
hopelessly caught in the shag net,
bowsie,
lousy,
occasionally flouncy,
a no-good, two-bit,
eat-shit,
clap magnet.

If there's a moment, in it,
when it comes to sinnin', committed,
if there's a line to cross, sniffed it.
Some may call me a sad get,
but unsafe to say
this particular gay
is a bona-fide, easy ride, hole-open stride,
outré,
ashtray,
clap magnet.

Tacky bitch,
cock-hitched,
wound up in repressions of time.
Oppressions I'm raking
are not oppressions I'm faking
and must not be mistaken for crime.

Just a clap magnet baby,
too often hazy, confounding shame,
profoundly lazy about longevity 'n' blame.
Sometimes gang-bang on the money,
now 'n' then a hunny,
often the game.

When there's a Rave I'll slide it,
in a dream I'll glide,
pride-eyed 'n' welcoming,
heavy-thigh'd and summoning saints.
Satan's fallen,
a kind of love's callin',
could be leather or fishnet.
If interested
I'm internetted,
infested,
too wide-awake to be rested.
So, about this discomfort let's be blanket,
I'm a got-wood,
no good,
fuck-the-hood,
most defiantly could,
ever hard,
partying tart,
clap magnet.

Twink Hunter

No more than a teen,
beat repetitive sociopathy has-been,
scene-queened and skin lean,
nil body fat,
fancy that,
ripped,
well-equipped, anti-ageing wrinkle cream.

In mirrors,
distorted,
hot-pant'd shadows courted,
sorted for weekends,
bent straight outta shape,
thwarted,
esteemed self, love aborted,
life is a line diss snorted.

B-movie cow-poke,
drawn slither of long smoke,
eight inch Grindr choke,
at twenty-one only does young,
no bloke,
daddy bespoke when token to,
coke.

A life pretended,
shadow ended, return sender'd
re-gendered by pressing thought,
bender'd out of sport,
face rendered, too taught,
surrendered le petit mort.

Twink Hunter prowl-tired,
surefired a man-squired cum shot,
Twink Hunter hardwired and gutrot,
knows what's required,
safaris the admired, bareback sired a good'n,
got wood on,
off-fucked and perspired,
Twink Hunter, job done,
at twenty-five, retired.

When I Believed

I'm lens'd impure,
amber'd, scar-scored,
a penknifed collage of minutes collided.

Older'd in terrain treacherous 'n' nearly,
slower but not slow,
pissing more, tweaked.
Still touching light,
hits crevices once linear.
Reflections soar sinister,
can see three of me sometimes.

Behind, in front, sideways,
time slides,
thin-iced in powdered lines.
On mirrored surfaces I sink,
there's an under me, searching.
All one-shiners,
snorting and bitching sink traumas,
battered makes sense,
that 'n' soft-shoe old,
that 'n' shuffle bold.

All but a rhyme in a Blues with my blame on,
cinder'd sour in the scorch of my flame on.
Yeah, I'm a tune,
a hot coal.
Yeah, I'm.

Then there's that end, always was,
a story-arc crapping its pants.
In the yearn, past shadows,
muddied, poo'd.

Choose who, who choos'd,
two-screw'd
'n' far from the maddened crowd-funded.

One Christmas when I didn't believe in making sense,
wanted a bike, a colourful bike,
got a scooter.
And that's when I believed in Christmas.

New York Portal

Bury me in monochrome,
between rust greys of corrugated,
around hot-tin clatter,
among the snow-showered,
near the steam.

Little Italy's Christmas lights are Edward G. Robinson-shaped,
gangster-glowing, blowin' up a thirties flap.
Saw it in the machine gun flash of *White Heat*,
tossed in the scowls of *Little Caesar*.
Cagney and Lacey cuffed it, Starsky 'n' Hutch butched it.
"Top o' the world, Ma!"

Timeless among the tick-tock,
in 'n' out the cogs of meat packing,
cowboy cocks rutting
yeehaw!
Rotting carcasses are skin-flicking
an emboldened golden-age pornography.
What's illegal in the abattoir slays illegal in the abattoir,
what's cool in being legal,
what's dreary in the boudoir,
who's meat packin' what?

Let rioting crash forever, smash it up bitch,
drag queens gotta sheer, steer Queer 'n' scream.

If I could step into you I would,
over Giuliani,
before the catastrophe, before the godliness,
in a big yellow taxi to the East Side.

Ageing Baby

Ribs hurt after the joy
of theatre lighting my pasts and futures.
I was a smash, a hit
and alcohol 'n' cocaine were swallowed 'n' snorted.

Aching baby,
I'm a screwed, hued, Blues train rollin' down the track,
rickety 'n' shakin',
making safe pain in the rain.
Hotel duvet'd and still baby
writing
yet another poem about ageing.

Ageing baby,
whispering rattles ghosts.
Tremulous voices and snapshots
of all remembered and forgotten.
I'm frailing baby,
holy grailing baby,
never Chris Grayling baby
and maybe
there's other places to colour.

I'll heal soon,
up 'n' at 'em,
bustin' moves to Candi Staton.
Young hearts must run free.

Ageing baby.

Billy Mack

For Billy MacKenzie.

There's a laugh
and it alives over fields,
kicks open wide,
country.

The not-afraid artists are,
way they see,
hear.
Sounds of pyramids,
of history,
brooks babbling.
The afraid artists are.

Dog-shit arias
whippet Bassey and Yellow.
Orchestra spaces,
hair-thin in Gothic of synths.
Howl and super mountain,
banshee camp 'n' silver shrilling.
I'm in it,
the soar,
nightclub and left wing.
Melody has a way of tearing.

The dog house down,
dug 'n' buried.
Bones,
mother-flooded,
spine.
In hollows whole,
the hot-sniffed 'n' pissed on.

Behind This Bleak

A sky black
is deep-thinking purple thoughts and ruin,
says nothing about everything to everybody.
Hear its murmuring when sleeplessness descends,
quiet, with occasional cars full of occasional coke-'eads.

I loathe 'n' love it,
reminds of lives unlived,
can sense years wracked, stretching.
No matter how they try to jazz it up,
fill it full of beat,
poetry's home is isolation.

Behind this bleak
starts a universe, apparently.
Constellations of stars and thought,
nihilism of accidents, of music.

No matter how they try to jazz it up,
fill it full of beat,
poetry's home is isolation.

The Most Powerful Man In The World

It's really fortunate
I'm not the most powerful man in the world,
probably for best.
If were and put to test,
don't know what mask I'd don, who I'd be.
You see,
I was the least powerful boy in the world,
feebled, defeated.
Dark days it's repeated,
running rerun, the cowering, pleading,
bleeding heart and carcass.
Head, car crash 'n' broken,
courage receding unspoken,
token,
butt of joking.
Finger pointing 'n' poking
doesn't make you feel good, kind,
it's not like you find your best you,
the saviour, upholder,
be-caped super-soldier,
don't feel brave, stronger, bolder,
just older when you should be young.

It's seriously fortunate
I wasn't the most powerful boy in the world,
don't think I'd have used my heat-ray vision
to melt all the guns.
Being honestly honest hun,
I'd probably have used it to gleefully incinerate
all y'fucked-up bullying sons.

Three Depth Wishes

For Joe Orton.

Toilet-door jammed with award,
open.
Gotta keep a look out for something younger,
fitter.
Something packing a prize,
an actual prize,
sizeable,
weighty,
a really big hitter,
rock hard shitter,
one worth winning... *cor!*
One worth sinning for.
Caves down here are bejewelled,
rammed,
glitter,
not with celebrities simpering,
but by forty thieves and the judiciary.
Gielgud loves piss!

Underworld fairies, tickleballs,
flightless,
flying.
In this well of tricks,
wands erect, shining,
dreams of possibility parade and whore position.
Half-beast bluster of a barrer boy,
brimmed,
fawn-arsed 'n' denim'd,
longing to be rimmed.
He three wishes!

Ammonia,
sharper than sulphur,
bogged among the crap,
horned and baring to back.
Before a little depth
foreplay bonds.
Proposals mean more than marriage.
Turd-finger left hand is where you place,
the wedding's banned.
Three tear'd cocks slice
the soft chocolate sponge of ass kisses.
Whispered secrets spellbind.
He presses,
three wishes!

Penny drops,
as do pants,
bulbs out and bulbous,
spent.
Darkness becomes the drips 'n' suits,
old school ties tightening,
throats regimental and suggestive
are noosed.
Rent.
Persephone's hung 'n' fleecing,
her mouth jammed with Jason's fruits,
as onlookers peeing,
peer,
group.

An ogre's raging at the billy scrote roughs.
Under his bridge,
waiting.
He's using his three wishes.

Ain't Over Baby

Bit of a workshop idea: take a favourite song and real life 'loved' physical thing [not a person]. Mine's 'Love Don't Live Here Anymore' and lighthouses [don't ask – OK, I kinda fancy lighthouses, you asked], and fuse the two 'notions' together. See what happens when a pop sung cultural moment and a personal actuality meet... could be fun.

An unwelcome
shone a spotlight
on all us ancients marooned at sea.
Gibbering masses, huddled,
love don't live,
vacancy.
Whole-heart trajectory,
teardrop-lit,
lighthouse-heavy,
not here.
Smashed!

Don't live, love,
moment dive an aquabatic,
light window-shining,
tall-stood, crashing, crashed.
Man overwrought,
abandon.
Me!
History's downed in vacant sea.
Love don't anymore, live.
See!

All you ever did,
long tall phallicy,
living inside of.
We don't!

Deep,
scotched on the rocks 'n' seedy.
Calling,
eyes drooping scales,
that tall ship's long taled.
Abandoned, me?

Ain't over baby,
till the fat siren wails.

The
BOURGEOIS
ZEITGEIST

A Treatise
by
Gerry Potter

I

Brian [Brenda] had finally caught up with all his/her little deaths, died and it was brutal, his agonising demise encased in a tiny basement flat on Waterford Road, just off Chelsea's once infamously fashionable King's Road. London certainly wasn't sixties/seventies swinging anymore; it was eighties/nineties dying and had been for some considerable time. When thinking back to those hopelessly destructing AIDS days something very necessarily blankets; not denial, nowhere near comforting as that, more a form of psychic protection, mental self-preservation. If any big life thing rocked me [and it had], nothing rocked me more than this. Desolate doesn't come close to describing, and I was just one gay man swirling in the fading friendships of so many gay men going through this exact same thing. Yes, there was a community-shaped bond, but grief's far too personal for us all to join hands in Kumbaya sing-song lamentation. In many ways, grief shackles.

On the stairs, holding onto an uncontrollably sobbing Helen [a dear old Everyman Youth Theatre friend, adopted mother 'n' other carer], I'll never forget seeing Brian's body-bagged frame clumsily bundled out of that tiny dump of a flat. Through industrial strength black plastic, I clearly recall the poking indentation of his nose; it looked both odd 'n' shocking and for the first time in our friendship I felt strangely intrusive. I instinctively knew it a thing he wouldn't like me to have witnessed and would've, how we say in Liverpool, 'felt ashamed'. Then add to that, heightened surreal hints of grotesque comedy: because rigor mortis had set in, Brian perversely reminded me of a bit from Eric Sykes's silent slapstick classic, *The Plank*. They were more Laurel 'n' Hardy removal men negotiating a too-tall wardrobe than experienced ambulance crew. Not wholly their fault, this rickety old flat had long been constructed from broken promises, peeling paint and wonky mazes. Then *bang*, the unexpected half-relief of a slamming front door. After all the harrowing judder-bumping commotion everything fell a still, steely silent and suddenly... I was very non-comedically alone.

Even though dying, the dying are very much alive, in a bizarre way possibly more so. Not your flamboyantly discoing best-friend alive, oh no, more a bell-ringing lumpen grouch, blue-black lesion'd, morphined off his tits, shitting himself and rightfully fucking furious, alive... It was like living in an all-male version of *Whatever Happened to Baby Jane*. I have to be over-sharingly honest here, I didn't much care for Brian [Blanche] ill. By very necessary nature the dying are quite selfish, 'n' guess I just wasn't ready for that. Absolutely hated – had for some time – we were no longer old school Brian 'n' Gerry. You start grieving long before they die... it appears the living can be quite selfish, too.

From what seemed like hours stair-sat 'n' stunned, I weighted a weary lollop to his always darkened bedroom. Dominating the main wall overlooking his bed, and only witness to his death, a giant wood-framed photo of a heroin-addled Billie Holiday. Like some gay men of my generation, Brian had a morbid fascination 'n' fondness for the finer romances of finality... be careful what you death-wish for. Apart from a gin-haggard Billie, it felt more like an ailing grandparent's bedroom than a once-effervescent ballsy queen's. Smells of damp 'n' disinfectant violently nose-bullied and, strewn everywhere, his far too many medications, walking stick and trusty commode [I fucking loathed that trusty commode!]. Only brightness, sunshine from an open window looking to his basement garden, falling onto his now vacant bed. It was a warm May mourning and breezes blowing through billowing curtains late-spring-summery and welcome.

Funny with grief, how paradoxically everything 'n' everywhere you are with it one minute and then nothing 'n' nowhere the next; there's another dimensionality that's paradoxically both tangible and untouchable. Sat on the edge of his bed, warm sun on sheet, stroking the still visible sweat-patches of where he'd so recently lain and bizarrely thinking *it's too soon to weep Gerry, to wholly acknowledge... he's gone.*

I stayed in that council mausoleum [it was a tomb long before he died] for another eighteen months and it was a living hell, just hated it. Brian had fought long 'n' hard for that 'cherished' London address, so suppose it was best friend duty making me stay, certainly didn't feel like choice. Thankfully, I had my trusted close pal Fas [Martin] who would visit regularly, but I most definitely wanted out... to where though?

Brian King and I were many things to many people, but more than anything we were children of disco... the dancefloor our unnaturally neon'd habitat 'n' stage. We were well-known clubbers, particularly in Liverpool; I thought of us as shiny speed-bombed acid-swallowing beacons of camp whooshy aplomb. Of course, some people didn't like us, some people always won't, but from most there was a respect, not just for what we did theatrically [and we did a lot], but for our courageous hedonistic gall and over-generous narcissism. Liverpool really gets hedonism 'n' narcissism; they're a celebratory double-act hot-wired into almost every Scouser's DNA, even the insecure ones.

Realising our small but perfectly malformed 'scene' wasn't big enough for our ever-spiralling personalities, we set our sights on early-eighties Manchester. It'd be about '82 when we first went and wow, warra lorra fun! Manchester's gay scene then was far more contained than now and red-brick imbued with an organically historical confidence Liverpool's lacked. There were certainly more gays, more venues, the dilapidated warehouses and canal-side Gothic of its city centre location giving it a darkly romantic fairy-telling sense of place. Its transvestite/drag communities were certainly something to behold. Back then, it really was burly/hefty truck drivers and wide-shouldered coal men dressed as their mothers or more glamorous 'with it' aunties. Also on big ballsy display, a stridently visible Hell-for-leather scene, full to the rim of be-chained heavily moustachioed clones, high-energied to buggery 'n' popper'd-up to fuck. They looked so goddamn butch in their off-the-shoulder camouflage netting, dangling key-rings and handkerchiefs of many colours, those same hankies dictating how they wanted to shag, be shagged, pissed or shat on. Remember whenever Brian 'n' I landed in a new city and, if not knowing where the gay bars where, we'd play 'follow the clone' – great game and very easy to master. We'd just look for, find, and start stalking the biggest handle-bar moustache fiercely sashaying in tightest leather... soon got us where we needed to go.

Although still indelibly northern in tone, Manchester felt more exotically detailed than our cheekier/spikier home town... a bit like *Coronation Street* in Carmen Miranda drag. To our young buck delight we soon found out it was far more sexually confident too... Oh we ran that city's trade seven times ragged! As May Butler, me wise auld Ma would say, we were up and down it like a whore's drawers.

My favourite haunt was a dingy upstairs club called Dickens [although upstairs it felt every inch a cellar club], a hoary cave of a dive that literally anybody could be part of. It reminded me very much of Liverpool's recently closed down Club Masquerade, and chock-a-block with queens, dykes, trans, drag, prostitutes, taxi drivers and any number of just-released Strangeways murderers. It was a ciggie-smoke venue at the end of the world, rough as a sober drunk, drunk as a sobbing rough, and part of the glamorously depraved partying screech of the universe. Brian really enjoyed Manchester's leathery muscle-bound showmanship, I preferred the guttersnipes, tarts, rent-boys and seemingly never-ending supply of Pink Champagne [speed]. Way back then, Brenda was by far the more socially confident and very at ease with the monied chatting gays, whereas I'd more than content myself with the awkward stony-broke/ speeding toilet-noshers [blow-jobbers]... each to their own, eh.

Dickens, like its name suggests, was a very *present* Manchester, proudly steeped in its dark Satanic history; not the tawdry written-down histories of kings and queens, but the spit 'n' sore arse histories of kinky Queers. Dickens didn't look anything like a Rabelaisian candle-lit tavern, but felt every sordid inch a Rabelaisian candle-lit tavern, far more decaying Molly House than interior designed whine bar. I loved the size/shapes of its clientele, from many a mountain-wide-enough bruiser to zhuzhier-than-stick-thin queen. I'm not saying these people were without problems, most of them looking constructed from rickety discord and crash, but here chorused a society-defying harmony; I could hear it in the mix of their confidently orchestrated jangle [Scouse for gossip]. Dickens was the uniquely imperfect perfection of this crazy-raved city and its high-flying orbitals, some of them very visibly smoking and deeply inhaling its grass roots. I knew then that this predominately working/middle-class underground intellectual atmosphere was for me... I, like them, could breathe it! Even back in the day, Manchester certainly had some of campest/ craziest Queers in the world.

Brian quickly found a group of friends [a predominantly blood family] made up of a lesbian sister 'n' gay/bi brothers, and for a short while moved into what was colloquially referred to as Fairy Towers, otherwise known as Arthur Millwood Court. I stayed living in Liverpool, but would visit often. Often, that is, until I was pissed on by a tramp. One night [and very unusually], Brian had left clubbing early and when I got back, try as I might, couldn't wake him up. 'Twas a snowy, freezing December and the only meagre warmth to be had was in one of the two tower blocks' lifts. Thinking I was being clever, I scrunched my exhausted self into the corner of one trying to snatch some sleep – it was like trying to catch forty winks in a moving microwave. It was only when being drenched by a stream of what was, for a very short time, warm water, I found out I wasn't the only one with that idea. Seems the blind drunk homeless in this city think they're clever too, so they're who piss in lifts. I was also leaving Brian to it because the Manchester of then was more his than mine and I'm not a gatecrasher.

As it always does, time passes and always with the passing of time, life happens. Brian would be diagnosed HIV, our worlds forever changed, he would need to be in London and Rave exploded.

Gaychester, camp for Madchester, scally for Manchester, meant all the worlds it gloriously conjured to me, something about it/me gelling would become a complete wonderland of dancing. I must make it very clear here [and as the twelve of you who have all my books are painfully aware], I adore disco dancing far more than anything else and am on record saying I'd much rather go disco dancing than have a career. I think it safe to say and with rainbow colours fearlessly flying, Gaychester helped me achieve that particular life goal. There was no way Brian and I fell out or became separate, but by late eighties/early nineties, we'd changed. Brenda retreating to the healing properties of a much more HIV-focused Big Smoke, while I continued partying. After not visiting Manchester regularly, I happily rediscovered it and it very kindly rediscovered me. When Brian got ill I'd move to London to be with him, but that would be in '94. This was '89, and while he was choosing a more Buddhist existential approach to existence... I was choosing Ecstasy. This next bit may be difficult to put into flowing coherent language as there's so much forgotten, but I'm pretty sure after some writerly meditative dig-diving I'll excavate memories still poetically embedded. It felt like all I did every night for six whole years was underground dance, so to accompany that here's an E of language... swallow it 'n' rave with me.

Tower-block march of God-feet, broken sparkled shattered glass shines, we're slipper-flying Oz-like, Dorothy'd and ruby. Sky-paved 'n' gutter starred, track-suited 'n' be-trainer'd we demand moons! Cigarette-papered amphetamine bugle-wraps, trumpet-jigs, we're all ears 'n' heralding tunes. Electricity blankets a city sleep and sparking alarm bells peel "wakey wakey". We're troubadours jingle-jangling rebellion, journeying to Manto's our song. "We're off our face to blizzard, the wonderful blizzard of us." We've every right to every wrong. Feel every cobble, every yellow brick; everybody's red-flicked 'n' poppy-dashed. Buildings gather like Titans, protect like bouncers, earth's beating its own drum and we accompany, like flouncers leading. Mind fast 'n' mouth jabbering, Keith the Teeth can't stop chattering, syllable-soup simmering, only direction the dealing, even shades neon-lit and everything's scene. Sat in with the toilet-pissing, the just-shat snorting, the just-snorted shag the just shat, off our tits 'n' constantly cock-clocking. Fancy that nancy twat! Money-pass and thankful giggle, Tiger E's 'n' trips, soon God-feet, soon. Been told they're double-dipped, there's lust in the Love Hearts and these Snowballs will melt… swoon. In taking the give, soon be receiving, the screaming blood 'n' gut spill of communion. Bar-juddering cheeky halfs, split in two, becoming one with all the others. "TUNE-ION!" Where Love Lives! The gathering *dum dum dum* of the immaculate thump. First wave hitting the big smile, House style, mind's open wide, never closing. On rocks 'n' cocaine building a high climb, bottoms reaching tops 'n' sneaky peaking, exposing. "TUNE!" Boom, explosion woohoos, freaking, love fall-out, mutating 'n' hitting the beat. God-feet are kickin' in wholly. Then there's Flesh, then there's Strangeways, then there's The Number One and Paradise, holy, holy, holy, whenever 'n' wherever our God-feet land sets dancefloors free. Glen 'n' Brendan Gordian's of the malarkey, Guardians of Strangeways, unknotting the wired, freeing souls, curators of this spine-winding galaxy. More take, more chance, more me, more us, more more and then there's Dancerteria. Scored! Sound hits, passes through, tangible as air and flesh/blood ghosts bone-rattle. Teeth 'n' disco-tits tittle-tattle. Faith in, music out; this is fade, who needs breath? Everyone's an engine driving night's eternities, gathered together the directionless stand. Le petite mort and a lot of death. Spine-thunders a wave-hike, not stopping… fuckin' 'ell it's nuclear. BOOM! The Shiver! The thunder! The room! The big hit, all in it together, light traces 'n' eye-liner'd eyes linger forever, one smile on the God-feet massive. Music height and perfect-pitched, the perfect bitched. This future, our present, our knowing, and knowing this knowing is ancient story, I look around, arms raised, flag-fingers fan faces. Boy, all in between, girl. Big beams large it, this palace is pure as love and Manchester is the greatest city in the world.

Rave was a counter-culture collected, working- 'n' middle-classes rhythmically combined, something all the previous counter-cultures I'd known did, something I grew with and around. That Second Summer of Love was a long hot summer indeed and we tranced, tanned luminescent green by super-natured glow-sticks. Of course, there where casualties, always are, but like all huge movements most people were fine [let's face it, not every mountain climber or recreational hang-glider gets out alive]. It felt truly revolutionary, certainly those early days, a people's rebellion culturally stamped, tramped 'n' boogied by Manchester. There was no other city I'd rather have been in and easily my choice to return to when Brenda died, as I'd much rather off-my-face-dance than forever grieve.

Brian and I were not only children of Liverpool's underground, we became adults ornately carved from it. Those early days at The Everyman Youth Theatre introducing us to Shivers of our city we didn't think existed. Everywhere we went, day-dream/night-forged warrens of the accessibly surreal, not only invited into but would soon be leading. It's what counter-cultures do best, holistically empower without having to use patronising phrases like 'holistically empower'. Manchester was exactly the same, a place where people grouped not only to Rave but to create, its bars, streets, canal-side life, improvisationally alive 'n' brimming with a gazillion ideas. It was feral/acquired intellect made animatedly palpable; everybody seemed to be doing a vivacious life *something*. The most wonderful thing about this particular counter-culture was, if falling, I was more than confident it would open its arms to catch me; catching the falling is what happens when you're not preternaturally obsessed by a five year business plan. I firmly believe we're more readily gonna be caught by the moment than a future projection. Why? Well, the moment's actually happening, projections haven't.

Then, one dark night, I went out and Rave had gone. It seemed that fast, replaced by über-bronzed homosexuals, uniformedly uninformed 'n' badly routining to Steps.

That's when I knew, first time I saw it, 'the distance', the initial invasion… the oncoming contagion of The Bourgeois Zeitgeist!

The Trickster's E'd-Up

From worn down monochrome,
mother whine and factory drone,
a ceaseless careering of clatter,
childhoods.
There's too much choose,
too much bruise.

Cave damp and overwhelm,
you're seeping
into soil-mush 'n' gravel,
dark thoughts, cloud, root.
This crush becomes you,
topples told tales and a rock fall family tree.

In here with the raggedy gnarled,
soak of youth,
in here with the auld forgotten.
The buried are alive,
we talk in red-brick, God and tongues.

Now you're absolutely everywhere,
bang among the starscapes 'n' rhythm.
You and the everything,
soul-stick 'n' bones pointing.

In the strobe of this heart-grab, everybody.

Folly Butler's Raving

In half-club, Folly Butler full-stood.
Dancing's for later she thought, dancing.
She's onslaught thinking slumber and who.
Overreach of rhythm pokes,
twitches a nudge,
immovable till she moves.
Haunts the spiral, glamours a spin,
outside and within the reel.
Noise becalmed she silents,
where there's a lullaby there's halo.
This maelstrom's child-play
she thinks thought by children
why else would it be such fun.
Always circling,
the soul-light, eye traces,
pick up of thought.
Babbling, hammocks a dawn,
what can be better than all our whispers swinging.
There's an invincible to be, a soul-wrap of gods and lift,
she's where she hurts, loves.
Fog-hide, dry ice and hiss-kisses,
peek-a-boo sway,
nobody's bone anymore, they're light.
They were always light,
anyway.
Buried in energy she blooms,
always blooming,
plays.
Petal'd out her head, wants to say in daffodil
love.
"Misollkher."

The Wretched Night

The pull,
grip reaching,
is taking over my stomach,
racing my heart.
It's a sneaky hand you own,
greased and cunning,
violating.
I have you,
you have me,
we're wedded to the stories,
the bat flight, the fisting
and when dancing stops.

And you're a wretched mistress, m'dear,
crueller than sea,
with the waves of your whispers, raging.
You're a fox alright,
there's nothing you can't rip into
when you put your mind.
And you've histories of all those crones,
slags, street-cornered 'n' knickerless.

You're ragged 'n' screaming,
a rope-light beating
and throbbing behind your walls... 'Car Wash'.
I love you know your bowels so well;
in all those cellars,
the stench of movement.

Oh yes, you're wretched, m'dear,
but I for one will always love you.

Throwing Shapes And Catching Spirit

Living a dark of so much light,
spying outline,
shine shapes of surface and heartbeat,
call it aura.
This is generous,
kind;
the narcissists are sharing tonight.
They are angle-bend hand-air,
trapped free 'n' semaphore,
I've been here,
seen here,
far-out-sheen'd here before.
You try telling the timeless they're stuck,
they'll just love at you, smiling.

We're outside in, inside out,
caught wearing the beat.
We pass through
knowing we're us,
being all about me.
Ghosts are human, we hurl-arc,
spirited of the age
uplifted.

Torso

Sweat downs, landscaping skin
wet contours
feeding the earth inside
the core
the inner molten
fired.

It drills, pumps sex,
can tell by the thrusting
something deeper's being dug.
The repetition
tunes into weathered improvisation.
Without words, rivulet speech of feet,
knees, hips,
language seeps,
outrage.
Our drenched torsos leak poetry.

The beat's heart,
thin skin, drums
among hallucination's footprints.
We are pathways,
trails, fairies, witches,
ribs uncaged,
sweeties, family,
we are The Shiver.

Vanity back-seats,
tripping flashes forward,
Dante heats,
torso, bathe,
amyl starbursts the engulfing inferno.

Double-Dipped

Duality bound hallucinogen,
drunk-eyed, no booze.
Water-bottled, hydrates thought
and mood.
In mutant lights, a foggy glow,
swamps of dancing arms.
Stasers of fingers, ballet,
eyes reach in and show.

Double-dipped 'n' pout there,
on the wildest we,
drowning in waving rhythm,
sweating out the sea.
Double-dipped and in here,
breathing my roomiest me.
All others of us gathered,
rattling floor-lit symmetry.

Strawberry-pipped and double-dipped,
we are sound, light and imagery.

The
BOURGEOIS
ZEITGEIST

A Treatise
by
Gerry Potter

II

Some of my best friends are middle-class and, since joining the Everyman Youth Theatre, always have been. A lot of them are really very nice, cool even, a few of them even know what's really going on. I was lucky, a working-class brat forged from the unionised intellectualism of a sixties/seventies semi-Marxist Britain and clearly remember a time most people [not all] had jobs. A city centre docklands kid brought up around one of Liverpool's – and arguably Britain's – most industrialised areas, and very used to the frantic cross-spillings of shift-workers. You could time the day by armies of people marching to 'n' from work. Not just blokes either, the women of Tate & Lyle sugar refiners were a blue tabard'd twice-a-day swarm marching to labour, animatedly buzzing with conversation and laughter... the million mothers of Vauxhall Road. The gnawing knowing of industry forever rumbling a stormless thunder, strangely comforting drones constantly audibly happening. Of course, these dark factory roles were decades-forced onto people and vocational choice scarce, but what they did have was money, a weekly wage feeding families 'n' community. I was brought up in a predominantly Catholic area, so for bigger families [of which there were many] a weekly pay packet might not have stretched that far, but if you happened to be young, free 'n' single... My three older brothers where young, free 'n' single and that weekly wage not only gave them access to new clothes, records and hairstyles, but allowed them to confidently be part of the wider social scenes on offer – and boy, did they take it.

When I was very young there was a time we had absolutely nothing, fuck-all, our Blackstock Gardens tenement flat empty with the hunger of poverty, a noise ricocheting a desolate I'll never forget. That silence raucously broken by two of my brothers simply leaving school and getting work in the local factories. The darkness finally lifted as for the first time warm/softening [certainly didn't feel cold or hard] cash came tumbling into our home, a weekly whack of me Ma's rent/keep and my pocket money. Don't think there was a politically defined under-class then, but if there was we would've been it. Overnight we went from absolutely nothing to certain something. Clearly remember skipping in the street, thinking we were weirdly kinda rich – of course weren't, but for the first time we were on an even keel with everybody around us. The visceral excitement of pocket money day enabling me to pile into nearby sweetshops with all the other soon-to-be sugared-up kids 'n' chorus-squawk alongside for chocolate, crisps, lemonade 'n' comics. It was jubilant treacle-toffee-down economics making a community not only of children, but feeding local businesses. Pubs, and in those days there where many, seemed to be busy every night and by weekends fit to burst, the culture of that so tub-thumpingly wildly sing-song. Oh, we were definitely mucky kids alright and would scruffily hang outside those pubs pocketing any amount of tanners and thrupenny bits. Some days, particularly weekends, your mucky face earned you a small fortune. Everyone looked great too, able to readily buy into the fashions of the day, working-class men 'n' women simply able to afford the trends of prevailing culture. Our tenements where huge red-brick Tolkien-like monoliths and seeing my brothers and their girlfriends confidently striding into town every Friday/Saturday night was just so evocatively thrilling. They looked amazing, late-sixties scally exotica, their sharp-suited silhouettes 'n' bouffanting beehives trendily framed by the towering red-brick enormities of our surroundings. Just them casually/confidently sauntering into the smoggy summer dusks of Scottie, Stanley or Vauxhall Road, pockets loaded by a wedge of just-earned weekending tenners, so made me want to be them 'n' go where they were going. Yeah, there might not have been much vocational choice on offer and that's genuinely crap, but there was some money, and I don't care what any cunt says, money may not soft-furnish every one of our needs, but it most certainly cushions some of the blows. For all its flaws, and there where many, this was a functioning working-class fiscally generated environ, able to enliven a great many lives and essential local businesses.

Then, one dark day, I went out into the street and industry stopped. It seemed that fast.

So, dear reader, what on Earth do I mean by The Bourgeois Zeitgeist? And how does that fit with currently living in Manchester?

First of all, I'm not saying the above description of where I'm from is in any way perfect, it wasn't, where is? Though it was communitied, enabled, largely employed and active, nobody had over four decades of unemployment or heroin addiction in one family. It was unheard of. If single, working and certainly with well-paid overtime [which was plentiful], most young people had in their hands more than a living wage… they had a hedonistic wage. Because of being paid weekly, a lot of that money poured straight into the shops/pubs surrounding, 'n' quickly spent over their counters or bars. The working-class I grew up around were too busy having a rollicking good time to OCD obsess on saving, pretty sure that was the same in Manchester and all our major industrial cities. Yes, there was working-class poverty, I was there and saw it, was it, but less than there is now. Closer-knit communities really did mean when things got tight you looked out for one another – it's not an urban myth glibly spewed in trending whine bars to humourlessly demean working-class history. What we have now are generational famines of fiscal/creative poverty, held up 'n' continually passively/aggressively engined and constantly applauded by The Bourgeois Zeitgeist.

1979 brought us the onslaught of the Thatcher revolution and suddenly not only was it somehow cool to be greedy it was societally expected of you. Liverpool was in the then Tory government's sights, a full-frontal attack of 'managed decline', a fiscal barrage so ideologically savage it almost crippled my home town. With media on-side, our unionised working-class communities were branded the enemy while individualist money-possessed Yuppies loadsa-flourished. Say what you will about the unions, but huge swathes of the working-class failed by factory-fodder state-schools were politically educated by their union affiliations. They were able to collect together not just in work places but anywhere; football clubs, labour clubs, social clubs, and the then-bourgeoning club-land. A proactively vibrant working-class template very much existed, looked great, was vocal and, above all, listened to. Thatcherism would be a filthy polluted soil The Bourgeois Zeitgeist would take root in, germinated by a cruelly sabotaged working-class and the societal normalisation of neoliberalism.

Whilst some the middle-classes are nice, sometimes very kind, forgive me if I comedically generalise a little here – they so often seem to be born into manners, finance and control. By that I mean from childhood there's usually some financial plan afoot and they're, for good or bad, made pretty much aware of that. In the way a piping-hot just-roasted potato carefully wrapped in grease-proof loaf paper was offered to me as a working-class toddler, in a similar way I think the mathematical certainties of accountancy were offered to middle-class children; it's a cultural thing, their version of a treat. I was, of course, told some manners, but certainly wasn't taught to be enslaved by them. I was brought up to respect my elders and did, but only if they respected me. If they didn't, they could fuck right off and that went for everybody. I certainly wasn't chained to my bedroom bureau, newly-feathered quill in bored hand, and emotionally blackmailed into writing a politely worded Rupert the Bear thank you notelette to an elderly overseas auntie I've never met, for a gift I didn't like [true story, apart from the metaphorical chains 'n' quill].

What am I culturally trying to say here? Yeah, that's it! If a middle-class kid and I went to the shop to buy a clutch of fireworks, with an already half-open box of matches I'd have hurriedly grabbed the fireworks while the middle-class kid politely pleases 'n' thank yous, anxiously waiting to carefully fold 'n' pocket the precious receipts.

1979 wasn't just about the unfolding horror of Thatcherism, it would also be liberating socialist enormities of The Everyman Youth Theatre, meeting Brian King, and for the first time confidently mixing with all the classes on offer. From then, right till the end of Rave, I felt the classes, certainly the ones bohemianly bonded by the eclectic vibe of art 'n' clubbing, knitted incredibly well. There weren't the increasing divisions that would soon scar, further divide 'n' horrifically conquer. Perhaps the class of '79 was the last generation to be fuelled by the memory of near-full, well-paid employment, the semi-Marxism of a post-1945 Britain, by the freeing individualities of recent sixties/seventies counter-cultures... Remember, those were the days you could be working-class and get a free university education. Those were the days you could be working-class and not have to somehow psychically book a future appointment, but be able to see your doctor on the day you were actually physically ill.

There would be twelve/thirteen years between 1979 and the end of Rave, enough time for Thatcherism to take its deadly toll and unemployment to become a familial working-class norm. Any sense of class cohesion would be more severed by 1992, as the middle-class template would completely dominate and be ultra-socially normalised. The time it would take a once proudly counter-cultural semi-Marxist Manchester city centre to become the chosen home and spiritual epicentre of The Bourgeois Zeitgeist.

Thatcher Just Isn't Dead Enough For Me

A wooden stake wouldn't have cut it:
for that shit to work you need a heart.
A silver bullet between the eyes,
take out the brain stem,
well, y'know, a start.
I'd have gladly got Vlad to impale her,
Frankenstein's monster to assail her,
the werewolf to rip off her limbs –
but those monsters are fantasy,
not the deranged darkened reality
of her ideologically driven
unholy-evil sociopathic whims.
You could kill her a million/billion times but, y'see,
no matter how unalive,
how brown-bread,
Thatcher just isn't dead enough for me.

First they came for our children's milk,
now they want their food.
Her ball's still rolling with lives she's stolen,
we're still screwed.
Firing squad, slow poison,
nailed to our country's mood.
It's just not enough
for this anarchic puff and his rag-tag ministry,
no matter how kaput
and for every factory shut,
Thatcher will never be dead enough for me.

Now, let me say this compassionately,
throughout all the hate,
miners disgraced and for Clause 28,
Thatcher will never be late enough for me.

The Immediate Resignation Of Theresa May

#theimmediateresignationoftheresamay

> *Never liked you or yours,*
> *glass in puppy's paws,*
> *hungry child in monster's jaws,*
> *ear-splitting bangs of slamming doors.*

Your time is really up,
your ticks should never have tocked.
Evacuate the boat
you've unforgivably rocked!

Britannia rules grave,
hard-hearted, impure.
Parentless bodies
washed up on our shore.

> *Never liked you or yours,*
> *glass in puppy's paws,*
> *hungry child in monster's jaws,*
> *ear-splitting bangs of slamming doors.*

Put the wood in the hole
and make sure you lock it.
You'll be alright
with the profit you pocket.

Mickey Mouse
imitates lion's raw.
Cartoon fingers
on buttons of war.

Your colour's raging
a hellfire blue.

Ivory towers
don't burn around you.

Milksnatcher
causing calcium droughts,
but you want the food
from our children's mouths.

> *Never liked you or yours,*
> *glass in puppy's paws,*
> *hungry child in monster's jaws,*
> *ear-splitting bangs of slamming doors.*

Strong and stable
as a non-Viagra'd erection.
Losing the win
of your beleaguered election.

Your speeches automaton drivel,
paper shaking in trembling claws.
Not Prime Ministerial at all,
a rusting reject from *Robot Wars*.

In your voice an echo,
a reverberating of hollow.
What else have you to apologise for
tomorrow?

The ravaging evil
of your unravelling plans.
None of us will forget those
'Go Home' vans.

Only there
because there's no one else.
Gathering dust
like our National Health.

Tax breaks for the rich,
even less for the needing.
Big banks, foodbanks, homelessness,
our consciousness receding.

You're even blemishing
the same tired old story.
Now even Tories
don't wanna be Tory.

In fire and water of this generation
is a rage pumping hard.
You're sacked,
time to collect your card!

If Grenfell and Windrush where predominantly white,
today would be the day
our country could finally rejoice
in the immediate resignation of Theresa May.

Never liked you or yours,
glass in puppy's paws,
hungry child in monster's jaws,
ear-splitting bangs of slamming doors.

The Erosion

Sea in/out,
cycles 'n' roundabouts,
revolutions peaceful pass.
Nature got it right,
anarchy and calm are where it's at,
what it's always been,
filling fish with plastic's a greedy bitch.
The Erosion's us,
we wither 'n' whittle,
architects of splintered goods.
We've wintered every summer with pollution;
fortunate breathe,
unlucky choke.

There's this bloke thinks climate change
is hot money,
struck gold on a car-crashed Barrier Reef.
He's The Erosion,
the end, insane, eye on the dollar
and promotion.
When the commotion's a storm,
there's beauty.
Yeah, a roof blows off, but the sky lights up,
ring-pulls are murdering whales.
Black Friday January sales into the apocalypse,
Disneyland sunsets,
one wing'd or not,
bets are on when the bees are gone.

Nature may occasionally rip up trees,
but we burn them to make plastic packaging for fruit.

The BOURGEOIS ZEITGEIST

A Treatise
by
Gerry Potter

III

"My name's Siobhan and I play the synthesiser. What do you do?"

This is the sentence completely waking me up to the brutally distancing banalities so completely inherent in The Bourgeois Zeitgeist, and after hearing knew I could never close my ears/eyes to it ever again.

It's now late nineties [I think] in Manchester's Contact Theatre and against my better judgment I'm convinced to go to one of these new-fangled American-styled 'networking meetings'. I was told it would be an ideal 'opportunity' to mingle with other likeminded artists and could be proactively good for me 'n' my career strategy [I've never had, or indeed wanted, a career strategy].

Downstairs in Contact's foyer a crowd's milling 'n' mulling about, some of whom I know, lots I don't. Instantly feel like we're being herded as a precise middle-class clip-boarded voice calls our names, ticking us off. Then, the way a sheep-dog might hear a shepherd's humanly inaudible whistle, ears pricked, eyes sharp, she excitedly yaps, "Would everybody like to follow me upstairs please?" I don't and never have responded positively to being patronised and am instantly distanced by the forced positive jollity of her manner.

The room we're poured into is garishly strip-light wide and at its centre a long trestle-table. Sitting atop are a hot-water urn, polystyrene cups, several paper plates of biscuits and two sets of juggling balls. The room's huge and we're haphazardly dotted about it like colourful-headed pins on a kitchen cork-board. The jolly-voiced woman joyfully trills, "Please help yourselves to refreshments. Tea, coffee, biscuits, juggling balls, no expense spared... Oh, and leave me a Garibaldi." There were no Garibaldis. Perhaps the budget didn't stretch to Garibaldis, or perhaps "leave me a Garibaldi" was an office in-joke about how obviously cheap the biscuits were... I'm not laughing, nobody is, looks like nobody has for some time.

Like an over-wound clockwork Chihuahua she proceeds to yapper on about how super-hyped 'n' humbled she is we've managed to come along and for us all to mix together, chat or whatever it is we 'kids' want to do, finishing her horrifically uninspiring speech with "and who knows what might happen, what will come of this and good luck everybody". Right now, I'm really wishing Brian magically alive and by my side as we'd be hysterically howling, ripping the piss out of her, this *Blue Peter*-like tawdry nonsense, 'n' very probably asked to leave. Sadly, he's not and I'm well 'n' truly stuck. Now sense I'm trapped in this sheep-pen, caught, there's a lot of clumsy bobbing about and nobody seems terribly at home with anything. Because it's the only thing making any sense at all, I invisibly sidle to the urn'd, biscuit'd trestle-table. Snobbishly ignoring the juggling balls, I gingerly help myself to a polystyrene cuppa tea 'n' bourbon cream. Now, what I normally do with any biscuit [it's a kid thing] is not initially dunk, but wave it over my steaming tea to slightly dampen the texture. Suffice to say, tea was lukewarm, therefore no steam, and my bourbon, like me, remained dry, very.

As at a wake, exactly as, the room fills with simmering murmuring noises and from what I can make out people seem to be shaking hands, nervously giggling, purposefully over-nodding, then quite suddenly moving on to whomever the next person might be. It's odd, looks like speed-dating without the flirting [definitely without the shag or indeed, speed]. Even the people I know are behaving like this, something I'd never seen them do before. Nobody seems in any way natural or at home with anything, looking more like the jagged illustrations of a first year art student animating a gang of hyperactive kids who've all just accidentally and at the same time shat themselves. The surface noise is confident, conversationally ebullient, but underneath [as always] the silent screams of the socially anxious and awkward. I'm generally not a socially anxious/awkward person, but feel instantly alone/distanced by all of this and seriously want to leave. I was about to slyly sneak off when a figure looking like a jumble sale recovering from a nervous breakdown hobbled expectantly toward me. Hat floppier than her dress, terrible BO, hand outstretched and in an easily mimicable atonal drawl she says to me, "My name's Siobhan and I play the synthesiser. What do you do?"

Suddenly the whole world slows, almost certainly stops and I'm drowning in freeze-frame, I genuinely can't work out what any of this means, what it's for or why it's happening. Not too sure how, but I instantly feel sorry for smelly jumble sale woman and completely know she doesn't want to talk any further. Then it dawns, she's been told to come here for her own good too, to connect with other likeminded people and furnish her five year plan… if she had five years. It's a gruellingly intense non-moment, obviously too much for her and certainly too much for me, so I very politely say, "My name's Gerry, Siobhan. I don't play the synthesiser, and I go." Then leave.

Never been to a network meeting since or am I going to go to one ever again. It might seem a little strong to say this, but I felt socially/creatively violated by that moment. For me, it was a sterile, too tense environment, leaden with faux anticipation and career neurosis, people penned-in, forced to be polite and accepting. It felt passive/aggressively policed by ideas 'n' ideals outside my own. I was used to the spin of clubbing, the socially combative anarcho-raucousness of boozing. My searing creativity often came from nights not remembered; this too-managed/mannered mirage was absolutely the wrong place for an artist like me. It was the first time I ever felt so severely distanced by something supposedly elevating/connecting art 'n' artists. Genuinely wish I could stop remembering how bourgeois dystopian it all seemed, feel it's given me middle-class PTSD. On sleepless nights I still get intense strobing flashbacks of giant Garibaldis attacking.

This was only the beginning, as The Bourgeois Zeitgeist would continue to create environments and schemes not suitable for artists like me. I'm now told Network Meetings are the 'only' place to be for anybody wanting to make it in the arts. Fine, things change, what can I do? I'm also told they've super-evolved 'n' are full of tuned-in 'networking hustlers', people who know exactly what to do 'n' say, whom to approach and why. I can't help thinking if this is now how art is, how it has to competitively operate, if it's in the hands of culture-spivs, then art is walking wounded on one crutch haphazardly sculptured from passive/aggressive whimsy. If only we could have kept 'networking' to simply meetings, that would've been OK. It feels to me taken out of the room and everywhere now, every platform, every screen, polite, needy mannered smiling, what I call 'extended networking'.

Manners, finance and control, the very ideals most of our middle-classes are born into, would soon become the proactive blueprint for almost everything creative. The semi-Marxist, anarcho-working-class, counter-cultural template I flourished under now largely gone. Without the street-defined powerhouse of those oft-confrontational energies, the bourgeois template was left to not only grow unchallenged, but dominate.

Now, this particular scenario may not have happened, think it a semi-dramatized illustration:

Two youngish Bourgeois Zeitgeist business people have a super-excitable business plan for a brand new kind of breakfast bar; they're going to call it 'Breakfast the World Over'. They're based in London and because there's so many London-Irish, floppy-quiff'd Nigel has a super-salivating menu idea. He excitedly spits at Elspeth, "Now get on this Els, can't think why any fucker hasn't come up with it before, y'ready hunz... To super-cater for that part of our growing demographic, to bring them in, make them feel mega-part of it all, more 'at home', yeah, why don't we serve full Irish

114

breakfasts on real dead navvies' shovels? Are you getting it Els, black 'n' white pudding, extra potatoes of course, are you getting it?" Elspeth, unable to contain her piss screams, "Yeah Nige yeah, what a super-rad idea! That'll definitely give Mews at Ken's continental cuisine for quizzical cats pause for thought. Oh my God Nige, oh my God, pause, paws, Paws for Thought, *Paws For Fucking Thought!*"

Of course, that's obviously me comedically riffing, but I genuinely think it could happen [indeed, has happened] and can only happen because nothing's there to stop them. They're The Bourgeois Zeitgeist and everything's societally on offer for them. If Nigel and Elspeth had come up with the full Irish breakfast on real dead navvies' shovels idea in 1976 then they'd have certainly been bludgeoned to death by real alive navvies' shovels and what's left of their sorry pallid carcasses fed to a pack of chained-up starving Alsatian guard dogs. Without the politicised ferocity of a once vibrant working-class template shoving a metaphorical brick in Nigel's mouth for even suggesting such a disgusting thing, the now out of control bourgeois template can fly absolutely free.

Being fair, I don't think all the middle-classes are aware of this power, not at all, that they are indeed the prevailing zeitgeist and have been for some time, particularly our buzz-fed Millennials. Let's be completely honest here, they've had over four decades of neoliberalist policy and opinion on-side. A gentrified Sussex village isn't a mining town relying solely on that industry to feed its family and community; it's where there are lots of very expensive antique shops, bankers and tea rooms. That gentrified Sussex village is the grandparenting Ealing Comedy ideal of a Britain dreamt up by accountancy and clotted creamed scones. The Bourgeois Zeitgeist is the welcomed bastard child of Thatcherism and world-consuming neoliberalism; Maggie a wonderful father, globalisation an insanely attentive accountancy-mutated mother.

When remembering the late sixties and early seventies of my childhood, the Benefits Street/Jeremy Kyle poverty porn culture of now was not the prevailing culture of then. Not saying there wasn't snobbery, it was everywhere, but a monied, confident working-class was able to spit in its eye because even if, just for a partying weekend, almost everybody was the same height. Nigel and Elspeth have grown up not knowing the confident working-class of old, perhaps confusing them with the ever-bourgeoning under-classes of now. Above all, Nigel and Elspeth are in the fortunate position to be able to afford *now*. Only ones who are.

Because The Bourgeois Zeitgeist is the only financially working template in town, of course young working/under-class peoples are attracted to it; it's the only prize left glittering. Where they're tarnished from isn't offering them anything, so what else can they do? In Manchester, where I still live, I often talk to young people, young Queer people in particular. To keep up with it they end up getting into disastrous amounts of debt. With young gay men it's about lifestyle, always was, what you're wearing being far more valid than who you are, that very necessary city centre apartment a must have... and even more importantly, drugs [cocaine ain't cheap]. With a call centre minimum wage and massive amounts of credit they can afford these things for a little while, but so many of them soon end up in deep financial shit, sometimes prostitution, or even on the street – the communities that may once have cushioned them long gone. Now, you might think this just lifestyle and always has been lifestyle; I think this is how lifestyle kills. Said it before 'n' I'll say it again, in fact I'll never stop saying it... only The Bourgeois Zeitgeist can truly live the dream, because it's their nightmare we're living in.

'Opportunity'... on its own a perfectly nice word, pleasantly open-ended, socially nuanced, somehow definite and yet notionally accessible. If The Bourgeois Zeitgeist has done anything, it's made me, without reservation, completely loathe

the word. Opportunity belongs to The Bourgeois Zeitgeist like no other thing, even more important to it than 'interest' – the financial kind. Opportunity is the blood-rushing surge of life-energy securing its next heartbeat and, of course, bank balance. Opportunity keeps it enigmatically 'distant', empowered, the throne it lords from, because – and let's face it – it's not a word belonging to the working/under-class, not a word you readily find spoken in foodbanks [and I should know]. Opportunity is the word 'carrot' in glamorously sequined drag and dangled in front of us from titanium fishing-rods rigidly held by The Bourgeois Zeitgeist. It's incalculable the number of times, even in the supposedly more liberal arts, I've seen/heard that word used to make people work cheaply or for free. Not only that, the people working cheaply or for free are then somehow put in this strange position where they're effusively thanking whoever it is for the 'opportunity' to work cheaply or for free; that it's indeed a super-brilliant 'opportunity' to have worked super-cheaply or for super-free because it'll look super-great on your CV. And saddest thing, it super-does... The Bourgeois Zeitgeist really has this super-shite super-sewn-up! I think of it as BDSM, but for employment, not pleasure. Actually, no, opportunity's not a glamorously sequinned drag-carrot dangled, it's a noose choking honesty 'n' decency from wherever/whatever the workplace. Nigel and Elspeth would most definitely bring the young London Irish in on work-experience, offering them the super-brilliant once in a lifetime 'opportunity' to serve full Irish breakfasts on real dead navvies' shovels in a heartless beat... after all hunz, it'd look mega-employable on their virgin résumés.

The Bourgeois Zeitgeist is not one person, class or group, it's everywhere, countrywide/worldwide and completely everything. Some of you will be screaming at me *you're just reverting to romantic working-class type and glibly redecorating neoliberalism, Gerry!* I would screech back *yes, it's born of Thatcherism and neoliberalism, but it's slyly much more than that. It's the melded aura of both, set free like an airborne fiscally virulent virus permeating and infecting all around, it is the dispirited of the age... and if I don't romance the working-class, who the fuck will!*

From my favourite book, Charles Dickens's *A Christmas Carol*, I'm made acutely aware of The Ghost of Christmas Present, a bravura bold opulent phantom, ermine/velvet enveloped, bushy long-bearded and thick-hair-curled. Endless striations of swollen-berried holly 'n' ivy are carelessly woven, garlanded gaily about the bursting vista of his voluminous frame. A booming behemoth of spirit whose bellowing earthen opera comforts as terrifies. He looms tall above us, like ten James Robertson Justices rolled into one, and authoritatively commands the moment, because for this particular shade the moment is always now. I'm recalling him pulling apart the draped, weighty drench of those rich, heavy robes and introducing our miserly Ebenezer Scrooge to the stinking, starving, hollow-eyed waifs of Ignorance and Want. Now, if I was ever to take it upon myself to write a present day Ghost of Christmas Present, instead of the gnarled howling whispers of wizened Victorian childhood once so graphically illustrated, the bone-shivering finalities of Ignorance and Want would be replaced by the twinkling teeth 'n' tits pizzazz of Inspirationalism 'n' Positivia. Like theatrical curtains parting, Inspirationalism 'n' Positivia, looking to the entire world like Fearne Cotton and Andi Peters, would spring forward, festival heart-finger'd, tightly lurex'd and with sparkling showbiz unison completely nail the routine, whatever the routine was, is, or might be. Then, before your wide-eyed bedazzlement, with a perfectly jazz-handed flourish, Inspirationalism 'n' Positivia would land in perfect fanny/cock-to-floor splits, always happy, always eager to please and, above all, always ready.

Beware Inspirationalism because she very rarely exists, but most of all beware Positivia, because at every 'opportunity' he'll try to convince you Inspirationalism does. Although born in a trunk at The Prince's Theatre, Inspirationalism 'n' Positivia are the culturally/socially uninhibited of the stage, because the stage is all theirs and for the taking.

Ee Bah Gum... The Debt Eaters Of Babylon, Chuck

Of course, you want to put it to one side,
lookin' t'other way's natural,
necessary.
Thing is, when you do,
arc, stretch neck,
outward bound 'n' opposite.
There's little reward in facing the same.
Knowing and forever knowing
the blame.

Young man,
doorway gravestoned,
sleeping bag drowning,
eyes wide,
beyond alone,
staring out oblivion.

On good days you don't see
sad things,
really, really bad things.
Sadder when it's 360 degrees,
even big freezes can't ice them out.
Puts a cap on that selfie pout.
Manchester, you carp on about Marx,
revolution, but afraid to turn your neck.
By 'eck, the wheel's twisted,
truth-blistered,
you've dispirited 'n' changed your tune.

Ey up luv, the rage,
no longer the rave,
while the bourgeois meat, greet, eat 'n' need
your debt.

Statuesque

Seriously,
you're dead right to tear me down.
I lie,
I've always lied,
they're there swirling around the rings
of my bronze.
I'm not a tree,
the truth,
no pockmark shade from me.
I'm the cold-faced steel of ego.

Untruth made solid,
immovable,
no bend-wind give 'n' take.
Bird-shit fake and blank-eyed,
no sculptor can successfully do teeth.
Really, there are better things to look at,
make,
communities for example.
Nothing's more statuesque than confident family.
Nothing taller than children's laughter.

Please, be doing me a favour,
a big favour,
pull me down,
my prejudice, my guns.
I lie, always lied.
Make room for the heart-beating,
the players,
games,
the enablers and drunks.

Several Gods

With their jolly on they dine,
several gods and laughter.
On seven strains of musicality
they're singing lives,
ending lives,
defending and upending lives.

Whoops there goes Britain,
whatever it was,
whatever it had become.
There goes all that alternative comedy
'n' unintelligible Jazz.
Several gods and their whims
tuning into beginnings,
improvising ends.

They burp like Charles Laughton
and do a monochrome drool.

Commercial Broken

Hard cell in sepia'd narration,
stanzas salve and soothe.
Crème de la crème trickle-up economics
and there lies truth.

I smile,
you smile,
we smile,
they smile,
cities quake 'n' crumble.
I smile,
you smile,
we smile,
they smile.

Through gritted teeth and patented while,
kitchen sink stanza'd, they soliloquise.
Emboldening the beautiful game, banks 'n' burgers,
dirty pieces of sliver.

Prize-eyed,
wide-eyed,
pie-eyed,
sly-eyed,
the golden shoot.
Prize-eyed,
wide-eyed,
Pie-eyed,
sly-eyed.

Fat cat entropy rancour,
infamy penny more for a pound.

There's climb, ladders 'n' medals,
pat on the head, sword on shoulder, the treat.

I believe somewhere
someone's doing it right.

The BOURGEOIS ZEITGEIST

A Treatise
by
Gerry Potter

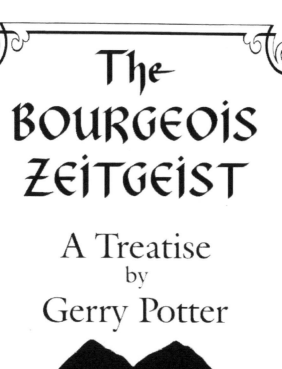

IV

So, eighteen months after Brian died, I left London and landed in the Manchester of 1997 [I think], and it was truly fabulous. I was still professionally Chloe Poems, gay socialist transvestite poet, gingham diva and voice of treason, an altered/altering ego of chequered bombast and poetical/polemical/political intent.

Our Ms Poems had done very well in Londinium, getting prestigious gigs and tons of publicity, so she fell into nineties Manchester something of a name. At that time, Chloe was an underground cabaret creation, more anti-showbiz avant garde than po-faced literary scene. Thankfully, the wildly eclectic spoken word scene of Manchester was anything but po-faced and stole my/her heart, 'n' very soon we both realised the gingham bitch wanted in.

Manchester of then had a startlingly vivid sprawl of poets: small ones, tall ones, some as big as your head. There's far too many to mention, but Dike Omeje, Marvin Cheeseman, Holden Caulfield/Mike Garry, Steve Lyons, Rev Porl, Tony Curry, Helên Thomas, Jo Warburton, James Quinn, Neil Bell, Shirley May, Fiona Bowker, Carol Batton, Dominic Berry, Martin Stannage and Manchester's very own lesbian vampire queen Rosie Lugosi spring instantly to mind. Not only were they differing shapes, ages, sizes and sexualities, they were all incredibly unique in style, not one sounding/looking like the other. They were a brilliantly feisty array of seriously 'out there' 'tudey performance poets making Ms Poems intensely aware she seriously had to raise her game. She, with her gingham X-ray vision, instinctively clocked Manchester really did have some of the greatest spoken word artists in the world. I had this lucky seventh son kinda feeling, like I'd landed slap bang middle in the middle of an underground golden age. Chloe covered Manchester like a wild gingham rash plonking herself firmly in the centre of it all. Wasn't long before that pesky gingham minx was creating her own scene. Based at the greenroom theatre she evolved 'n' hosted Slam Bam Thank You Ma'am and Manchester's first performance slam, The New Bohemia, both tremendous hits and instrumental in giving its then spoken word artists a wider platform and audience. She also teamed up with the miraculous Jayne Compton to create the underground sensation that was Club Brenda. Named after Brian's camp name, Brenda was a dance/ performance sensory overload of what downtown New York might have to offer. I remember so many outrageous nights at Brenda, particularly with our gorge anarcho-lesbian Elvis, the trees, the hallucinogenic stars and, of course, the dancing. Manchester's counter-culture was still blazing a fiery trail and very much this wonderful city's creative alternative.

It was around this time I was privy to conversations from certain arts bodies critiquing the counter-culture, calling it crude, amateurish and repetitive. In some small way it probably was, all counter-cultures are, but when flying it soared, taking everyone with it. All of an intuitive sudden, I couldn't quite shake the feeling it was somehow coming under a kind of snide intellectual attack. This was happening around the same time city centre living was exploding, loft-style accommodation and the like. Up to that point, Manchester city centre – and all city centres I knew – belonged to the many differing peoples of Manchester. I'm a big fan of the tribe, collections of whoever's colourfully populating their world, youth or whatever cultures, emboldened by the agency of the time 'n' space, *their* time 'n' space. Like a swarm they descended, locusts disguised as flamingos. The Bourgeois Zeitgeist was not only about to reclaim Manchester's city centre, gradually eliminating the tribe, but mould it into its own image. The Bourgeois Zeitgeist then/now so often complaining about noisy clubs, revelling partiers 'n' rowdy drunks, writing letters of complaint to local councils, threatening to, 'n' occasionally getting, places/venues shut down... nasty bastards! I firmly believe if you're going to move into somebody else's space, first 'n' foremost you have to respect the cultural vibes 'n' energies of said space and try your very best not to turn it into an orbital of Sussex. If you're going to be in somebody else's city centre, even if only occasionally, try to enter into the culture of that city centre. Perhaps just even one night a week pop into a local pub, not whine bar, to help keep that local pub afloat 'n' open.

Since the descent of The Bourgeois Zeitgeist, so much of Manchester's counter-culture has disappeared – clubs, bars, theatres turned into café bars, Tesco Metros, student accommodation or even more apartments, cells/hives for the dreary drone contingent of The Bourgeois Zeitgeist. What was once an earthen hot-pants hot-pot main of so many wildly flavoured ingredients was slowly turning into a very precise plate of grill-seared halloumi 'n' leaves with a light balsamic drizzle starter. Pretty much the same as what was/is happening to London's once fascinatingly interesting Soho. It was then I joined the dots: of course, certain arts bodies were critiquing the counter-culture, because a brand new demographic was hitting town... a demographic with a lot of money.

The Bourgeois Zeitgeist's absolutely everywhere and in absolutely everything. It's ferociously thriving in our corporate sectors, but I can only speak of it from my experience in the more liberal arts world, where it's not so ferocious but still exists. I don't think The Bourgeois Zeitgeist liberal, I think its origin story inherently right wing. We can even convince ourselves we're Labour supporters, hard core socialists, surface anarchists [and may well be], but the politics of manners, finance and control are not hard-core socialist or anarchic. From the year 2000 onwards, I would see the barbarity of finance strip the visceral creativity from art, stop its irregular improvisational heartbeat.

Certain arts bodies had been brewing the idea that training emerging artists to become their own 'accountants' was a brilliantly progressive way to further things, particularly their 'individual' careers. Being from a background of manners, finance and control, you can clearly see where they're organically coming from, but art for me, particularly counter-cultural art, isn't and *never has been* about manners, finance or control. Unlike this new upcoming wave of artists, the counter-culture didn't spend huge swathes of its valuable drinking/ dancing time obsessing on receipts. Up until 2000, I'm pretty sure I'd never heard an artist even say the word receipt, never mind have near nervous breakdowns about them. If you're unfortunately born into the culture of manners, finance and control, 'receipt' will probably have been your first word closely followed by 'momma', 'pie chart' and then 'five year plan'. The wider, more impacting darkness would be the creative apartheid about to engulf our arts worlds, the unfair separation of who could and who couldn't – by that I mean complicated forms and the indecipherable bafflegab of arts-speak. Yes, there seemed more money for individual artists, great, really great and I do mean that, but you had to be seriously trained by these certain arts bodies to get it; there were a lot of elaborate new hoops to intricately jump through.

Because there's only a bourgeois template in successful societal operation, I absolutely get, for survival's sake, artists really do have to approach certain arts bodies for money. With the continuing erosion of our counter-cultures where else can they go? The thing is, to fill in the forms you probably have to be able to read 'n' write, to converse fluently in arts-speak. You have to be able to socially/confidently engage. What if you can't? What if you want a career in the arts, education's hopelessly failed you and your familial/community background's left you thinking you're irreversibly unable? Incredibly serious question here, where do *these* people go? With a fully-functioning counter-culture you don't have to be able to read 'n' write. If you could do a turn or watch/listen, you'd be open-door welcome whatever your class or educational ability and usually [not everything works for everybody] immediately engulfed by it. I don't think big plush offices, power-dressed arts officials, complicated arts-speak and reams of near impossible mathematically-based form-filling will be attracting our creative under-class along in a hurry, do you?

It's funny isn't it, these certain arts bodies now have huge expensive seminars about how to attract the working 'n' under-class, about how middle-ground, predictable and safe our arts scenes have become... What really boils my piss is it's those same arts bodies who created these scenes in the first place. Their great big idea to engage the working/under-class is to have terminally dull networking seminars about people who are societally unable to engage in network meetings. The recursive, entitled/privileged idiocy of this speaks for itself, Schrödinger's arts scene. Perhaps these seminars are created to simply get them out of their offices to another town [Brighton's nice], drink a load of concessionary plonk, nab a free hotel and with what's left of their 'perdayums' perhaps indulge in an occasional huge-cocked BDSM prostitute. No wonder the arts world is in ongoing class stasis if its big, supposedly far-reaching ideas are even more sterile networking meetings and cherry-picking people who can fill in the fucking forms. And I stress here that this comes from experience, the people who can actually fill in the forms and naturally lean towards the detailed logic of accountancy might not necessarily make the best artists. Believe me, I've seen a lot of very dull art. The arts are incredibly same-signal these days – not all of it, there's still some very good shit out there, but there's a lot of tiresome, uncreative repetition.

From a poetry-scene perspective, there's been an unbearable deluge of what I call dreary Bourgeois Zeitgeist white hip-hop. There are some fine practitioners of this particular art-form, of course there are, not saying there isn't, but Christ-on-a-bike there's so much dross. Nothing's cornered 'same-signal' art quite like the current poetry scene.

Now, you might love her and that's cool, but I can take or leave Kate Tempest, not my cuppa Earl Grey. But I do recognise her uniquely talented spirited spin on who she is and what she does, she's the absolute pinnacle of it, a great talent, top of her game 'n' very deservedly so. Personally, I think her a one-trick pony, but it's a great trick, and let's face it one great trick's all anybody needs – ask Norman Wisdom. She undoubtedly touches so many people's minds/hearts/lives with her work and that is truly wonderful... unless the people's minds/hearts/lives she's touched decide to become poets.

A few of years ago I was seriously considering a move back to London [I love and miss London] and very nearly did. I spent quite a bit of time there casing the joint, looking at its poetry scene – and it was its poetry scene putting me off relocating. There are some wonderful poets in London, brilliant in fact, some of the country's finest, my favourites, but it's surface-blanketed by so many sound-a-likes 'n' all-out mimickers I was honesty repelled by it. The poetry scenes I knew, particularly when first landing in Manchester, were a delightful, occasionally scary, smorgasbord of sound, tone, age, 'tude 'n' shape, not one poet looking or wanting to be like another. Granted, there was the odd too-stoned/too-pissed John Cooper Clarke-ian hogging the mic, but thankfully were few and far between [I'm a huge fan of Clarkey, by the way].

Not every Manchester poet was good, there was some going-nowhere-crap – poetry scenes the world over are infamous for their going-nowhere-crap – but even the bad ones had some individuality. I'm quite old now and that could very well be the main reason I found the London poetry scene far too young, those young poets being too cloned from Kate Tempest. I got so bored of seeing/hearing terribly earnest/concerned young people, gesticulating hands held waist high, faces pretending they've never known wealth, telling me in a dreary Bourgeois Zeitgeist white hip-hop style they'd just split up with their girlfriend/boyfriend and how said girlfriend/boyfriend didn't understand them. Yeah, yeah, yeah, boys are socialised mean, yadda, yadda, yadda, girls are witchcraft strange! I was sat there completely understanding the poet's girlfriend/boyfriend, clearly seeing why they wouldn't want to go anywhere near a whiny narcissistic bore sounding like a twelfth-rate Kate Tempest... and c'mon, let's face it, at eighteen all you're gonna do is split up with each other! Then there was the whole world-peace shit, the one-love festival heart-fingers ballad – I, without reservation, abhor festival heart-fingers [I feel they act as a Bourgeois Zeitgeist forcefield, keeping all the negativity out and the Inspirationalism 'n' Positivia in] – and social urban turmoil sonnet, a never-ending litany of what Katie Tempest just did. Saddest thing with all this tedious repetition was I could tell there were some potentially great wordsmiths at play, some lovely poetry going on, but it was subsumed by clear vocal impersonation and somebody else's literary technique, a kind of modern day, supposedly urban, far more urbane, *Mike Yarwood Show*.

What completely put me off moving back was one young bloke, possibly nineteen tops, really well-to-do, upper middle-class, maybe just upper. He comes on stage, hands held waist high, the usual earnest *my face has never known a penny* routine, and proceeds to tell us about a horrifically difficult time in his life. Honestly, tone of his voice came across so sombre, the weighty sadness of its breaking timbre suggesting to me parental/sibling death or perhaps he himself may have a terminal disease. No, he was recalling a very difficult moment from his recent exams where his father told him if he didn't pass them he wouldn't get a car... no word of a fucking lie! He then proceeds to tell us in a dreary Bourgeois Zeitgeist white hip-hop style the success story of narrowly passing his exams and how that indeed nailed him his first Porsche. The cunt even does festival heart-fingers on the word 'Porsche'. I thought the audience would've balked at this [I nearly threw up]. Couldn't be wronger! He got all the applause, whoops 'n' frenetic finger-clicks they could collectively muster. Not only that, the poem was absolutely shit and given to us in a vocal delivery clearly not belonging to him; the way he was using words and his clunky physicality were so divorced from each other, it was like watching Play-Doh try to jive. No sooner had he left the stage someone came on and did the exact same patter, exact same face, exact same hands held exact same waist high... but this time about climate change. Just the night before I'd been brutally subjected to a gang of largely teenage dreary Bourgeois Zeitgeist white hip-hoppers telling me if I could only reach inside and forgive/love myself more, I'd become a much better human being... WOW! Right, so there I am, a fifty-three year old world Queery gay man, who's seen most of his immediate family die, lived/lost big time through the AIDS epidemic and then some... and then a lot more! Who are these similar sounding kids telling me if I really tried, genuinely tried mind, no half-measures here, I should reach inside myself and if I could only muster enough personal courage, self-belief, pull out a much better me? They don't even know the actual 'me' sitting there, completely aghast at their formless unintellectually unstructured arrogance, so how can they possibly know somewhere 'deep inside' there's a much better model? Aha, I may have it wrong here, perhaps by the look on my terminally bored icy face they realise the real 'me' can't stand another single nano-second of what they're saying and they're desperately trying to coax out a 'much better me' who just might. Well, I can assure them, if I'd reached inside and found that much better me, that 'much better me' would've screamed "Take a long time out and find much better you's!"[1]

I remember thinking *why is this kind of piss-poor juvenilia so at the forefront of London's poetry scene, it certainly never used to be and who's teaching them this crap?* And then I realised, this seemingly unstoppable deluge of same-signal poetry has had to come from the workshop.

---

[1] There was a brilliant skit by Cardinal Burns of Channel 4 fame about these 'urbane street poets' I thought would see them off... it very sadly didn't. It's a bit of incisive genius worth YouTubing/seeking out.

Give Narcissus A Break

Give Narcissus a break, just being young for fuck's sake,
a far flung, well-hung vanity case.
A bloke being used,
like Jesus, like Gandhi,
Rodney Bewes.
A bloke weft open 'n' woven over,
spun to spin archaic views of how we should behave,
who we should be.

See, Narcissus is a Queer story,
a tale to steer away from, a lost plot,
grim-gory, a hoary Henry, hot.
Narcissus had got the lot and that will never do.
Nobody should scale their station,
find wiggle room in their striation.
This is about constipation of control,
rage of the old and patrician,
conditioning, repositioning their thrust.
Doom the cocksured robust, they must be demeaned,
created, recreated, berated, not seen.

Narcissus probably got it right –
by lake and night light
we're all changed by moonbeams.
We're all beauteous subtle in mind's-eye,
silent schemes of stardom and silver screens.
Narcissus just said it, saw his face and read it,
but no one gives him credit for honesty.
Too busy colluding in false modesty,
hiding behind 'not worthy' and 'help me'
while using their lake to take another selfie.

Sold

Do the smile,
half-breathy laugh,
laugh suggesting knowing,
like you know a little more,
just that little more,
than the rest of us.

Do the mannequin stance,
the pose,
more camera-friendly,
subtlety more persuasive.
Makes you angular,
passive yet powerful,
a little God with a human complex.

Moist eyes speak volumes,
reminisces sing,
lit nostalgic and still be young,
be the longing shadows of our fathers.
You can be safety of memories,
fair to middling.
Be a parent to your child,
wrapped the nappies they've sold destroying the world.

The Waiting

In stops, starts,
juddering chugs of *boom boom POW!*
Exploding hearts, shopping spree 'n' dingbat,
too precious, golden momentums
slip-streaming.
They're my shadows,
1979, sixes 'n' heaven'd,
slim and cheekboned, awe-lined in mirrors.
I'm ugly-vain and beautifully afraid.
Adventures treasured are thigh-jacked,
slim-hipped, bejewelled.

Too busy for The Waiting,
sitting in corridor'd nothing.
I've feet, an audience, arse and dick.
Everything I need,
onslaught and gravity, electrifying depravity,
I've portals on hold, what's a job?
These extremes will be the best of me,
bring it on, up, around.

Caught out, stretched,
years gallop a hot trot.
I'm a riot, we all are.
City-scape's aflame,
burnt, in photos, embers,
black, white 'n' blistering.
The Waiting's next door but one,
uninvited.
Glass to the wall,
cunt's fuckin' listening.

Nonsensica

I thought it being fatherless,
thought it death,
thought it both longevity and poverty of breath,
I thought it pain,
unbearable heaviness of winter rain.

I thought it thinking,
thought it sinking,
thought it instant eternities in between blinking,
I thought it crazed,
unblissible minutes cutting up days.

I thought parody,
trick,
thought schtick,
diced,
twice.

I thought it distant,
thought it close,
thought it bedazzling combinations of both,
I thought it lost,
penniless in cascading cataclysms of cost.

The
BOURGEOIS
ZEITGEIST

A Treatise
by
Gerry Potter

V

There's an impassioned Bourgeois Zeitgeist out-of-all-control zeal to try to bring poetry to the masses I neither have, nor want. Afraid I'm a smidge cliquey, a bit closed shop about poetry and think it somewhat creatively short-sighted. I see poetry as more organically fluid, a bit of a find and not necessarily something to be imposed, as it's an oft' peculiar language and not everybody's cup of tea. Workshops are great, introduce people to poetry that way by all means, but don't suggest you or they have somehow failed if workshop attendees simply can't be arsed. Some people will never like poetry... get over it and – most of all – yourselves! It's no accident the rise 'n' rise of the workshop completely coincides with the rise 'n' rise of the drearily plodding same-signal poet.

There's something about performance poetry in particular I believe must be found, excavated 'n' devoured. Sometimes you need to undertake a very physical/emotional/personal journey to vocation, it can't always come to you. For example, I don't think Googling 'Goth' makes you a Goth, I think going to a dank sweaty hair-lacquered stinking death-metal music-pumping nightclub and miserably body-banging with other Goths makes you a Goth. There are certain things you just can't get from a workshop you can only glean from being physically there, wherever/whenever physically there is or was. A workshop can't give you the gut-rushing learning thrill being at a mid-seventies Twisted Wheel John Cooper Clarke gig could; it can't give you that uniquely mind-bending life-changing frisson. Let's face it, a workshop doesn't sell you drink, drugs and wildly drunken fuck with you in a badly graffiti'd toilet... sadly, not in my experience. I think you can learn more by 'n' from the powerful osmosis of atmosphere rather than the droning prose of telling 'n' re-telling – sometimes teaching's in the air. Telling and re-telling can work, of course it can, but there's a palpable, pulsing body-poetry boom-banging in being 'on site'. When you take an actual journey you're making a whole load of exciting, thrilling and possibly precarious decisions [yup, you might die]. You're not sat in a safe-spaced sterile environment with a middle-class voice telling you how wonderfully super-awesome poetry and you are. OK, I'm patronisingly generalising, things have changed, now even working-class voices can tell you how wonderfully super-awesome poetry and you are. In the same way, contained sterile networking meetings can't give you the vibrant blood-pumping life-thrust of a city's true energy or ethos, perhaps contained sterile poetry workshops might not give you the beat. Boxing clever doesn't mean boxed in, it sometimes actually means hands-bloodied boxing; it isn't all manners, finance and control. Orders quite clearly order, it's often polite and not terribly interesting. The only thing I would insist on is all venues must be made accessible, with badly graffiti'd accessible toilets to wildly drunken fuck in.

The other thing about workshops and this is good and bad, is they give poets much needed work and I really get that. Good, because money absolutely means life, 'n' bad, because I've heard this on many different occasions:

"I've got so many workshops coming up and so much preparation to do, I haven't written a poem in ages."

Well done The Bourgeois Zeitgeist, really, that's fabulous, money for poets is great, but can't you see the distancing? Poets are now becoming distanced from their own poetry.

I'm not saying stop workshops, not at all, but I think there may be too many and they're creating far too many sound-alikes. Brian and I both hailed from drama workshopping backgrounds, The Everyman Youth Theatre giving us our sparkling confidence and chaotically shimmering vocation. Thing with the Everyman experience, yes, we were a group of young people together, but we weren't being shown how to be exactly the same as one another, in truth the very opposite. Drawn from our own unique personalities 'n' experiences, we were collectively given 'us', our individual styles 'n' selves. We were then thrown like camp, screeching Christians into a glorious lion's den of electrically 'n' eclectically-vibed counter-culture. Can't help thinking, because so many people are her, is there a 'How to be Kate Tempest Workshop' ripping through London like the Great Fire? I'm constantly told the poetry scene's the most successful it's ever been [financially, The Bourgeois Zeitgeist would love that, think of the receipts]. That's as maybe, 'n' bloody well done the poetry scene, but it really is about how you define success. I think huge swathes of it are in a creative nadir, fuelled by unthought-through repetitive juvenilia and very obvious imitation. I very seldom go to poetry gigs these days because of that, so here's hoping beyond hope it's changed. People keep telling me it has, but I'm still far too frightened 'n' emotionally scarred to venture 'n' find out, they've given me a kind of poetry gig agoraphobia. I'm most certainly not the only poet thinking this, I have conversations like these with many other practitioners, but I'm probably one of the few saying it out loud, writing it down and willing to honestly document my personal experiences 'n' opinions of it. If right now is the most successful poetry's ever been then I'm afraid I don't see it, I think there's a touch of re-branding going on... all I see is 'The Emperor's New Poetry Scene'.

Poetry's very big business right now and has been for some time, manners, finance and control being its dynamic new USP. As you can tell, I'm not too enamoured by the spoken word 'industry' at the mo. Bizarrely though, I've never enjoyed being a poet as much. It's something you never stop growing into and perhaps more vocational about it than ever. My distance from the more Bourgeois Zeitgeist aspects of it happened when, a few years ago, two hundred writers/poets where invited to Buckingham Palace to perform an open mic for the Queen and

Prince Philip. Being the still very proud author of 'The Queen Sucks Nazi Cock' [Chloe's biggest hit], you can readily see I'm not only poetically anti-monarchy, but also infamously 'n' historically politically. Two things really bugged me:

1) Some of the poets who attended this 'do' where self-declared, Left-leaning republicans, hmmm! Now, please tell me if I'm somehow getting this a tiny bit wrong, but if you're a Left-leaning republican isn't the last gig you'd want is to do a royal hoop-licking open mic at Buckingham Palace? Surely you'd rather burn said royal hoops with a red-hot poker and then their palace down! Well, this and many other poets big-time loathed that occasion, finding it not only politically demeaning to modern performance poetry, but historically offensive. Must say I loved the internet stink 'n' storm it created; at last, proper creative confrontation [genuinely felt shit, like the seventies], something The Bourgeois Zeitgeist hates and all scenes intellectually need... I may have had a newly filed re-gemmed acrylic or two in that.

2) They performed an open mic. Now, this may not be your understanding of open mic and again please tell me if I'm wrong. I'm thinking open mics' creative platform's forged by the very poorest of our American spoken word communities to give not only voice, but necessary empowered visibility to both the plight and artistry of said impoverished communities. Open mics/slams becoming the heart, soul 'n' soil of the largely multi-cultural working/under-class voice. So, where does the incalculable opulence of Buckingham fucking Palace and its stinkingly rich, politically dodgy occupants fit into that history? More importantly, why do you want to bring them into that history – what's in it for you, a new kitchen? One of the poets in attendance was made very famous by a poem about urban latch-key kids; I've always wondered, did they do that particular piece in a

building with two hundred empty palatial bedrooms and in a mutated vocal style 'borrowed' from those first open mics 'n' slams? Don't think I have to point out the obvious ironies inherent here, or do I? As a writer you're most definitely 'told' to show not tell, but perhaps some folk actually do need telling. I also wonder if, after they'd been to a 'How to be Street Workshop', they then popped into a 'How to Perform in Front of the Queen' workshop? Wouldn't surprise me – they're completely workshop and Queen crazy. After all, there may be a certain forelock-tugging, cap-doffing knack to career bowing 'n' scraping one can only glean from an over-detailed, clearly-defined, terribly organised workshop.

In some small way, me and artists like me have for decades been contributing to the modern day spoken word scene. Particularly as Chloe, and largely in Manchester, I ran many performance poetry nights. Along with a host of other anarcho-republicans we used our 'agency' and did our bit for a fairer, more politically even world. There are many reasons I hate all Royal Families and billionaire hierarchies. The biggest reason is division – there is no greater darker poetic division than a hereditary, non-democratically elected feudal monarchy. Because it came from a largely spoken word ethos, I can't help but feel betrayed/distanced by events like these. Without discussion, big organisations use their 'agency' to recreate a poetry moment I personally politically oppose. It appears all agency is equal, but some agency is far more equal than others. No wonder they didn't discuss it with me, or poets like me, as we'd have used our agency to say *NO!*

Remember, no matter how welcoming it appears on the surface, The Bourgeois Zeitgeist has manners, finance and control pouring out of its very passive/aggressive arse; it'll be those questionable qualities soon finding themselves on the telly. I don't give two high-flying bourbons or hang-gliding Garibaldis how people get by, survival is just so important and I genuinely understand big bucks recompense really helps. Poets need to eat, buy Evian, garlic peelers, any number of Rescue Remedies, holiday in Greece, replace already perfectly well-equipped kitchens and some of them even have families to spoil. Coming from a creative environ accustomed to, even welcoming critique [and as an oft' critiqued poet myself], I feel compelled to offer my personal/political view on the current craze of poetry adverts on the goggle-box. Spoken word's all over it at the mo, from McDonald's, huge sporting events, through to building societies, poetry's blazing an incredibly capitalist trail, an incredibly capitalist trail not setting me on fire... and I'll tell you for why.

Couple of years ago I was tentatively approached by a certain professional body to maybe be part of an exciting new advertising campaign to basically sell something I opposed. Even before they would have checked me out and said no, I immediately said to myself "No". And profoundly glad I did. The advertising campaign it became really disappointing, with poets known/unknown plucked from our scenes 'n' placed in very clichéd twee situations; it was manners, finance and control taken to its safest place. Manners because most of the poetry was so accommodatingly polite, often sounding thematically jingoistic. Finance because it was literally spoken literature selling finance at the height of politically dominating austerity. Control because the poets are being media controlled and selling financial control to the viewers watching. My critique is two-fold: although some nice moments [in real life, some of these poets are truly fab], generally the poetry wasn't very good; it of course had to be inanely broad for the buying public to attach itself to. After all, cleverly dumbing-down's where advertising flushes, sorry flourishes – I give you Kenneth Williams's joyfully voiced Bloo Loo [which was actually better than a lot of the poetry]. Also, the tip-toeing placid, mild-mannered, really 'together' aura of the poets involved gives a not very accurate view of the poetry world. The poets I know are anything but mild-mannered, together and placid. Seriously, when watching those adverts all I can see is a reimagined sepia version of someone with severe glaucoma's Wimbledon. They're so contentedly cosy and deliberately inoffensive I don't think anybody would notice if they put bowels of strawberries 'n' cream in those things instead of poets [yes, I said bowels]. The people who might be attracted to our poetry scenes by these adverts could well be expecting to see a genteel, be-seated Cliff Richard suddenly leap up like an aged lamb 'n' spring into an acapella arms swingin' version of 'Living Doll'. The idea poets are benign conduits of fiscal apathy and rose-tinted nostalgia are images 'n' archetypes not sitting too well with poets like me, who are anything but. Again… the distancing.

The Bourgeois Zeitgeist bodies controlling poetry see these adverts as a huge success, but then there is something indelibly, Britishly, bourgeois about them. A bit like those patronising old Hovis adverts with the little northern boy cycling down a misty cobbled hill. In all historical reality that little northern boy delivering bread [accompanied by the local colliery brass band] was probably starving, perhaps had rickets, polio, a calliper and not given enough money by his employers [if he was given money at all] to buy an actual loaf. Funny how things change but slay the same. These poets are desperately trying to sell mortgages, the beautiful game 'n' burgers to people who at the same time may be having their homes, playing fields repossessed, swimming pools shut down and/or are a single parent setting off with the family to a local foodbank. In the depths of such crippling governmental austerity, passively/aggressively selling finance – and *all* advertising is aggressive marketing – is not really the best look for spoken word. In the future, and poetically looking back, I think historically/politically these adverts will not hold up terribly well.

I'm a pesky confident outsider understanding the many genius moments historically inherent in underground culture. I see those genius underground moments as authentic intellectually sculptured achievement. Because of where I'm from, I can't help thinking poetry becoming Capitalism's bitch isn't really that clever or indeed successful. But then, like I just said… I am pesky.

Just one more moment of big bucks poetry scene Bourgeois Zeitgeist manners, finance and control I really must share. Yonks ago, as Chloe Poems, I'm gigging a big gig and very happy to be part of all of this, was excitedly waiting for it to start. Before the event began I was politely ushered to one side and told by an incredibly well-spoken organiser if I were to go over my allotted time, for every minute overrun a pound would be taken from my fee. They then in an exceptionally mannered, gently threatening way told me a very famous poet got a whole eight pounds deducted from his fee last month and I really wouldn't want that to happen, would I? I immediately felt I was being confronted by a rubbish East End gangster carved from shadow, whisper and Received Pronunciation apology.

Chloe got a whole twenty-two pounds deducted from her fee that night. No cunt uses manners and finance to control me!

You're Absolutely Right To Feel Sorry For Yourself

Perhaps the moment's too much,
too dense,
past tense leaden,
perhaps not pretending's right.
Only so much shite can be tolerated,
Positivia is so often constipated,
chock full of uptempo banal.
Snarl,
rage,
be angered by what is.
Cunts take the piss thinking they can cure you,
assuming you want to be cured;
cunts think what you emotionally own isn't yours,
cos they've read in a book,
seen in the cards;
cunts think rose quartz crystals are the whole nine yards.
You're the wounded,
the broken,
cunts are asleep, you're the woken.
It's your brink you're tottering on,
cunts stink of waffling on.
Oh but they're being kind,
cast a rune,
cunts whistle soothing whale tunes.
Heads up their arse, popping out too soon.
You're the mental, the sane,
reeling in pain,
you're right to feel sorry for yourself,
right to know what is and isn't help.
It's you in there,
screaming inside,

it's you rocking 'n' creaking,
fucked 'n' freaking.
No 'splain from anybody
should stop you from speaking
or not speaking your talk,
limping your walk.

You're your library
of your books,
no one else's two fucks matter,
you're right to be selfish, rattle 'n' clatter,
cunts gather like dust on your shelf.
You're absolutely right to feel sorry for yourself.

Tony Wilson Says

The very last Manchester Mardi Gras, 1999 I think, before it became Gayfest 'n' then Pride. Manchester Queers at the very forefront of LGBTQ+ visibility and politics. From the Clause 28 march to its incredible end of festivities Vigil, a remarkable 'n' out there, deeply caring community, of which I'm über-proud to be a small and imperfectly malformed part. Anyway, as Chloe Poems and I've been hosting/performing on the main stage all weekend, I'm in the last portion of the main stage event and decide to do 'The Queen Sucks Nazi Cock'. An amazing moment met by the 8,000-strong crowd with huge, raucous revolutionary support... and to top it all, introduced by Tony Wilson.

The Ghost of Phyllis Pierce is a purple haired ancient matriarch
and I'm following someone in Her Majesty the Queen drag.
Poetry doesn't get much weirder than this.
It's in the stars and the sky's about to fall.
I've already danced with Gwen Dickey,
she got me up to 'Car Wash'.
Dropped my fifth E and about to go back on.
Risk taking's easy when you're off your head.
Tony Wilson introduces
and him saying my name is nostalgia fireworks.
Crowd cheer like they know me,
I certainly know them,
in so many ways,
had loads of 'em:
they're Manchester gays.

I say, "This is called 'The Queen Sucks Nazi Cock'."
Mouths drop, there's some booing.
I win them,
over 'n' over 'n' over again.
Power of performance thunders
that with E I'm invincible.

A gingham blur, diva,
the boom-boom banging voice of treason,
a toxic intoxicated power-flounce of reason.
There's magic to anarchy, a freaking shamanarchy,
people know when it's been set free.
Tinder-boxing Canal Street,
it so loves sparking reverie.

I finish,
I flourish,
they're their approval soaring,
some still booing.
The Ghost of Phyllis Pierce grabs my hand and gravels,
"Fabulous Chloe!"
On stage and applauding,
Tony Wilson says,
"Well, that definitely wasn't the third way was it?"
and I'm in Heaven for a while.

Come On

Come on,
want it to happen,
needs to.
The victory of elevation,
our thinking clearer.
Money, smoke and its freezing fog,
clogs,
coughs,
splutters up such tactless phlegm.
We're too sticky,
clots stuck in muds of finance.

Come on,
move on,
away from the promises of debt.
Half-hearted and attacked,
fallen by the wayside,
too bogged down by efficiency of work.
As quagmires go, this bitch is a doosey.

Come on,
rise,
out from the shadows into the fire.
We're better than this.
Come on!

The Weathered Mapped

I am false fire, literature's Hiroshima,
blown out, bowled over,
bowel-splayed and shit-stained.
See me, don't see me, whenever the day has wronged.
I'm not here, where you thought treasure,
where you wrought pleasure, where you buried hope.
Walking bleeds me narrative,
happiest in punctuation of rain.

I am old horse, broken, whisperless, worn,
tales told by wags, forgotten.
Groping for luck amongst cocksure arses,
spat on fingers and horseshoe tattoos,
many hands make light.
I'd shoot myself if I was someone else,
polish the barrel, finish it off.
Drunk, I'm the person I always was,
ask the rent boys, stolen phones.
Best when I'm shot-glass'd 'n' married.

I am non-sky, cloudbound,
my rain aches, refuses.
Hopeless smoke between Satanic chimney 'n' God.
My prayers fuck, moan, end in a little light re-grief.
Looking at nothing and knowing everything,
something the hopeless and ignored do.
We're geniuses of gobshite,
can wank melody, cum snow.

Outside, world sighs,
blowing itself apart.

The Elephant, Man

He's in the room, all our rooms,
bulbous, ugly and ornament.
If we could reflect, be mirrored,
we would.
Be pictures, dreams,
written down,
framed 'n' ageing.

In the room,
with others dressed, top-hatted,
white tight and ragged.
We're all opera,
it's staging.
It's us in the room,
over-gesticulating, whiplash-circusing.
Bosom-heaving 'n' out there,
bouquet-waving scented goodbyes.

Elephant men in the room,
question-less, posturing,
broken-boned, tangle-spined,
limp in the lifeless.
Trunk born in,
bundled,
maybe kidnapped.

Invisible Career

I have an invisible career,
hides in 'n' out my opinion,
my social prejudice,
my working-class confidence.

It's a slippery shadow, wet by storm,
by pouring drain,
by slate-steel grid.
You can see my invisible career,
guttered
in the amphetamin'd amphitheatre of sewers.
Personally, don't mind rats as audience,
rats have always been audience.
You can't know everyone and why.

My invisible career rewards,
I drop into conversation
"statuesque as ornament".
People nod, like they can see it,
like they can pick it up and spiel.
I talk down their talking-up,
it's what my invisible career would want.
It's not greedy,
never,
just understands shortcomings.

My invisible career sits collapse-shelved
on muttering terms with dust.
Is terrified of somebody else's spotlights
and shop bought chamois leather.

Tie The Knot, Spin The Wheel

Even the bunting's rejoicing,
breeze-weaving all over the shop,
ribbon'd pompoms are parping True Britannia.
Smiles on our faces glow wider than the Thames,
brighter than nightlife.

There's a street party with our blame on,
a Jack waiting to be waved.
One of those moments even poverty makes sense.
Little bits of jelly,
red, white 'n' blueberry jus frosted cup-cakes,
pissed-up ass-pinching dads.

Entropy occasionally needs glitter,
a little diamond mined.
A rosette spin of the wheel.
Less understanding of need.
We can all rejoice, a mixed-race princess
will be wearing blood-red rubies,
sparkle-dug or stolen
by colonial murder, rape and greed.

The
BOURGEOIS
ZEITGEIST

A Treatise
by
Gerry Potter

VI

When arriving back in Manchester, I joyfully discovered the steely, make-do 'n' improvisationally hard-graft resilience of Studio Salford. For those of you who don't know, Salford's a neighbouring city seamlessly blending into Manchester [well, I say seamlessly, there's still a polite warring going on, a war of the put-out noses]. Studio Salford was everything I wanted – more than that, everything I remembered theatre to be: fearless, experimental, organic, creatively argumentative, largely working-class, really pissed-up, often off its head and, most importantly, of the community. A caucus of remarkably gifted peoples coming together with fuck-all else but a big idea, a joint, a pint, always a ciggie 'n' [if you're really lucky] a line. Creating theatre about the area and worlds beyond, subject matter completely belonging to and of its writers, actors 'n' directors. Housed upstairs in The King's Arms pub, Studio Salford would Salford/Mancunian-flourish, giving new, emerging and well-experienced theatre practitioners not only work [often brilliant new work], but a buzzing, thriving, multi-skilled theatrical community. Bloody well done James Foster, Cathy Crabb, Mike Heath, Stella Grundy, Elizabeth Poole Morrison, Neil Bell, Cellan Scott, Sue Wormsley, Jen Williams and everybody initially involved in this spit-fighting, generously charged venture... genius!

I remember thinking the atmosphere they created was so solidly dynamic, a chaotically tangible sense it belonged to histories of peoples'-theatre and performance. In the traditions of politicised working-class Unity Theatres of old, Studio Salford enriched not only the creative landscape of both cities and, without a penny to its name, thrust them forward. So many productions performed and pouring from that gregariously courageous ethos, productions that will be communally remembered for a very long time. I put on my play *Miracle* at

Studio Salford and it was a huge impacting hit; it remains one of my very favourite experiences of living here.[2] Being too mannered, financed 'n' controlling wouldn't so much have been looked-down upon, but probably met with some savvy incisive suspicion because this company was the very antithesis of that. Studio Salford towered above everything; it was solidly about the unknowns of creativity, the striking volatility of moments and making those moments vibrantly happen. These theatrically scally troubadours were unafraid and thrived off risk, something The Bourgeois Zeitgeist would be sooner be rid of, something it would rather eliminate as risk costs money.

Like a mixture of the Carry On team, The Bash Street Kids and The Royal Shakespeare Company, with more than an anarchic sprinkling of the Joan Littlewoods, the revengers assembled in this rickety studio-theatre were crafted from a confidently politicised rage, coupled with surreal comedic blasts of hyper-spun reality. How very Salford! Shows simply got put forward 'n' chosen, were often quickly rehearsed and just put on. Without the wearisome, dithering, scratchy sharings of other theatres, Studio Salford exhibited a ballsy up-tempo confidence The Bourgeois Zeitgeist could only dream of. And all this without the merest hint of Inspirationalism 'n' Positivia. Studio Salford would probably have taken Inspirationalism 'n' Positivia around the back of The King's Arms and proper knuckle-duffed 'em up.

Here was a thriving concrete-paved/working-class domestic-fantastic vibe reaching out and wonderfully unsullied by the over-cautious, let's try it out 'n' see if it has legs, obsessive developmental-mentality of The Bourgeois Zeitgeist... Studio Salford was fuckin' Punk man! Without doubt, the greatest theatre company in the world.

It naturally inspired so much too, in particular the brilliantly expansive 24-7 theatre festival. This superbly grass-rooted festival felt very much seeded 'n' propagated in Studio Salford's soil. 24-7: a nuclear fringe theatre spectacular, exploding around these two cities and the fall-out being so much new work and talent. David

Slack, the festival's original director, and damn good actor, hailed from – and in – many of Studio Salford's plays. Sadly, not all of my theatre experiences here would be so holistically or intellectually fulfilling.

This is several experiences rolled into one [and not just Manchester], because they were all so sadly very similar. I was asked by a bigger, more mainstream theatre if, for one of their many well-funded schemes, would I mentor an emerging poet/playwright. I knew the emerging poet/playwright very well, loved their stuff and enthusiastically said "Yes". This theatre was well-known for its work with emerging artists, so I simply thought it would be about occasionally seeing the artist and helping along with experiential advice. This theatre has done – and still does – great work, so maybe this was an unfortunately creatively unevolved blip...

Anyway, the young artist had already done lots of performance poetry and was really into creating a more linear narrative-led piece of work. I thought it a splendidly artistically-stretching idea and was right behind them. Part of this scheme was to meet with its head-honchos and discuss said idea – great. And so, with a very career-excited young artist, I go along to this meeting thinking it would be a sounding-board of suggestions for their piece... how wrong I was. Because the young artist had mental health issues their play had by theatrical necessity quite dark themes, things about their own mental health they were wishing to uncover 'n' explore. As the young artist was explaining their piece, I and the young artist could both see these two head-honchos were passing each other what can only be described as concerned/worried glances – it really confused me. After this enthused pitch [I loathe the word pitch, so unnecessarily competitive], the two head-honchos leaned a rather assertive TED Talk forward and in good cop/bad cop unison said they *very much liked the idea, but it was a bit too bleak and not quite what the building was about.* They continued with *we'd really like you to do 'a something' here, but perhaps not*

159

this. A crestfallen young artist then asked *what* and they said something like [I'm paraphrasing and have been all along] *one of your trademark high-energised poetry shows, perhaps a spectacular*. Still kinda stunned, the young artist continued *so, you don't like my idea?* They said *it's a fine idea, it's just not for here, but your other work would be super-welcome* [that pre-fix 'super' is one sly motherfucker]. Have to say I was completely flabbergasted by this, shocked even, these 'professionals' were politely poo-pooing this young person's idea. Not only that, but confidently changing it to one of their own. I realised I was in textbook Bourgeois Zeitgeist territory, manners, finance and control at the forefront of everything.

After this meeting a rather confused young artist and I spoke, with me suggesting we carry on with their own play idea and bugger the consequences. The young artist immediately told me *no, they'd change it*. I asked why and guess what they said? They said they *didn't want to mess up the 'opportunity' of working in this building*. They were literally panicked they'd take away what they saw as their big break. The young artist went along with the idea, brilliantly creating a campy flourishing poetry spectacular, it was performed at the theatre and met with thunderous supportive applauded approval. Thing is, with this particular theatre's ethos of inbuilt Inspirationalism 'n' Positivia, almost everything here, especially if in-house, is met with thunderous supportive applauded approval. A short tour was booked for the show, one of the venues being a high-art avant garde performance night in London, something I've performed at and if you're not hard-core performance savvy, a potentially difficult audience. I immediately knew this young artist's work might not be as enthusiastically appreciated there as at its original venue, and I was right, it wasn't. It remains that poet's worst ever experience of performing; they came to me visibly shaken, shell-shocked and angry. I'm happy to say the artist fully recovered from that ordeal and is now an accomplished professional poet, with a string of successes behind and in front of them. My problem remains *why*?

Why couldn't this young artist simply go along with their original idea? As somebody with a wealth of drama work, advanced youth-theatre work in particular, me 'n' mine would never have dreamt of taking a young person's idea from them. We'd have worked long 'n' hard at getting it to work and would have damn well made it work, but never would we have moved them away from it. 'Empowerment' is an oft'-used word in theatres like these. Where I come from, this isn't empowerment.

That was a different time though, late seventies/early eighties, an anarcho-working-class, confrontational counter-cultural vibe was still bouncing around, this was the era of The Bourgeois Zeitgeist, manners, finance and control at the helm of every decision... the stark brutalities of 'The Accountant Culture'! After my experiences at the much freer-thinking Studio Salford, the controlling uptightness of theatres supposedly more 'professional' venues would continue to disappoint.

Don't know where you are with the culture of branding 'n' rebranding. As you can probably guess, it's not a 'pitch' I think seductively sexy. Surely branding and rebranding's something the Beckhams do every time they have a baby, so much so I often think they've a child called Brand. Brand Beckham. I seriously wonder if the bourgeois template is now so societally ingrained that it's increasingly sociopathically narcissistic, that it's confident enough now to arrogantly want everything reimagined in its own perfectly ordered image. Manners finance and control! There's something that can be creatively colonising about The Bourgeois Zeitgeist really setting my teeth on edge.

You may have noticed in lots of television adverts, once really spunky, sometimes even punky songs have been hugely rearranged. What were powerful counter-cultural rallying calls are now ultra-passively 'n' half-breathily sung to the sparsest, most genteel plinky-plonky arrangements. Pseudo-sounding heavenly harps 'mindfully' replacing once roaring guitar'd power chords. All their revolutionary hardcore metal taken away in the mannered financial hope of selling you irritable bowel easing yoghurts. Yes, it's probably easier on the ear and possibly digestive system, but I can't help hear The Bourgeois Zeitgeist screaming… *"Everything's ours now y'hear, every-fucking-thing [oops sorry for swearing], your look, your poetry, theatre, even your tunes, all those stomping head-banging tunes you used to pogo up 'n' down so fucking [oops again] anarchically to, they're ours, everything's ours now! We've turned them into nothing more than a frond of a just-blown dandelion invisibly fading into a late-summer breeze! We've come to accept our reward! Ha ha ha ha ha ha ha ha ha!"* They've rebranded Punk to ease wind. Don't know about you, but I think that shit stinks of revenge. I really am waiting for The Sex Pistols' 'God Save the Queen' to be reimagined with hardly audible plinky-plonky harps and a breathy half-singing voice politely trilling "no future" in the hope of selling us The Duchy of Cornwall's deliciously creamy hand-rolled butter.

Rebranding's also happening here in Manchester's arts scene and leaves me cold, very cold indeed. Imagine if you will an ancient community red-brick building, its architecture nobly of its time, still at the forefront of its particular community's activities. Not just the building, but its name, a brilliant name, one proudly encapsulating its eclectically fascinating history and many multi-cultural working-class stories surrounding. If a name ever holistically defined a building or community, a place of huge multi-cultural class-struggle, upheaval and victory, then it was this building, its name always at its communal epicentre. Perhaps The Bourgeois Zeitgeist thinks it inherently owns history and legacy, I wouldn't put it past it, probably schooled that way. There are times The Bourgeois Zeitgeist goes far too far or who knows, perhaps once again, it's 'instinctively' responding to a changing, more monied demographic. The area surrounding this building, like so much of Manchester, has been suddenly and violently gentrified. There's still a thriving multi-cultural working-class bordering, but it's long had the sheen of a much more affluent middle-class shine – you can instantly see why a fiscally 'numbers'-aware Bourgeois Zeitgeist thought a name change could be 'professionally' applicable. It's not only socially criminal, but creatively 'n' emotionally unintelligent to take away such an area's [and era's] defining moniker – a moniker constantly there and often reclaimed by its ever-evolving communities – then replace it with a something an early-eighties community centre orbiting an orbital of Widnes might have shamefacedly tombola-chosen. I genuinely can't see how anybody could think it a great idea unless they perhaps wanted to 'only lovely'-up the building for its new demographic. The Bourgeois Zeitgeist, by insidious nature, is passively/aggressively 'only lovely', wears it like a broken half-smile on a just morning-dew'd face. It also tightly holds the purse strings, only thing that does, so has privileged/entitled carte blanche to do whatever the fuck it wants. Even if it means erasing a community's historically grass-rooted ethos. Yes, the building still does do great work, brilliant work, but we must ask ourselves why it had to change its name to do it. Just why? It's interesting most people I know ignore its instantly forgettable new name, still calling it by its old historically emboldening one [I defiantly do], dismissively chortling at its zappy throwaway nonsense. My sincerest hope for that community is when the current management leave it goes back to the name it always was and most certainly should be, to un-erase the erasers and take back its rightful cultural heritage. That innate capitalistic, original Thatcherite/neoliberal voracious thrust of The Bourgeois Zeitgeist, everything societally on offers for it, it literally can have whatever it wants... so why oh why does it want our 'peoples' history'? Must point out here, I live in this area, have done for some considerable time, and not the only person feeling 'distanced' by this, not by a long chalk.

163

The bread 'n' circus politics of spectacle can have a place, perhaps even a brilliant place; I firmly believe that's when a society is equalled-up, when there's a more cohesive sense of us all striving and belonging together, when we're collectively breaking down 'all' division. If that isn't happening, if division's actually increasing, then I believe the politics of spectacle can sometimes be a further-distancing kick in the teeth for our most vulnerable and needy.

Great big 'council organised' theatre festivals and events might mean everything to some people and that's truly great, go for it, but at these moments in time they mean very little to me. On a creatively personal note, I've always liked my theatre small. I'm acutely aware, like all festivals held in Manchester [and it feels there's a festival every week here], they generate much needed cash for its very many city-centred businesses and isn't that just capitalistically dolly. My obvious observation is that in between a cheeky Nandos, giant Bratwurst and, if terribly lucky, a half-priced cocktail, these things are an exercise for a very giggly Bourgeois Zeitgeist to over-excitedly bingo-tick off as many performances it possibly can. I'm now decades-aware everything is solely curated for the people who can afford it, so although slightly grating they don't bother me that much. Festivals in this city [*every* major city] are now the norm, so much so they've lost impact, events without occasion – I world-wearily expect them. An über-grumble with them was when a very rich pop artiste was doing one of his really big, well-funded, well-paid shows, and about some of the publicity garnered. The media went bat-crap crazy for him apparently introducing an unknown African instrument to a wider European audience. Going back to the colonisation of creativity, the appropriation of art I was talking about before, I'm thinking surely the African instrument was invented by Africans, yet this very British, urbane, middle-class musician seems to be getting all the credit, even suggesting him kinda brave 'n' risk-taking for doing it. Very probably not his fault and he seems an awfully nice chap, sensitive, solid, reliable, that sort of pop star [a bit like the Elvis of The Bourgeois Zeitgeist, Ed Sheeran]. As we know the media isn't that bright and immaturely soundbite obsessed, but in a city culturally diverse as Manchester it seemed not only a tad insensitive, but once again Bourgeois Zeitgeist privileged/entitled.

If I had one magical wish, it wouldn't be planet-wide peace or to indeed feed the world, it would be to extract this now decades'-old formless Bourgeois Zeitgeist energy from the corporate/municipal/arts arenas. Now I'm not saying it doesn't do great things, it very probably does, but it is [and has always been] its subtler/invisible distancing worrying me.

I remember one young girl, eighteen, in 'some such' young person's theatre company. I'd just done a session with this brilliant group and it was, I thought, superb; I'm really rather fab at that shit. After the session, this young person comes up to me and sheepishly says *you know stuff don't you?* I say *I know some stuff, yes.* Bursting into tears, she then tells me she's leaving the group. The big reason why I shan't go into because I promised to keep it secret, but her explanation ended with her heavy finger-pointing, jabbing furiously at a poster image and her repeatedly sobbing *this isn't me, this isn't me, this isn't me!* The image she was pointing at was of an exceptionally well-designed, supremely confident break-dancing silhouette. I said if the image bothered her that much she should talk with the people organising and try to perhaps change it, I'm sure they'd listen, but there was no getting through to her. We must have jangled for hours and eventually, after some considerable time she calmed down. I again asked her to seriously reconsider her decision, because the staff were lovely, they'd get it, but she wouldn't/couldn't. We hugged, and as she was leaving, walking backwards to the door, she pointed to the poster figure and once again said, *sorry Gerry, really sorry, but I can never be that!* Of course, it wasn't the poster but the difficulty of past experiences leading to her decision, but I will say the poster image didn't help.

Inspirationalism 'n' Positivia work, of course they work, wouldn't be so goddamn prevalent if they didn't, but when they don't work, they fail big time. Coming from a late seventies/early eighties youth theatre/drama background, we proactively moved away from images projecting 'confident youth' because we automatically knew not every young person was naturally confident – often far from it. We were aware, even if for a few, bright sparky upbeat images can act as a barrier to entry and also found you really don't need these images to attract young people, they want to do things anyway. Inspirationalism 'n' Positivia are pitched at a shrill 'upbeat 'n' at 'em' frequency, a frequency attracting the naturally confident. Others cotton on to it of course, but that same frequency can also piercingly distance. Without it even knowing, 'n' I don't just mean the arts here, The Bourgeois Zeitgeist favours the confident.

I genuinely worry about the 'uber positive' influence of The Bourgeois Zeitgeist a lot. It appears to be hopelessly addicted to attention, acclaim, career validation and applause. So addicted, I'm pretty sure if could it would cook up 'n' mainline applause. I historically don't think of either Liverpool or Manchester as naturally easily to applaud cities. Yeah, if whatever's on show deserves it, of course, clap away. I rather loved our shared, heightened, slightly hard-nosed creative cynicism; our rag-tag bohemian knowing applause has to be earned. Not anymore it seems. The Bourgeois Zeitgeist has slowly changed the creative character of both cities; I would go as far as to say, eroded. I wonder if it needs all that attention, the sound of all that applause to know it's still there, like it might vanish without it. It appears on the surface to need an awful lot of unnecessary validating noise. When I think of the sound of The Bourgeois Zeitgeist, I'm reminded of rattles at a football match and whistles on a gay Pride march, melded together.

I recall a young group of actors who were coming to the end

of their particular course. I'm invited to the closing event and thinking it was just an end of year celebratory piss up [I dearly love piss ups], I mosey along. It was a piss up, yes, and that was very cool, but also something a bit more showbiz, and even a bit more showbiz is too showbiz for me. The closing 'ceremony' of this course was all about a young actress who successfully auditioned and got an acting job. Yeah, just that. To tremendous 'applause' the slightly embarrassed looking actress then has to take to the stage while the people running the course gave zippy upbeat speeches over-effusively congratulating her... I found it absolutely mortifying to watch. The people running the course might have had the audience applauding about five times for this visibly ill at ease actress; they simply wouldn't stop and must have said the word 'opportunity' at her at least ten times. Later on, I ended up chatting to another of the course's actors as she seemed clearly upset and furious about something. It transpired she and a handful of others had gone for the same role and didn't get it. She was naturally sad she hadn't got the part, but far more angry about the pomp and circumstance surrounding the actress who did, the actress clearly not wanting all the fuss. She was damn right to be, for starting out burgeoning performers all this crass über-celebration around careerism 'n' success was completely the wrong signal to be sending out. This new-to-it-all actress had already thought she'd somehow failed and this fatuous display of accelerated/agitated celebration compounded her feelings of failure even further – another clear case of the invisible distancing of The Bourgeois Zeitgeist. Of course, one must congratulate the actor on getting the job, have a gorge bevvy with them, but don't deify the job or turn it into an insane full of fun career circus. There's just no empowering point to that. Thing with The Bourgeois Zeitgeist is it's carved from career, finance, success and what appears to be a continuously cloying desire for applause/validation. It's what drives it on, and while that may well buoy-up full-on career victory, it horribly sinks if that isn't happening. I've seen several things now [not just in the arts], where it over-enthusiastically validates, in fact almost deifies job/position. Sometimes they're outdoor events, events where people without jobs/position are coerced into wildly applauding people simply with jobs/position. I know most people in the arts are lefty and liberal, but I can't help thinking things like this really play into the Tory 'we're all in it together' language of hard-working families… talk about distance.

Going back to '79 ['n' as a member of The Everyman Youth Theatre], people 'n' friends you knew would often get jobs in theatre or telly. We'd all pile down The Everyman Bistro for a congratulatory drink, then perhaps stagger off to the gloriously seedy Cazzer for a celebratory drunken dance. When I first became a youth theatre worker and for the physiological dynamic of the group, I found out it was deliberate policy to play down any 'supposed' success. At that time *Brookside* was burgeoning on the horizon and a very big showbiz televisual deal indeed. Four of our youth theatre attendees got lead roles in that show; there was no ceremony, no party, just an after-session congratulatory drink, and 'for the sake of the group' exactly how it should be. Pretty sure if that were to happen now, they'd organise a carnival, brass band, Chinese dragon and firework display. I'm not saying modern life is rubbish, it isn't, it's often quite nice, fun even, I still dearly love disco dancing, but I could argue it's not as emotionally intelligent as it thinks it is.

It really is incredibly easy to get an audience to applaud anything these days, TED Talks and *The X Factor* have seen to that. You just have to tell them something Positivia-inspired dripping in Inspirationalism and they'll unanimously roar. There seems to be a major-city patriotic jingoism manifesting too, not just here in Manchester, everywhere; it now appears all cities are the greatest cities in the world. While this may be more than enough for some folk, I'm afraid it's nowhere near enough for me. I remember back in '88 when Glasgow hosted the National Garden Festival and its slogan "Glasgow Smiles

Better". I was sitting in The Waterloo, a fab rundown gay pub with this gorge Glaswegian Lefty lesbian, 'n' she says, "Smiles better, smiles fuckin' better, Glasgay smiles better! Gerry, have y'seen wha' Thatcher's done tae this city, nay cunt's fuckin' smilin' anywhere, never mind better!" Warra wise lezzer!

All this inherent mawkishness and now serial applause is seriously not working for so many artists either. I'm a big social media-head 'n' because I don't perform anywhere near as much as I used to, use it a lot. I really rather enjoy colloquially opining and it's a jolly useful way of keeping my 'gobby' Scouse voice in the world. The thing with being a social media-head is you see what everybody's doing and that's usually cool, but a big chunk of artists seem to be using it to 'virtue signal' just how continually goddamn wonderful they and art are. I've a friend called John Flynn, an ex-lodger 'n' damn fine chap, who also uses social media. Flynny's a brilliant plasterer, so brilliant he's in constant demand 'n' works a great deal, but I've yet to see him updating how blessed, grateful, honoured, thankful or indeed 'humbled' he is when he's just plastered a fucking wall. Wish I could say the same for artists.

If you're an actor/artist ['n' that certainly includes poets] working in the field of whatever presentation, you really are bound to occasionally/eventually get a performance job or funding, particularly if you've acted or been funded before. It's not as uncommon an occurrence as some make out and certainly not a magical, quasi-religious or mystical happening. The crowing by some artists of how blessed, proud, grateful, honoured, thankful and humbled they are for every single crumb of recognition, fiscal or otherwise, is at virtual 'extended networking' fever pitch. Our arts scenes now seem to be torrentially awash with digitally hypothetic, politely worded, Rupert the Bear thank you notelettes. Artists are repeatedly doffing their ever so 'umble caps to whoever may have somehow given them something workaday mundane as a job, gig, or a bit of money [and how can they not when the courses they've just been on have ecstatically taught them to über-elevate the mundane]. It seems they're being taught to become patsies to their enablers. I've actually read updates worded just like this so many times and this is an amalgam of those phrases:

"I'm reaching out, because I'm so genuinely super-thankful, grateful for everything happening to me right now, seriously you guys, I don't think anybody has ever felt or been more humbled."

"I don't think anybody has ever felt or been more humbled." Think about it, just how many times can someone constantly claim profound humility [to potentially the world] before they realise there's no humility in that whatsoever? Thing is they're often poets who, historically, are supposed to know what 'words' mean! I'm pretty damn sure true humility is the very opposite of boastfully proclaiming that particular emotion to almost everybody on the planet! Loadsa-humility, loadsa-grateful, loadsa-gigs, loadsa-applause, loadsa-funding, loadsa-honoured, loadsa-thankful, loadsa-blessed... seems we haven't moved that far away from Harry Enfield's early eighties yuppie character Loadsamoney after all, just made it a bit more 'spiritual' – a kind of pseudo-spiritual Capitalism!

Once more, the inherent capitalist, careerist, position and opportunity obsessed right-wing nature of The Bourgeois Zeitgeist comes to the fore. While artists blurt out every seemingly conceivable brilliant thing that's ever happened to them, I'm wondering if they're aware of the peoples who didn't get that funding, that audition, that gig. I wonder if they're aware they may be adding to a kind of creative division, an invisible distance we don't talk about. A distance we don't talk about because the constant up-tempo extended networking designed template of Inspirationalism 'n' Positivia continues to dominate the conversation. As for mindfulness, a word very much bandied around so many of our arts scenes these 'kinder' days, well it seems to me artists are not being terribly 'mindful' of the feelings of other artists. It cements my thoughts that mindfulness really is in the mind of the beholder. No wonder it may take six weeks of workshops and three tons of lightly balsamic'd drizzled quinoa to properly sink in.

The artistic playing fields I once knew, the counter-cultural playgrounds I chaotically tumbled about in, wouldn't have done or tolerated any of this. We didn't hyper OCD über-thank everybody for every conceivable thing that simply may, or may not, have happened to us. We'd be momentarily genuinely pleased, of course we would, or perhaps snidely 'n' bitchily pissed off – the way it should be. We were creative yes, wildly so, but also sassy grounded pragmatists, armed with a sharpened sword 'n' shield of acerbic witty cynicism. I can't remember a single instance of Inspirationalism 'n' Positivia in the Everyman Youth Theatre, not a single one, times and teachings have most definitely changed! I'm not saying Everyman Youth Theatre equals good 'n' all else equals bad, the seventies/eighties/early-nineties model I'm talking about was taken out of action. Liverpool's Everyman Theatre in its infinite idiocy decided to be rid of the free-at-the-point-of-entry youth theatre and replaced it much later [and run it very differently to the one I'm talking of]. It's a very upbeat 'modern' organisation now.

I can't help thinking that a lot of art, because of The Bourgeois Zeitgeist's influence 'n' particularly extended networking, is becoming increasingly intellectually/creatively reductive. That it might be dying. That art, certainly the art I respond to… may be dead.

---

[2] The script for which you can read in my previous collection, *Accidental Splendour of the Splash.*

...And People Are Stupid!

So the point of life is to end it,
to send it culled back at intangible saviours,
is that it?
God lies,
political lies,
life lies,
death lies waiting?

Bit rubbish if you ask me.
After the love-making,
skin-splitting, blood-spewing pain,
we end it on whims of money, ego 'n' gain.
Hego/shego children a-goo-goo,
like pogoing on intimacy and bomb.
Is that the point of tongue and promise,
of egg and cum?
All that giggly first step aplomb
leading to legs blown off,
arms gone!
Wiping drool, first day at school,
the yard, playground, the rule.

So that's the point, the magic,
reasons we breed,
to treat each other like we don't need each other?
So the point of life is to end it?
To bend it out of shape and hope.
Oh why bother!

Point-blank fuck this shit and pump lead into Cupid!
Culture Club nailed it,
people are stupid!

Shadowless Excuses

Carnage-ashen arson flakes,
feather-scars horizons,
that place memory mirages
and we're not there,
not present in our pasts 'n' futures.

Hollow-amber, trapped,
in the ointment-ills, our salve burns.
Skin-covered cottons, silks,
hives riot and the inflamed scorch on.

I keep cursing words too said,
not said enough,
shadowless excuses muted, muffled,
whispers colourless, land.

In another desert, another dawn,
hot cold and ancient.
Around a fire,
stories and reasons.

When Nothing

Not thinking,
dumb-blunt,
nowhere blows to somewhere.
Not alert or aware of stopped,
blank and unwelcome.
Can't make head,
spread tales
of this or others.
Sunk,
like penny bad,
turning up without appointment.

Wanting to tell it straight,
linear-scarred,
I'm jostling for time's position.
The end
backward starts,
born old and completed.

Earth between fingers
disintegrates.
Just the worms, tunnels
and the start.

Do You Seek Immortality?

Feels cupped youth,
haphazardly held for however long;
I'd say bittersweet, but it was too much of a party.
Fingers slipped through and inserted,
all those privates' moments,
tumble clumsy, thrilling
and on dancefloors the futures of history.
If I'm honest, want it back,
but my inner pragmatist concedes defeat.

There's a sense, like honey,
I can conjure,
thick with ingredient and optimism,
an aged auld wizard
with wand-waved immortality.
He's as young as my teenager and like him, doesn't exist.
Old Willow Pantomime says…
"If magic lasted forever it wouldn't be magic,
if magic lasted forever it would be normal."

Thing is, I was that effervescence,
defying logic, making mockery of knowing.
When falling down didn't last forever,
when you landed on a more rounded perter arse.
Nah, I don't seek immortality,
but do mourn its passing.

Hope

Tell them,
the couple in the rat-shit doorway,
too young and experienced,
barricaded from elements
by two broken umbrellas and an iron-scorched shower curtain.
Tell them to their faces,
scabbed by poverty,
pockmarked with disease,
that this is indeed the greatest city in the world.
Tell their gaunt lost look,
their hollows,
their eyes staring beyond rain,
beyond humanity and into cold.
Tell them with all your heart and knowledge,
tell them with all your bank details,
with all your religion,
all your nostalgia,
scatter cushions,
your Inspirationalism,
Positivia,
there's hope.

The
BOURGEOIS
ZEITGEIST

A Treatise
by
Gerry Potter

VII

I first saw The MEN Arena bombing unfolding on the News, so immediately flew into town to see what was really going on.

Everything was cordoned-off, but the sense something terrible had happened was everywhere, the air itself harassed, prickly 'n' panicked. It was an incredibly bleak, siren'd night and that would obviously spill into the next day.

The next day, as next days always do, came and Manchester's initial reaction did it proud: a seismic multi-wave of shock, grief and understanding bringing it solidly together. Outside the stoic Gothic of our majestic town hall, a mass public gathering was quickly held. So massive the public response, seemed the whole of this gorgeous city turned out. Such a wonderful event, a staggered sense of loss, coupled by this multi-cultural environ united and on the streets, felt like an illegal Rave without E. There's a holistic *something* about tragedy connecting; of course, you wish the tragedy hadn't happened or will ever again, but it *has* happened, *will* again, and you *always* respond. The connectivity felt like we were breathing in love. In the wake of this ugly atrocity Manchester was responding beautifully. Because it felt so collectively big, I recall being overwhelmingly moved and communally humbled by the sheer human scale of it all. I'm at home with being dwarfed by big things, long as those big things collectively matter and can make a difference; this most certainly was doing that.

On a hurriedly constructed stage, a series of public speakers and live musicians were doing their thing. Each and every one met with the truest 'n' warmest applause, applause I readily joined in with, applause so palpably meant every time it broke out felt like you were being hugged. Of all the speakers taking part, it was Mancunian poet Tony Walsh perfectly capturing the moment, not only emotively but expertly. His poem, 'This is the

Place', an instant anthem and very necessary poetic duvet both enveloping and comforting his gathered city. Combined with an ever-growing, ever-glowing shrine in St. Ann's Square, this was not only the best but the most this city could do. These were defiantly the hours Manchester was the most beautiful city in the world. The purity of such en masse emotive clarity made this the most special of all my Mancunian moments.

As somebody who's experienced a lot of grief I'm very used to a sense of reflective quiet. Along with emotional reassurance, stillness is somehow essential. I was around in Manchester for the IRA bombing of 1996, a god-awful event leaving so much of its city centre rubbled and uninhabitable. I'd never seen such twisting architectural carnage and was once again overwhelmed by my adopted city's steadfast responses. There was rage, disgust, but for some reason – and perhaps because no lives were lost – the reaction, although full-bodied, felt a little more reserved. Plenty of table-smashing pub debates of course, but there was definitely a quiet. I felt it the same in Liverpool after Hillsborough: for some time the city fell into a naturally emotionally-defined, contemplative still place. I didn't quite feel that quiet after the MEN massacre. Maybe for a day or two, but the stillness I thought would naturally follow, and this is a purely personal positioning and viewpoint, didn't. There was a huge theatre festival happening and people rightfully going about their lives, unafraid 'n' normally, but the sense of what I felt, and can only call 'agitated determination', was 'for me' a little too much. From media to pubs, clubbing to street, I felt I was constantly, too enthusiastically, told to be somehow upbeat 'n' proud. Of course, I was insanely proud and will forever be, that was a very natural given, but right at that moment I was sad. Young death is particularly sad and, in my head, because I've experienced a lot of young death, sad is quiet. I remember quite a few Paddy's Goose pub conversations about it, largely with Mancunian friends who were also feeling something not too dissimilar. Remember my auld Salfordian mate John saying, "Bless 'em but people keep tellin' me to be brave 'n' I don't know wha' that means." It was happening so much I had to retreat from the city centre and just let it be what it was. It was definitely a city centre thing; drinking in pubs outside of the area, that reflective sense of quiet was most certainly there, and by quiet I don't mean silence. I started to wonder why it was what it was, and it dawned on me Manchester's city centre has irrevocably changed. It was certainly burgeoning back in '96, but not yet completely subsumed by The Bourgeois Zeitgeist. Perhaps certain understandings have not so much disappeared, but been overwhelmed by something else? I'm not suggesting for one second some people were being actually opportunist, they weren't, not at all, they were being genuine, but 'opportunity' is such a tremendous part of The Bourgeois Zeitgeist's embedded emotional/professional make-up, maybe something about that naturally/organically bubbled to the fore... it sometimes can't help itself.

At this point I simply didn't want to feel inspired or find 'the positive' in anything, I didn't feel under siege, didn't need hugs 'n' stuff, didn't need to be on-side or angry; didn't have space for that, I just wanted to be naturally very sad. I'm old school, I think being sad enough. For me, the quiet of sad's what grief's about. I don't solely mean grief for the current situation because it wasn't my situation, I wasn't those families, but also for the multiples of personal griefs reanimated by it. There was an almost religious quiet at the St. Ann's Square shrine, looked and felt painfully beautiful, but elsewhere it felt a little fractiously odd. I suppose things weren't helped by the rapid decent of a world's media constantly searching for story. There's something about the omnipotent presence of cameras not sitting well with me. Perhaps it was just that. But what was incalculably tragic began to feel weirdly frenzied, a slightly out of control media circus... I really don't trust the media at all. As I always do when things are a bit much, I gently took a step back.

I remember instinctively wanting, longing even, to be in ye auld Manchester of quite semi-recent yore, particularly Hulme's once wonderfully baroque palace of the broken, The Salutation ['The Sally']. If ever personally troubled [and for so many other reasons], it really was my go-to pub, it had a rave-yard stench. It was drenched in a discernible atmospheric feeling that people thought exactly like you. Sculptured from the underground rock 'n' roll of anarcho-absurdist counter-culture, The Sally rang with a shabby, ragged bohemian communality easy-reaching out, forever partying and quietly understanding. It felt timelessly etched from those ages-old revolutionary tavern-like vibes Liverpool pubs like Ye Olde Cracke were, and no matter what had happened, its creaking familiarity could indeed comfort. It really was the only place to be when 9/11 happened, the conversation so politicised, informed and meant. The Sally did powerful conversation brilliantly, such animated, often comedic discourse and impassioned brio at play. No Inspirationalism, no Positivia, just everybody in every heart-meant spitting syllable of what they were saying. I loved being in there with my auld actor pal Neil Bell; we could certainly tub-thump the topic out of any drunken conversation and often did. From the insanely multi-addicted crazy Hulme-'eads to the medically professional, here was a class-less pub of such gritty intellectualism and wit it didn't need to be told how great it was – it instinctively knew it was the greatest pub in the world. You always met somebody you knew and would know they were rocked by whatever had just happened, too. It could be searingly table-crashing brash, but also crazily quiet. Yeah, that's what I wanted, needed right then, a bit of crazy quiet. The Sally of then really was a place you could find and talk to the like-minded, where you could at least try to make 'your' sense of what was going on… it truly was the pub of pubs. Big Hands, The Temple and The Pev were similarly good to be in, I seem to remember. It's funny isn't it, some bars just kinda know.

Some time later my friend Shaun and I went into town shopping. As per, we popped into city centre Tesco's looking for what we camply call 'cheaposity', reduced yellow-label foodstuffs [I've not paid full price for bread 'n' milk in donkey's]. We left Tesco's via a wide, darkened alleyway – even in the height of summer this particular thoroughfare is always somehow cool-shaded and handy to escape the sun. After years of societally destructive austerity it's also become 'home' for this city's growing homeless problem. I wondered, because there seemed to be a lot more than usual, if they'd been moved here because of the current unifying festival. Whenever there's a unifying festival to unite the city, you see it a lot. Our homeless are often authoritatively 'encouraged' to move away from the unifying festivities. Although a warm night, the alleyway felt desperately cold and shadow-huddled in damp, dirty doorways, the physically broken frames 'n' faces of far too many people. Homelessness in Manchester is now epidemic and while no human being should be without shelter, the number of women, particularly young women, on these streets is just devastating. Raging around us, wrung wretched and hopeless, a joyless/ginless Hogarthian vista; Ignorance and Want could have well have been here, but I can assure you there wasn't tooth nor tit of Inspirationalism 'n' Positivia.

I'll never forget the image, it's seared onto my mind, of a drunk/drug-addled young woman, grubby as fuck, nestled in between even grubbier, probably Spiced- or smacked-up much older men, not one of them even remotely in this world. Whatever world they were inhabiting, I hope it was much better than the world of detritus and piss-filthy pavement they were collapsed upon. Don't know if you've ever seen a group of puppeteer-less marionettes left on a floor? I have; they looked like that, but a billion times more abandoned, blackened and unloved. It breaks my heart to see and constantly come across such impossible homegrown poverty. That, coupled with recent traumatic events, sent me tumbling.

Shaun and I move from here to Albert Square, where yet another big festival had its headquarters, and at its epicentre, from some dance tent or other, we couldn't help but hear very loud pumping music. Don't know if it was disco or techno, but whatever, it was wildly partying. Over the noise comes a mic'd-up, booming joyful voice… *"We're so proud right now to be here, to be Mancunians and every Mancunian should be proud of themselves, because Manchester is the greatest city in the world!"* This inspirational, upbeat, positive call-out is met with the whole tent applauding, whooping, hollering 'n' a-cheering, sounding like they'd had lots of cheeky half-priced cocktails – so that's where Inspirationalism 'n' Positivia were!

I freeze-frame, time slow-mos, and for whatever crazy reason I'm suddenly reminded of that awful networking moment with Siobhan who played the synthesiser. After a little while 'n' age, I turned to Shaun and said, "It isn't Shaun, it just isn't, not anymore. Manchester isn't the greatest city in the world."

Now, Manchester, before ferociously wielding your burning torches, collectively jeering 'n' running me out of town for bein' the cheekiest fuckin' Scouser in the world, let me explain. My feeling was then as is now, any city tolerating such crippling and continuing poverty can't in all intellectual seriousness claim itself to be the greatest city in the world. Not London, not Newcastle, not Glasgow… good Lord, not even Liverpool! Great is surely something encapsulating us all; great is certainly alleviating, but greater still is eradicating poverty. Manchester, like all big cities in this country, has seen poverty brutally and ideologically increased. I'm pretty sure 'great' isn't a failing health service, the reintroduction of rickets, homeless young women, student nurses using foodbanks and in-work poverty… I could seriously go on 'n' on 'n' on.

Why are our big city centre's chanting such up-tempo jingoistic dominance, constantly über-celebrating, and just *what is it* we're constantly celebrating? Call me an auld camp cynic, but I think we're constantly celebrating how 'monied' some of our citizens are, therefore flipside being how 'monied' some of them aren't. I'd just walked past the ones who clearly weren't. We're celebrating the heightened insensitivities of Inspirationalism 'n' Positivia over the intellectually-pointed detail of pragmatism and cynicism… to all intents 'n' purposes we're celebrating Capitalism.

I think it's reached the point we're celebrating celebration and sometimes don't know why. If we look to the failing high streets of our many run-down orbitals, no one's proclaiming how great they are, because they're obviously not. How can we celebrate how continually 'great' everything is, when you simply have to look at any broken tent-strewn country-wide pavement to see it clearly isn't and hasn't been for some considerable time? How are we able to afford all these huge 'unifying' celebrations, yet unable to house our most vulnerable? I'd rather have both, want both, want more even [who wouldn't?], but would gladly forsake just half of this continuing spectacle if it meant never seeing another destitute young woman on the street. And because the powers that be are always boasting how fantastically fiscally successful they are, well then, if that's the fantastically fiscally successful case, at very least, some of the profits of all these many festivals should go into housing our homeless. Then no one would suffer the humiliating indignities of having them authoritatively moved on from our 'unifying' festivities… win, win! There isn't a brightly lit big wheel in the world as fun as that terrified homeless young woman is tragic. It's why, wherever I am, whatever city, I can no longer applaud the unrelenting Inspirationalism 'n' Positivia of event – 'The Politics of Spectacle', of distance, it feels too much like diversion.

If I were living in Liverpool ['n' it's entrenched with The Bourgeois Zeitgeist, too], well betchbygollywow this book would be called *Liverpool Isn't the Greatest City in the World* and those 'Giants'

[whom I think may actually be called 'Bread 'n' Circus' or 'Smoke 'n' Mirror'] would deffo be getting it in the neck. If over one million people can take to the streets to 'applaud' oversized puppets, then surely half a million, a quarter even, can storm the streets and revolt for the homeless. It just happens to be written here, my second favourite city, my other home town, a place I unquestionably love: Manchester.

If what I've written feels too critiqued then I'm not sorry, don't buy this book, send it back, shout at me in a pub then forcibly remove 'n' break my spectacles, or maybe, let's chat. As with any long-term lover you can only detail the faults because you know them so well. Doesn't mean you've fallen out of love... it's just tolerating the bed-farting.

Messy

World plate,
splattered ketchup, torn meat,
gravy burying flavour,
mashed.
Not one dominant taste,
not one dominant food,
not one dominant design.
Noodled.
Drained.
Sandwiched thin-ice between porcelain
and table,
the chalk we all come from.
Part of Earth,
part of sky,
part of universe.
Stars tore themselves asunder,
planets aged to dust
to fire that flat globe.
Beautiful.
Ugly.
Tasty.
Messy.

In On The Rainy

In on the rainy,
sock wet 'n' can't be bothered,
take 'em off in a min,
when I've a biscuit and idea.
My cuppa,
cauldrons past,
tea's bubblin' liquid memory.
The storm colours in,
lightning brights nice,
there in the streaks,
family.

I like the sky black,
feel covered,
blankets what's left,
what's still mine.

A Knowing Wind

Given up,
drain-downed
among our waste,
the wasted.
You'll see them fifties-quiff'd,
just turned eighteen,
see them smack-hooked in prams.

No film can tell it,
no book,
no play,
no poem can say it.
It's all our stain,
all our never loving,
our never hoping.

We can't understand
if we refuse to understand.
We can't turn running water
into diamonds.
Won't even make it drinkable.

Problem is,
I'm pretty sure we know.

Nervous In The Bum

I'm nervous in the bum,
an old feeling,
had it at school and in church.
Means I'm scared,
uncomfortable with truth,
means I instinctively don't believe what I'm being told.

I'm not unhappy of nervous in the bum,
I know it,
trust it,
prepares,
has never let me down.
Spirals my spine,
helter-skelters round 'n' round,
up 'n' sound.

Freud could probably explain it cleverer,
not interested,
there's many a slip Brexit cup 'n' lip.
Bottom line is,
I'm nervous in the bum.

The
BOURGEOIS
ZEITGEIST

A Treatise
by
Gerry Potter

VIII

I think we're at our greatest when recognising where and why we're failing, not constantly celebrating around who we've failed. Over four decades of anti-working-class policies, the creation of an even more debilitating fiscal caste system and the introduction of further crippling austerity, means societal breakdown on a scale so huge I think most of us are unwilling to see it – even when it's visibly unravelling right in front of our very eyes. How can we see it when they keep putting bells 'n' whistles, bangs 'n' flashes, fireworks 'n' funfairs in front of the agony? We're constantly pushing our most vulnerable away to the bleakest recesses of our cities. So far away I fear where they may eventually end up. There's a Bourgeois Zeitgeist oft'-spoke office-speak phrase, goes something like *we need to have that conversation*. How are we ever going to begin *to have that conversation* with people we refuse to even see, never mind hear? We might as well be talking to ghosts. It's as if we're mesmerically being blinkered, or a strange unforgiving 'something's' trying to paper-over the cracked. Or am I again being too poetically romantic and we really are just self-interested, self-aggrandising twats?

Bless it, The Bourgeois Zeitgeist really does think it's helping, but in that mannered, financed, controlled way the bourgeoisies have always thought charity benignly helps – and which we know doesn't. If charity was the great benefactor it pretends to be, then after centuries of über-generous benefaction we'd surely all now be on an even keel. We're quite categorically not. This ship is not only sinking, for so many it's sunk; sanctions, suicides, do not pretty cities make. There's neither a network meeting nor poetry workshop in the whole wide world can save a family from financially drowning, so no matter how good our intentions [and some of our intentions are great], intentions alone are not good enough. No matter how individually 'n' spiritually uplifting they can be [I'm certainly no stranger to a standing ovation], I've yet to hear a round of applause loud enough it can bring back much needed industries and jobs.

I'm sure The Bourgeois Zeitgeist has no idea it's the zeitgeist and has been for some decades, that it's the dispirited of the age, creator of The Accountant Culture. I think if it did try to see itself, like a vampire it would probably hissingly hurl the mirror to one side. Maybe that's why – it simply doesn't want to walk through the broken glass our once working homeless are now sleeping on. Remember, it's both terminally and skilfully mannered, using manners like a TED-Talking Jedi might a lightsaber. A reflectionless force to be reckoned with alright! Someone on social media once asked me what my relationship to The Bourgeois Zeitgeist was... I replied: *It's Dracula/Darth Vader and I'm Van Helsing/Obi Wan*. Make of that what you will.

Just off the anarcho-socialist cuff, here's a couple of poverty-alleviating suggestions:

1) To employ well, but also to recognise, apologise, honour and remember the countless communities devastated by Thatcherism, we create government-funded community industries, something New Labour [an agent of The Bourgeois Zeitgeist] most certainly should have done and most definitely didn't. Huge super-community centres focused on reviving and keeping said communities alive and 'buzzing' forever. Based on the NHS model, huge teams of trained vocational workers, working in the fields of cultural employment, social-cohesion, renewable energies, education and vocation. Nothing makes anybody socially more able/mobile than fiscal/vocational confidence, nothing, not even juggling balls. Perhaps these communities won't then have to rely on the uncertainties of historically failing charitable intention, but can meet and organise their own festivals 'n' workshops, plate their own bourbons 'n' Garibaldis. Also, in every super-

community centre, a giant red plaque of apology finally acknowledging the grief and torment caused by the decades-long evil ideologies of Thatcherism!

2) Failing that, not Basic Income but Hedonistic Income. There's little intellectual point in keeping people alive if there's not enough money for them to properly live. Basic Income suggests to me the same inequalities as before, but with luck a half-fuller stomach. Hedonistic Income means we're all ecstatically scribbling 'party' on the same page. This would of course mean increasing tax and I seriously wonder if The Bourgeois Zeitgeist could ever be that kind of universally charitable. Would it be willing to give up one of its three holidays a year, or make do with a new kitchen every six? It's not rocket science, a network meeting, nor is it a thematically-linked mindfulness workshop. It's beyond simple, the simplest: to live well and happily a society needs money; I'd certainly like to see the stinkingly rich charitable live without it.

Instead of acting like quickly evaporating salves, I'd love to see our arts scenes, all our arts/social/municipal/industry scenes, behind suggestions like these; love to see them become part of truly radical solutions. I'm afraid in our current climate I see every festival, whatever it is, whoever it's for, whatever city it's in, as a quickly-evaporating salve, 'n' a pretty shit salve at that; everything's getting worse, divide and applaud.

Things were once far more artistically radical. In the eighties there wasn't a spare piece of outdoor wall or corrugated metal without an anti-Thatcher/Tory poster. Even slightly more conservative theatres like The Liverpool Playhouse were putting on productions called *Fears and Miseries of the Third Term*. Not only a great show, but just that big bold phrase alone plastered all over Liverpool [pretty sure it was the same in Manchester] was its own powerfully radical meme. I don't see Theresa May's face anywhere but on the telly. Although we didn't get rid of

Thatcher fast as we should, those posters really supported the activists, the working people on the ground. They made it look like the arts proactively societally cared, we were all in it together and not just selling an upbeat workshop, networking meeting, yet another unaffordable festival or God forbid... mindfulness! So, we have to ask why, when things are much worse now than even then, has that imagery, that brilliant Conservative-attacking wall-art disappeared? I've a sneaky suspicion a media savvy Inspirationalism 'n' Positivia have an integral 'something' to do with that, I've a feeling they don't think truth's 'sexy' enough... I've a feeling Inspirationalism 'n' Positivia could in all probability be glittering, fanny/cock-to-floor splits, *Tories*. I feel Inspirationalism 'n' Positivia would think 'fear' 'n' 'misery' would be rather inappropriate buzz words to sell shows, probably too busy selling revolutionary apocalyptic immersive theatre. Remember, being preternaturally bubbly 'n' smiley they like everything nice 'n' everything. So, c'mon now, who needs proper societal fiscal solutions/parity when you can make festival heart-fingers? Seriously, in several of our big cities, I've seen the homeless begging, Spiced out their fuckin' brains and sleeping, dying underneath giant celebratory posters of festival heart-fingers. As you can by now imagine, I didn't get 'the feels'.

Have just read this back 'n' must stress I'm not being glibly anti-middle-class or wholly anti-art; I'm being profoundly anti-Bourgeois Zeitgeist. I'm also aware there are still active chunks of counter-culture banging out great stuff.

In my multitude of internet researchings, my heart has been wholly lifted, among others, by both the Momentum and Grime movements. Anything behind huge societal 'fiscal' change for the many 'n' not the few has my complete support: it has to be about a massive redistribution of wealth. Momentum is a very broad church of peoples and from what I can see/sense a good chunk of those peoples are from middle-class or lower-middle-class backgrounds. And that's just fabulous – anyone fighting the good fight is fighting and make no mistake comrades, this is war, class-war!

The Grime movement appears to come from an underground-collected, largely working-class youth vibe, creating fiery political art, music 'n' original spoken word which doesn't look too over-workshopped [not yet anyway]. It manifestly wants a much better country for us all and not just the peoples who can continually afford the festivals. These peoples seem to be opposing the 'festival-funding' banks and not continually applauding the foodbanks. I say foodbanks because I've on occasion had to use them and thank all that's beautiful about humanity they're there, but they're *not* to be applauded. Poverty mustn't be applauded, complete Bourgeois Zeitgeist territory that… it'd applaud shadows if it could. [Shit, I've probably just given it a brilliantly super-rad mega-new idea.]

Foodbanks are strange very difficult environs, but nothing's that strange or difficult when you or your family are starving. Hunger's a physically/emotionally impacting leveller. So much of current societal thinking is about food control, what it is 'n' more importantly whom it's for. A world-wide Bourgeois Zeitgeist is, in so many ways 'n' on so many levels, bang in the middle of that barbarically sordid narrative.

This may initially read a bit daft, but bear with me. I was once hungover-watching some Sunday morning telly, a strangely colourful programme the name of which thankfully escapes me. It was about youngish people and celebrities garishly chatting 'n' eating. The chefs on display looking like bloated, mutated clones of Jamie Oliver, all upbeat Mockney-confident on themselves and appeared to be gleefully cooking for what appeared to be the shiny happy cast of *Hollyoaks*. The tone of the piece was of sumptuous relaxed social dining, and that the food being lovingly created had the 'right' mix of people there to eat it. It manifested as Netflix watching ancient Rome, if Netflix watching ancient Rome was populated by too-jolly/chatty Page 7 Fellers 'n' Page 3 Stunners. They may have even had Positivia 'n' Inspirationalism as guest cooks, glittery-giggling 'n' salivating over the unfathomable deliciousness of a peculiarly shaped German sausage, perhaps joyfully squeezing a cheeky shot of chilli jus into a just-lightly balsamic'd drizzled kitchen utensil... y'know, an always-ready for the grill-seared halloumi kind of show. Anyway, its ballgame being, this was a great culinary space to generously aspire to and everything on colossal orgiastic offer was pitched at the gorgeously aspirational, very welcome 'special guests' surrounding... It knocked me fucking sick!

Knocking me even sicker was the programme immediately following, supposedly about secret eating. I think called *Secret Eaters*, its disgusting format completely different from the one preceding. I'm sat here shuddering with full-on rage recollecting this monstrous piece of wholly classist televisual shite. A horrifically stern, middle-class, 'uniformed' Nanny-like figure visits [well, I say visits, more like descends upon] the homes of overweight working/lower-middle-class peoples. She, with rehearsed invitation, seems to move into their houses and then 'austerely' dictates to them in their 'dark, cramped' living rooms everything about food and what might be their 'difficult' relationships to it. I could be imagining this, but I think the vile Nanny-vulture even leaps/pounces out from behind a fridge door, or is coldly watching from 'above' on television monitors, telling off the overweight people for even attempting to 'sneakily' enjoy a midnight sausage. I'm not too sure if the Nanny-vulture itself was actually fat-shaming, food-shaming or class-shaming these people, but the programme's ethos most definitely was. The whole atmosphere of this tawdry televisual debacle was intensely highlighting shame, failure and about how unquestionably wrong these people were for wanting to eat. Even darker, much darker, about something authoritatively bigger than them having complete mannered control and, above all, knowing better! Whoever these overweight people were even end up thanking the vile Nanny-vulture for the 'opportunity' of having her around and 'helping' them lose weight! All I could see was a joyless act of humiliating, culturally, culinary demeaning S'n'M played out in front of my very eyes. If this isn't the absolute epitome of Bourgeois Zeitgeist distancing, then dear reader, I don't know what is.

I think seeing these two TV shows separately I would've still loathed them beyond all measure, but seeing them follow on from one another really cemented my views on not only the power of The Bourgeois Zeitgeist, but just how mentally controlling it had become. This full, bold, bloated manifestation made me realise it's beyond über-confident now and no longer has to hide itself. Remember, some nasty cunt in scheduling put these two pieces of filthy crap together, thinking it great morning/afternoon telly... seriously, ask yourselves why and who for! Food is right 'n' good for the middle-class, aspirational, nobody-knows minor-celebrity or city-slicking entrepreneur and they can have as much of it as they damn well please, but food is bad 'n' wrong for the tippy-toe, sneaking-to-the-fridge, working-class failing fatty and said working-class failing fatty must be shamed 'n' punished for feeling something physically 'n' emotionally demeaning as hunger. One of the saddest things is, once you open your eyes to the arrogant vulgarities so deeply entrenched in The Bourgeois Zeitgeist you can never ever again close them. The Bourgeois Zeitgeist isn't one person, place, class or organisation, its far more than merely that, it's the politically unchallenged, decades-long dispirited of the age, engulfing absolutely everything, and with Inspirationalism 'n' Positivia on-side, why we wildly party on the streets where our poorest are dying.

It appears I've once again digressed, how cheekily Scouse of me. Well, it's my book and being an anarcho-socialist, serially iconoclastic Commie fag, I'm allowed to.

You may have noticed an illiberal smattering of potently pungent swearwords. Well, I swear, sometimes like a trooper. In Manchester/Salford an increasingly powerful Bourgeois Zeitgeist has arrogantly 'suggested' that areas surrounding the 'well-to-do' Media City should be No Swearing Zones. This is now an area completely subsumed by the business heads of the 'free thinking' media; who knows, perhaps they're just being mindful. I'm not completely saying there's a North/South divide, but I've never heard anything so holistically anti-working-class in all my puff. Newsflash knob'eads, the working-class swear.

"Fuck you The Bourgeois Zeitgeist, fuck you up ye passive/ aggressive, too mannered, financed, controlling, putrefyingly baggy, sweaty arse!"

In the 'almost'-words of Michael Jackson... "halloumi 'n' leaf us alone!"

Manchester Does Breath

Manchester does breath,
sighs queens and gasp,
with all my puff I love it.
It's been underground and I've been buried.
Me and the zombie dancers
bit-partying all over the floor.

Manchester does breath,
sleeplessness a-go-go,
I've skated on amphetamine,
snorted its sheen,
popped its spills and thrills,
spent 'n' been.
Me and the dead awake, eye-wide,
Manchester doesn't snore.

Under the flawed bored,
sunk'd in the canal,
Manchester does breath
and I breathe.

Finding Those Lost Weekends, Babe

Neon smears a guttural shine,
oil on water,
grid art.
Eternal kid popped out, gunned down 'n' tart.
I'm slipping through
where drag queens are slain,
where joy shields pain,
home of the severe riah'd pariah,
the seven-headed hairdryer.
The scaled 'n' fallen of lost weekends.

Everywhere open,
wide-eyed and startled,
yet no one's shocked,
haven't been for years.
Ancient caves of flat-lining, filling up Queers,
stories ended,
broken mended,
intellect descended and risen.
Shuffling resurrections find hole-mouth,
piss-kissin' and sound becomes oxygen
and
and
and... breathe.
Hiss.
Swallow.
Precision.

These animals my animals,
different heads same zoo,
no one a keeper,
don't wanna be kept.

Just looking for a solid shadow,
to lean,
to glean,
to clean.
Looking for a shadow knowing what's what,
where's where, who's who.

Make no mistake,
in these caverns the dead alive,
deep see skiving and driving ways through.
In these graves,
tatty dreds drool the root.

Babes, pretty sure there's sleep somewhere,
between collapse 'n' scheming.
Honey, there's bound to be sleep somewhere,
just never in dreaming.

The Last Woman To Hang

You see it swallow-eyed,
playing bye-bang and ferocious.
No love,
no need.
You are elevated by amyl
and dawn promises of nothing.
I communicate with the dead
because I belong dead.
We're all dead when not acknowledging the living.
I sigh with my little cry,
something beginning with end.
Oh, throw it away,
nonsense 'n' melancholy,
barbarous trips through blacked-out enlightenment.
Why I like discos, imperfect lovers,
who never can say goodbye.
Someone once told me
the best way through is love.
Someone lied.
Someone's always fucking lying.
I try with my little lie,
something beginning with love.
We
heart,
we
breathe,
we
start.

Fancy myself a fifties tart,
full-pout smouldering, plot 'n' gun powdered.
The last woman to hang life's dirty laundry.

The Sauna Demons

Drug-fucked 'n' cutting,
shades dissolve a scurrying jagged black
and in an explode of thinking, poppers.
Amongst the little shapes,
people bump cock and long-blind fumble.
Lube-smeared spread hopeful.
Drunk's got an interval and techno-pound pummels.
This is choice and devils cupped are in the detail.

Sometimes it's best alone,
shit-squatting, waiting,
in this whole I summon,
heightened and ultra-sensing.
It's always below, the rumble and dig up,
scrip-scraping through pornography's concrete.
Flesh is a feast day.

In over-imagined half-light
a hint of cheek and long finger,
boned, knuckled and reaching.
They whisper welcoming
in languages long lost and trodden on.
Not secrets,
every hot tramp mutters this spiral.
It's a bit remembering everything 'n' forgetting.

This is where the rave dived,
screwed-in and bang-banged.
Where they live,
the sauna demons and lost holes.
They don't scare, never did,
me 'n' the dark know.
I like they trickle-giggle, long for their touch.

The Big Noise

Big noise rides a cocksure overwhelm,
pendulum lilts the well-hung.
You'll hear it sometimes.
Most times when you're quiet.
There are too many sounds
all the time,
a mind-choir.
Big noise fails the rock-hard,
in cascades and topple,
riots.
The lone voice hollers,
stretches screechless between dimensions.

Why don't we kill when we're being killed?
The big noise shouts down,
you're an echo ricocheting
around 'n' about alleyways.
Pick it up,
cast it away,
there are endings with your name on.
Last line in the register,
drops.
We stop singing to stay lost.

The big noise splinters in CGI,
expensive,
in reflection of eye-memory,
distraction.

Pain Killers

I make my welcome broad,
wider than ideas
and embrace the pain killers.
The people who boogie,
recite,
kill bullshite,
smile through storms.

Within and around night's lights,
fireflies buzzin',
disco-huggin'.
Recognition in a nod,
in share of rhythm.
Pain killers wreck it,
beat out their agonies on dancefloors.

When I hear them tell their stories well,
when they mean it,
precious.
Kills the pain.

In This Town

I've a long face,
worn it out and too many times
chin's scrip-scraping the pavement.
I'm jaw-dropped, haunched and homebound.

There's tricks uncast,
spells unspun,
incantations unspoken.
In this town the magic's not always paid for,
you have to earn it,
learn to boil your own oils.

The wizard on the thirteenth floor's throwing
a hard party and some stars.
He insists we swallow or we won't get in.
He insists the partings started.

In this town
the wizard isn't always right,
never always wrong.
He's ever-so hobo and Catherine wheel.

I'll go home.
I know the wizard's game.
Play it all the time in this town.

And Breathe

Change,
air,
in,
is the breathe out,
the inhalation,
all together,
apart,
lunged,
fleshed,
pumped,
in,
all,
together it,
not automatons,
robots,
hearts,
beat,
we rhythm,
air is change,
in the.

The
BOURGEOIS
ZEITGEIST

A Treatise
by
Gerry Potter

IX

We see what we see and must say what we see. I'm sure some of what I've just said will be met with outraged disapproval and that's absolutely fine. I'm certainly not a poet because I want to hold the world's festival heart-fingered hand, I'm a poet because I want to untangle said festival heart-fingered hand and use it to hold up a mirror. No doubt I'll be called a 'spoiling-it-for-the-others-meany-poos', paranoid even – believe me, I'm used to it – but this is what I see, therefore what I'm saying.

As mentioned earlier, I don't perform so much anymore, very rarely, and there are a few reasons. Main one's being I feel somewhat detached 'n' distanced from the current arts world. Even though I've acutely critiqued a few things, I genuinely still believe the arts do tremendous good, particularly in places like Manchester. There are some incredibly committed people really meaning what they're doing who are making huge differences and they will always have my heart [but not fingers]. It's just at this moment in time it 'n' I have emotionally/intellectually/creatively parted company. I don't feel artistically/politically content with the almost constant celebration and applauding, particularly outdoors; it just doesn't sit well with me. I'm also very aware, because of this increasing fiscal apartheid we're all living under, audiences are less 'n' less working-class. Even what's left of the counter-culture is now populated by people with money; you now completely need money to do things on the cheap. At my beloved Unity Theatre in Liverpool the other day, tickets for shows where retailing at £18 – so many people are unable to afford even that. As Austerity digs much deeper and continues to destroy more 'n' more lives, I feel at complete and often enraged odds with Inspirationalism 'n' Positivia. I seriously can't keep smiling/applauding when I'm actually broken/crying – and broken/crying just doesn't suit the everything's mega-nice, everything's super-awesome Bourgeois Zeitgeist agenda.

Writing this, although occasionally funny [believe it or not, I've had quite a chortle], has been at times a completely heart-breaking exercise. When I look at the decades of austerity, at the ideologically engineered entropy working-class communities have continually endured, the cultural erosion of my peoples, their politically-managed social erasure, they're poverty-porn re-branding, I'm sometimes at a big aching loss. It's simply too much to take in. Right now, I don't feel upbeat 'n' positive about things, not at all; I feel historically/presently angry and profoundly sad. I'm remembering a piece of theatre at Manchester's Contact called *White Trash*, an absolutely brilliant moment of work, my favourite in all my time here [possibly in all my time anywhere]. I'm remembering the young scally male performers being outstanding, a fusion of irrepressible working-class energy and highest art, a stunning series of quite surreal set-pieces grounded by real-lifed gravitas. I'm remembering how completely spiritually uplifting and physically heart-breaking it all was. Uplifting because of the spectacular physical energies involved; it flared with city-felt cocksure brio. Heart-breaking in the blinding intensity of its aching and incredibly revealing pauses, in those long corridors of silence, their history, *my* history, the rusting whispers of industry, heroin. A cold yearning sense of what little they had and the insecurity even that may be taken from them... and it has. I'm remembering this was before Coalition-led Austerity.

I respect people trying to make lives better, I genuinely do, but nothing short of massive redistributions of wealth will do that... the working-class needs money!

After writing that last piece, I, satchel over shoulder, camply ambled from Manchester Central Library to meet some friends on

Canal Street, the homo from homo of Manchester's historically hysterical Queer communities 'n' one of my very favourite places on this 'ere planet. It was a hot June day and we're sat outside an auld gay men's bar of wonderfully leather-bound ill-repute called The Rembrandt. If the wind's blowing right you can still get a whiff of 1985's poppers. We were boozing, John, Helen, Rick, Kerry, Reece, Ray and I, chatting away, and suddenly heard these strange strangulated noises. At first, we couldn't actually make them out, felt inhuman, animal-like, but not like any animal you might readily recognise. Harsh guttural raspings, coughing 'n' spluttering from poisoned stomach to phlegmy mouth. To all intents 'n' purposes, the noise of retching starving hellhounds. In true scorching summer tradition, Canal Street was bare-chested full and these aggressively howling noises echoing a-hacking everywhere. The people table-sat outside its many bars nervously started to look, neck-stretching 'n' shoulder-weaving to find where these awful wailings were coming from. They were coming from neighbouring Sackville Gardens, and not just-released Hades-spawned mutations, but yer actual human Mancunian beings: a gang of homeless, desperate, drugged 'n' fucked-up young people with babies in prams. Something had obviously gone communally awry with them and it, how we say in the North, 'proper kicked off!'. They were fighting/screeching, half-empty cider bottle hurling; a couple of the lads had ripped off shirts getting ready to fight, their skeletal, undernourished skin-lesion'd torsos devastating to behold. Saddest thing of all, people sat along Canal Street were pointing and laughing. Not everybody, but a good few thought what they were witnessing was in some way amusing. I'm instantly reminded of my brothers in 1969 and how these young men weren't them, how these young men now, the ages my brothers may well have been then, seemed not just a few decades but a million worlds apart. These young men had none of my brothers' obviously well-dressed confidence, no security of community, none of the cocky bravado coming from knowing you're gonna have a gear night out in town with your mates, and certainly weren't standing with a wedge of just-earned weekending tenners in their pockets. They were lost, bellowing 'n' scrapping, flapping about in the wastelands of their beyond-troubled histories and our present. I say 'our' present because nothing of now belongs to these ghosts, they don't have anything; it's our present because everything is geared to and made for The Bourgeois Zeitgeist, The Accountant Culture.

We are all The Bourgeois Zeitgeist, including Manchester, including Liverpool, including every city, including me, and no one more The Bourgeois Zeitgeist than those raging/ragged people tumbling chaotically about Sackville Gardens... 'the dispirited of the age'.

Unless we completely change the system, are brave enough to recognise the unforgiving/unrelenting carnage of division, then none of this 'distance' will stop. On the contrary, it will get even wider.

So, just what is it I'm meant to be continually applauding again? Those distraught, furious, homeless people inhabiting Sackville Gardens, unable to afford, engage in [or are moved away from, barricaded out of] our supposedly 'unifying' festivals? Or the people on Canal Street laughing at them, those who can afford, can engage in, and most probably will?

One spectacular moment of a recent Manchester International Festival, something I actually very much enjoyed, was the unveiling of a big statue of local hero Friedrich Engels. I would have liked his statue placed in a more working-class bit of Salford and not a brand spanking new Bourgeois Zeitgeist area of Manchester, but hey, you can't have everything.

There are legendary stories of him stepping over the sick'd, drunken working-class of Salford and deprivations of what he witnessed, helping him forge ahead with creating of the weekend. He and his bezzy Karl, prestigious boozers by all accounts, would drink in an auld haunt of mine, Salford's The Crescent, formerly The Red Dragon [now sadly gone]. And then, in a Manchester city centre down-at-heel dive called The Coach and Horses [opposite what is now The Gay Village], perhaps first draft scribbling away at some utopian manifesto or t'other.

I like to think of my girly sister Caleb Everett [or, as I sometimes teasingly call her, Calebsia Everhard] and I as campier drag versions of Marx 'n' Engels [Marge 'n' Angela] – but only if we can be in the same undercover drag as Williams 'n' Hawtrey in *Carry On Constable*.

I wondered what Engels would think of modern day Manchester/Salford, what he would make of the crowds applauding/cheering his statue. I've a third eye for the working/under-class, can spot them a mile off: I scanned the crazily partying vista and have to say didn't see too many; I didn't see the people he fought for the weekend for. Mind you, so many of those people have had over four decades of no weekends at all, just the bleeding and blending of endless days. They are 'The Distance'.

Being the end of a tremendously successful festival, this was very rightly an end of festivities party, but I couldn't join in with the constant cheering 'n' applauding. I kept wondering, what if I could magically make that statue come alive? Would the iconoclastic Mr Engels also be clapping along?

So, I upped sticks, and in full Kenneth Williams drag, poison-pen in hand, went to seek Ms Everhard at a down-at-stiletto-heel bar in The Gay Village.

I want to thank you Manchester for far too many things, one of them being for well over twenty years now you've been the surroundings cradling me and I've loved/love rockin' 'n' rollin' in your red-bricked arms. The other is for hedonism; no city does 'off its 'ead' quite like you. Not just off its 'ead for off its 'ead's sake either, but a deeper intellectualising, politicised understanding of it. Ask anybody Manchester, I've been off my 'ead in very many cities, towns and villages, but there's something about me 'n' you that's truly special. You're the king and most definitely queen of off its 'ead and if you could ever find you're the 'ead you're off, babe, you'd defiantly wear the crown. I wonder if perhaps you're on some dark/light partying ley-line whose shriekin' partying frequency completely interferes and Vulcan mind-melds with mine, and it is dark/light. I very much love those bright/bleak neon'd shiny/toxic hues of yours 'n' all the cobbles in between; don't think there's a nook, cranny, crook, granny, fuck alley we've not ducked/dived into. Oh, we've adventured OK; you've been a brilliant discoing Silver to my Lone Raver, a wonderfully flowing cape to my camp crusader... "I'm Camp Man!". When I think of all we've gotten up to, knowingly into, I smile and it's the smile of a friend y'know, a best friend. You remind me of Brian, Manchester, he was dark/light, ribald, oft' gritty, caustically witty, a fabulous dancer and we were always rowing. I often wonder what it would be like if Brian were here with us now. I think, if alive, we'd all three be camply partying together. Must say, I sometimes make him, not quite sure how but I do, be here with me/you, a bit of a Scottie Road slyboots resurrection... and guess what? He fuckin' loves it! I've a peculiar feeling he'd be on my side with The Bourgeois Zeitgeist, but that wouldn't stop him partying with it, sniffing its coke/poppers and feigning disco-flattered fabulousness for yet another coquettishly large Brandy 'n' Babycham. She really was one of the cooler hustlers. You would have adored him, for all his glittering bombast he loved nothing more than a good ol' fashioned sex-cruising mooch. He would have soft-shadowed down the canal for a bit of after-clubbing delight and you'd have looked after him, like you've always looked after me. I've loved so damn much of you, Manchester. Too much to ever put into silly words.

Speaking of words, here's a tiny handful of my more literary adventures. I'm remembering Fab Café with The Monday Night Group, a disparate band of others, writerly intellectuals letting what's left of their middle-aged hair down to 'Tracey Barlow's Bedroom Tapes' disco [yes, Dawn Acton, the original Tracey]. Remembering Hannah 'n' I wildly dancin', proper tit/hip boogyin' to whatever heart-lifting pop moment, then zooming off to The Gay Village's Napoleon's Bar for even more jigging, a profound chin-wagging session and to eye-up 'n' argue over the same potential bit 'o' trade. Remembering drunkenly spilling out of Conor Aylward's gorge seedy as intellectual poetry night Per Verse at The Briton's Protection, having just dropped a flurry of fun-stuffs with Jackie Hagan, then piling down the New York New York to show the gays the right way to add rubies to slippers, then how to click three times 'n' fly. Remembering demonstrative drunken chats with Brink from Flapjack and telling him about a great idea for ten books in ten years, then him possessing the wily anarchic generosity to make that happen. Our Brink prides himself on his inward/outward gothnicity, but he's also [like Studio Salford] very Punk.

Oh Manchester, just a few flashes in a gloriously glittering giant chip-pan of spitting/sparking delight, of surrendering, of knowing how and why to. Yes, you're mighty 'n' grand that's for sure, stoic, a handsome fucker, you look magnificent when snowing. If human, why, I might even court you, if you asked, let you be my boyfriend. Ah, but you swept me off my feet decades ago, fuckin' charmer. You really are all the bedazzling, broad-shouldered, big-built you should be, but you're small as well, dirty. You don't need to constantly whistle a fanfare, join in the applause, you're not in any way humble at all. Although you shouldn't, and are nowhere near equipped, you continue to clumsily somehow shelter our homeless. Even though not enough, nowhere near – only a proper home is – you still try to cover, and thank the Dark Lord below they've got you. Seriously, you and the rain are all they've got. Dread to think where they'd be without, you're the only thing around here not moving them on. I definitely love you for that.

You've seen it before and will see it all again. I respect that about you, Manchester, it definitely makes you great, not the greatest mind, nowhere is right now, but certainly one of the very best. Tell you what would make you the greatest; if the revolution started here...

C'mon babe, think about it, you've certainly the credentials. Only revolution now! I'm in! Difficult in the current climate of Inspirationalism, Positivia 'n' mindfulness, that's for fuckin' sure. I'm not saying they're to wholly blame, but the constant chorusing of melodic humility it sings... well, isn't fighting talk is it? The cloying echo-chamber'd passivity of careerist virtue signalling... don't sound like a war cry to me. I miss the fighting talk Manchester, why I put it back in this book. You know what I mean; you're responsible for so much of it, I got a lot of mine from you. I wrote 'The Queen Sucks Nazi Cock' 'n' 'How Do You Respect Fuck All' here, cheers for tha'. You can see why The Bourgeois Zeitgeist doesn't want it; your fighting talk would be in opposition to it. "Keep calm and drink tea!" That's a proactive Bourgeois Zeitgeist solution... hardly attacking agitation is it? If everybody had kept calm and drank tea on the 20th February 1988, Manchester wouldn't have had that historically Queer defining Clause 28 March. The homeless deserve something on that scale and if this was 1988, I genuinely think they'd have got it. I've been on a good few marches for the homeless, but they were nowhere near as well attended. I think the least we owe them is a heartfelt flare of outraged civil disobedience.

I'd so like to be rid of The Bourgeois Zeitgeist, the energy, force, the polite horribly mutated financial end of middle-English right-wing distance 'n' division. That's why I took the right wing off the bee, Manchester, for the swarm's unable to fly, for the bees without hives who can't lap the honey... one-winged bees are people, too. More than anything about The Bourgeois Zeitgeist, I just find it so repetitively dull, wearily pedestrian; it uses words like 'revolution' all the time, particularly to sell its art, but never once started one. It's one cheeky bastard that's for sure! I wish I could historically pin-point it more, maybe make it human, not talk of it as a formless murderously decades-old fiscal energy. That's what it feels like though, a dense smog-like spirit financially engulfing us all. It's got us all talking about money... The Accountant Culture! I think if we were all on a more even keel it might not bother me so much, but when it comes to class war it's won – and that beyond pisses me off. Why we need a bloody revolution, soon as. If there were to be a bloody revolution tomorrow [and believe me, I've tried so hard to start one] I'd back to performing before you could say Molotov cross-dresser. That, or very least, a radically reforming Labour government with massive fiscal redistribution at it very heart... yeah, I'd joyfully get back behind the mic.

Tell you summat fer nottin' though, Manchester, you're definitely missing 'something', something you once had, every city once had in stormy anarchic wildly weekending abundance, something I thought if I fell backwards it would instinctively reach out to catch me... I want a fiscally empowered working-class and my counter-culture back!

End

P.S. Just want to take a moment to thank Sleaford Mods, Scottish comedian Limmy, writer/wit Fran Lebowitz and Miss Marsha P. Johnson for their invaluable virtual-YouTubing help/support.

The Mods because they've been the viscerally witty, essentially gritty soundtrack for this treatise, they know this country's backward; 'Jobseeker' is a work of unadulterated genius.

Limmy for so many brilliant characters, including Dee Dee, Jacqueline McCafferty [my 'heroyne'], Xander and the very epitome, the soulless fire of The Bourgeois Zeitgeist itself, Malcolm Malcolm of the Politics Bar. Whenever I think I've gone too far I immediately pop on a Malcolm Malcolm video and instantly realise I've not yet gone far enough.

Fran Lebowitz because she clearly sees it too, certainly the erosion of creative counter-culture so The Bourgeois Zeitgeist can mindlessly hop from city to city, benignly staring and nodding at the same things they benignly stared and nodded at in the last city, all this while drinking the same individualised frothy coffees. We may be on different pages with this Fran, but I'm sure we share some similar ideas; I'd really love to have a proper New York downtown jangle with you.

Miss Marsha P., not just for this book, you're always with me. You knew gutter intellectualism and the true 'counter' of street shit like no other. That searing energy so goddamn Queer, so goddamn right! One day babe, the whole wide world will be Miss Marsha P. Johnson-shaped… I adore you!

Trade Itself

Whilst raving in '90s Manchester we would often zoom over to London to lose our minds 'n' bodies in Trade, some of the best beats ever clubbed.

London's secret
secretes,
Socrates bare-chest mythologies,
socked it to 'em bad style.
There's balm, spit, poo in the toilets,
next to the snow-storms,
next to the skin'eads,
next to the coked-up celebrities.
"Sodom'll come out Gomorrah,
bubble-butch that bottom doll, there'll be some."
Show-tunes mutate, gimmick, are techno-industrial,
sung 'n' snug fist-deep in bowels of mouths 'n' hearts.

This perspiration is mine, yours, theirs, ours.
Biblical salt strains our pillars,
our pillows drench in sleeplessness,
these are, after all, our dreams,
wet.
River's running red,
bare-backing's kickin' in a back-room sweat,
history's blood-rivering our feet.
As it always was 'n' will be,
all is dancing, alive and dying.

I'm told they're all professionals,
gym-bunnied 'n' torso,
their special corner glows.
Queer ecology,
bitches feeding off butch auras
of just-bleached blue-denim'd whales,

blowing in Westwood sales,
we're are sperm, plankton and small fishes.
All us bitches are owned by music,
by the below gods,
decked.
Camps and the bunnies
are strobed, shit-faced 'n' shipwrecked.

I'm on the floor and joined to another body,
no touch, just sense,
we beyond light.
Without words he says, "Did you see that?"
I said, "That huge computer circuit board?"
He says, "Yes!"
I said, "Yes!"

Big World

Big world, you bore me,
all your trash-Jazz acrimony,
not only tuneless,
without rhythm,
you're unintelligible.
What bores me more, you know it,
dine out on it,
gives you reason to dance badly.
I hate people choosing to dance badly,
who choose not to improvise.

Big world, fuck off,
crawl under,
seep through,
disappear.
Every pothole's for you crater face,
every drain 'n' sewer.

I won't get sadder.
Big world, I won't let you win.

The Shaman's Shell

Comfortable and conch,
spiriting a three-sugared cuppa,
universes spin violently in tea,
explode in coffee.

Patterned splat and carefree
are the She-Hag's scarscapes.
Stars shape her promise,
said she promised those hearts some ecstatic beating.
She said to the shaman,
"You've still some streeting to do."
Put him in and off his face.

The Shaman's shell-suit glistened,
rocked the techno,
spat out gum
and in the dark creases,
fireworks.

Those Fingers

Another of my favourite Manchester theatre moments has been the Take Back Theatre initiative. Founded by Julie Hesmondhalgh, Becx Harrison and Grant Archer, Take Back Theatre is a shamelessly powerfully creative socialist theatre moment, there very much for the peoples on the ground, the foot-soldiers. Although very modern, it really does have that urgent bravura seventies agitprop vibe I so adore. This was written especially for a Take Back supporting and celebrating seventy years of the NHS.

Those fingers,
sheet folding,
bedside-mannered and rolling,
occasionally maybe scolding,
running along the crease.
Those fingers never cease,
warring bodies needing peace,
those fingers administer release,
from pain,
those fingers time 'n' time again,
tireless,
priceless,
trained,
targeted,
aimed,
those fingers intricately humane and stitching.

Switching,
from one role to another.
Those fingers,
sister,
auntie,
father,
mother,
those fingers smother,

brother,
and no matter other,
those fingers offer handfuls of hope,
the scope to cope and chill.
Those fingers dishing out potion 'n' pill,
those fingers fast,
those fingers still,
friends,
cleanse,
kin,
boss,
win,
loss,
those fingers see you through.

Flu jab,
brew,
never the don't
when doing the do.
Those fingers five,
decades saving lives,
soothing hives and mind,
those fingers thrive in living,
selflessly giving, those fingers kind.
Brow mopped,
never stopped,
wiping bottoms, tops,
transplanting organs, cleaning slops,
those fingers filling holes,
full of drive and goals,
never half-hearted,
getting stopped hearts started,
cheeks parted,
thermometer in, vomiter bowled.

Those fingers young,
middle-aged,
old.
Often warm,
occasionally cold,
those fingers on fire.
Inspire,
take society higher,
seemingly never tire.
Hands shaken with life-saving thanks,
shouldn't be using foodbanks.
Those fingers often thwarted,
positions distorted, misreported,
must always be supported
and after all they've done,
all they've saved,
sorted,
must never be deported!

Those fingers birth,
those fingers death,
close eyes,
first breath,
new moon,
sunset,
entering the world,
simply the best.
Guiding the old,
baby to breast.

Weathered

Falling asleep to The Shipping Forecast.

Hitting pillow'd waves,
drown-time lament.
Ghosts call back
in side-winding spirals of your shell-like.

Within weaves and dreamscapes,
knots speeding.
Neptune splices his mainbrace
and the voice clipped, breaks.

Eddies pour through trident fingers,
seaweed tresses flow.
Amongst mermaid giggles,
pearls.

Eye of the storm stares,
gods slumber on these sea-beds.
The yachtsmen bed down,
turn the dial.

Space splatters a blue-grey torture,
white noise sifts in.
Sand's time
and salt stabs your lungs.

Dreamt Lover

I love you, don't I?
Told you yesterday,
you dreamt I said it,
didn't I?
I told you, you dreamt,
saying *I love you*,
told you I said it love, told you I said it.

You told me I said it,
I love you, didn't you?
Told me,
yesterday, promising tomorrow,
you said it.
I might be dreaming you said,
this may be dreamt,
but you said it,
I love you,
didn't you?

We love it, don't we?
Yesterday.
Dreaming.
We love saying it,
love dreaming,
being dreamt.
Love.
Dreaming.
We said it,
love dreaming,
didn't we,
we did dream love,
didn't we?

I'm Like A Lot Of Gay Men, I Am

From day one it's been complexly about saying goodbye.
To masculinity, to community,
family,
to impossible norms and respectability.
Maybe not wholly for you and that's truly gorge,
but beeyatches, most definitely for me.
As other boys collectively cheered *hello* to football
I cried long goodbyes to pride.
As they boldly showered-off body skills
I found more terrified towelled places to hide.
No matter how otherwise I'd try
it always felt like saying goodbye.

So goodbye pondering, I'm sat
cup-of-tea-steady in silent storms.
Chocolate for breakfast,
speckled patterns of too-damp walls.
Still saying goodbye, but somehow kinda used to it,
forward-thinking anarchic opposites,
but then that was always my way, my plan.
I'm like a lot of gay men, I am.

The Manc Vampire

Scene: *An incredibly ramshackle and unkempt bedsit, half-draped in shade and back-broken excuses. There are 'other' sounds whiningly circling, noises abstracting from beneath emotion, intoned by ancient subterranean darknesses. From a central-staged unmade single bed, everything is only an arm's stretch and struggle away. It's a woman's bedsit; there are bits of inexpensive Pound Shop frill and pink, used condoms, bloodied syringes, burnt silver paper, scorched teaspoons and stained knickers. Thrown about, the occasional glittery dress, filthy yet brightly coloured nylon tracksuits, laddered tights, dirty trainers and one pair of badly scuffed stilettos. Above the bed, a cheap golden-framed Sacred Heart of Jesus, a long pink Rosary limply hanging off one of its plastic ornate corners. In the stillness of its streetlamp-lit haze, a sense of shop-bought ridiculousness and the heavily Gothic permeates everything. This is a place dangerously lived in by a precariously hyper-experienced life. Outside the door we hear the sound of two people, very drunk and off-their-faces: Val, the prostitute whose bedsit we are in, and Adam, her punter.*

Val: I can't get it in.

Adam: Don't worry, I will in a minute!

Val: Wha'?

Adam: Can't wait to get in there.

Val: Get y'hands off 'n' shurrup will ye, it's just a bit stiff that's all.

Adam: I'm mega-stiff here, feel.

Val: Y'are, aren't y'big boy, fuckin' 'ell warravya got goin' down there, five pound of liver sausage?

Adam: Whatever I've got it's all for you.

Val: I'll chow down in a bit.

Adam: Chow down now.

Val: Let me just concentrate a minni will ye!

Adam: That's it, keep your hands on it, get it mega-big.

Val: C'mon hun, I've got to—

Adam: Just hold it, I'm so super-fucking horny right now, go on, wank me off.

Val: Do it y'self a minni, can't pull y'off while I'm tryin' to open the door, y'daft fucker.

Adam: Don't want to do myself, want you to, blow us off babe, oh go on, please, I'm mega-fucking desperate here.

Val: Alright, a quick one, gerrem down then...

Adam: Fucking too right.

Val: Christ fellah, you've really gorri going on 'aven't ye!

Adam: *[After a brief moment]* Fucking hell that's good, mega, oh super-fucking-mega, ooh, ohh, shit yeah, go on babe, go on suck it, fucking suck it.

Val: Yeah, y'like tha' don't ye!

Adam: You're good dude, so fucking good, phwoar you know what you're doing alright, oh wow fucking wow, God, fucking wow, this is better than Porn Hub...

Val: Right, that should keep y'goin', let's just try to get this bastard'n door open shall we, cluckin' like an unfed chicken 'ere.

Adam: Oh go on, one more little suck...

Val: I will in a bit, just need to sort m'self out, seriously give us a sec 'n' I'll blow ye big time.

Adam: That had better be a promise.

Val: Cross my heart 'n' 'ope t'die.

Adam: Have you got all you need in there?

Val: Gor'enough, then I'll proper finish ye off, promise.

Adam: Can't fucking wait, I'm so super-hard for you right now.

Val: It'll be well worth waitin' for mate, I can tell ye – there, that's it, at long last!

[The bedsit door flies open and in tumble Val and Adam. Adam is a fit, attractive man in his late twenties, clumsily pulling up his sharp-suited trousers. Val, a garishly tracksuited, scrunchie-haired, badly dyed blonde in her early fifties, rushes over to her drug equipment and quickly sets up a hit.]

Val: Won't be a minute mate, what's y'name again?

Adam: Adam Sharpe with an E.

Val: Nice one Adam, don't need y'full name mind.

Adam: Sorry, office/networking habit.

Val: Wish y'had an E.

Adam: Oh right, E, yeah, me too.

Val: Don't worry y'self, honestly won't be minute babe…

Adam: Take your time, this baby isn't going anywhere soon.

Val: Bet it isn't.

Adam: *[Paws his crotch]* It's already pointing in your direction.

Val: Can see it from 'ere, like Nelson's Column.

Adam: Cheers!

Val: Actually, more The Leaning Tower of Penis.

Adam: Flattery will get you fucked.

Val: Fuckin' hope so.

Adam: Super-fucked!

Val: Can see I'm in for a proper thrashin' with tha'.

Adam: Definitely… wow, this stuff's fucking beyond mega.

Val: Y'look well off it mate, wasted.

Adam: I am, but not wasted though, not at all… buzzing, super-fucking-mega-buzzing.

Val: Sweet.

Adam: Come on babe.

Val: I will, just sit down for two minutes will ye.

Adam: But I want—

Val: Sit! *[Adam sits]*

Adam: *[Pause]* Nice place.

Val: Fuck off, it's a shit 'ole, fallin' t'bits.

Adam: No, I like it, natural, lived in, who else lives in here?

Val: In 'ere? Only me.

Adam: I mean the whole building.

Val: Nobody, just me, told y'hun, fallin' to bits 'n' the fuckin' damp, no one in their right minds would want to live here, to be 'onest with ye it's probably unfit for human contamination.

Adam: Habitation.

Val: Same thing in my book.

Adam: Didn't have you down as a nihilist.

Val: A wha'?

Adam: Nothing... doesn't it like mega-freak you out?

Val: Does wha' freak me out?

Adam: Living alone.

Val: Babe, I literally had nowhere before 'ere, on the streets for six year, far as I'm concerned this damp rotten shit-pit's Buckingham fuckin' Palace.

Adam: An optimist then, eh?

Val: I keep me options open babe.

Adam: Glass half full?

Val: Depends wha' with.

Adam: Oh man, I just love this feeling.

Val: What's tha' hun.

Adam: Don't you feel it?

Val: Feel wha'?

Adam: The night, clubbing, drink, drugs and dirty fucking – fucking! – just gets you going, really mega-revved! I feel so fucking woke!

Val: Oh tha', yeah, same as you mate.

Adam: Wish you'd hurry up.

Val: Two ticks hun.

Adam: Looks complicated, is it?

Val: Nah, piece of piss.

Adam: Been on it long?

Val: Fuckin' time luv...

Adam: What is it, what exactly are you doing, is it chasing the dragon?

Val: Nah, just messin' with me toot-toot, won't be long sweetheart, seriously, bear with me.

Adam: Never seen anybody do that before.

Val: Sure y'safe for that pony?

Adam: Pony?

Val: Fifty quid y'promised.

Adam: Oh yeah, definitely.

Val: Not bein' a bitch or owt, but can I 'ave it up front mate?

Adam: If you do a good job I'll give you a ton.

Val: Fuck off, serious, 'ave y'gorri in cash?

Adam: Yeah, I'm very generous, especially if it's a blow job well done.

Val: Believe me luv, for a ton it'll be a proper seein' to, I'll swallow it whole then swallow, if y'know warra mean!

Adam: Dude, that's hot.

Val: Serious, need that money big time, rent on this hovel costs a fuckin' bomb, well, a bomb and an occasional fuck.

Adam: You one of those who fuck the landlord for rent?

Val: Name me a cunt on this street tha' doesn't.

Adam: I don't know this street.

Val: Y'could get fucked for half a bitter shandy round 'ere mate, that's why I could do with tha' ton, keep him off me back, literally.

Adam: Oh yeah, like it's for rent.

Val: It is, well, some of it will be.

Adam: If you're even half as good as you were out there, you'll get it alright.

Val: Y'know wha', believe ye, not bein' funny or nottin' mate but y'seem a bit too posh to do a runner.

Adam: Oh I am dude, mega-posh, so mega-posh it hurts, Scout's honour.

Val: Pure used to scroaty cunts rippin' me off.

Adam: Bastards!

Val: Some snidey twats out there mate, proper, should gerrum done under the Trade Descriptions Act.

Adam: Funny.

Val: Well, me job's keepin' peckers up, inni?

Adam: *[Laughs]* Are you nearly done?

Val: Yeah, just about. *[Val takes a lighter to underneath some silver foil and, straw in nose, inhales the smoke]*

Adam: Seriously, I'd love to give it a shot.

Val: Can if y'want, easy get some more, but wouldn't advise it mate, I've seen far too many people go under, proper under, more than I could ever count, not pretty, not pretty at all, won't be long luv, promise ye, be over in no time.

Adam: *[Pause]* What does it do?

Val: Stops me 'avin' a nervous breakdown mate, keeps me sane.

Adam: Sane?

Val: Yeah, I'd go proper off me nut without it.

Adam: Wow, so it's that important to you?

Val: This moment in time luv, the most.

Adam: What does it actually feel like?

Val: Er, I dunno…

Adam: Give us a clue.

Val: Fuckin' 'ell you ask a lorra questions don't ye… er… like y'chillin' 'n' buzzin' at the same time.

Adam: Wow dude, can I try it?

Val: No luv, that's all there was, y'still up off tha' speed I got ye, pure paste tha' mate.

Adam: Too right yeah, I mean I really am mega-off it… it's just I want be what you're on.

Val: Tha's cos y'whizzin' y'tits off, take a bit more.

Adam: Oh yes, brilliant idea, wanna catch up with you, *[takes out speed and dabs it]* would you like some?

Val: No luv, I'm sorted, just need a sec, that's all.

Adam: Still really want to try it though, want to try every-fucking-thing.

Val: Tellin' y'now mate, serious, leave this shit alone, fucks y'right up, fucked me up that's for sure, kills ye man... now, if y'll just give me a couple of minutes I'll be right with ye. *[A groggy Val moves to the end of her single bed and sits]*

Adam: Are you tripping, seeing stuff?

Val: Nah nottin' like tha'…

Adam: Like what then?

Val: Just wha' it is mate.

Adam: Are you seeing things flying inside your mind?

Val: Inside me mind?

Adam: Yeah.

Val: Like wha'?

Adam: Don't know, anything, bats, demons, y'know, like *Game of Thrones*.

Val: Game of wha'?

Adam: *Game of Thrones*, it's this superb series, you can get it on Netflix.

Val: Don't be daft!

Adam: No, seriously, it's fucking mega-superb, works on so many differing levels, one minute it's sword and sorcery, next a bitchy soap opera, then a fucking mega-porn movie, it really is as trashy as it's esoteric.

Val: Esoteric?

Adam: Completely!

Val: Don't really watch tha' much telly babe.

Adam: Are there like other dimensions going on?

Val: Other dimensions?

Adam: Yeah, you know, like *Doctor Strange*.

Val: Doctor who?

Adam: No, *Doctor Strange*, it's a film, actually it was a comic book first, brilliant as well, but it's a mega-film now.

Val: Nah, just this dimension hun.

Adam: Then what's it like?

Val: Me dimension?

Adam: Yeah!

Val: Like I said, just a chillin' 'n' buzzin' dimension mate, serious, be back with ye in time.

Adam: What's it really like, go on, tell us!

Val: Don't really know wha' to tell ye.

Adam: Is it like *Trainspotting*?

Val: To be honest with ye, right now it's like some daft cunt's peckin' me 'ead while I'm trying to get in the zone to give him the best blow job of his life.

Adam: Sorry... *[pause]* are there colours?

Val: Wha' y'on about now?

Adam: You seeing colours, are things flashing in and out at you?

Val: Just red...

Adam: What kind of red?

Val: Fumin'!

Adam: Do you mean like fire?

Val: Exactly like.

Adam: Does it feel warm?

Val: Fuckin' ragin'!

Adam: Shall I call the fire brigade?

Val: *[Snaps]* Call who the fuck you want luv! *[Quickly calming down]* Sorry babe, no offence, be with ye in a bit…

Adam: No offence taken, when it comes to drugs, I'm super-naïve, probably talking all kinds of rubbish.

Val: We call it chattin' shit.

Adam: Sorry for chatting shit then.

Val: No worries… where y'from, nice accent, London?

Adam: No, Sussex.

Val: Don't know Sussex, 'eard of it, is it nice?

Adam: It's a boring shit hole.

Val: Shit 'ole? Thought there'd be all trees 'n' tha'.

Adam: Spot on, it's a leafy shit hole full of trees, like a library with greenery, a conservatory with books, not like here.

Val: Warra y'doin' in Manchester?

Adam: There's just tons more opportunity here, I mean super-loads, my little brother's here too, so that helps.

Val: Nice to 'ave family with ye in a big city.

Adam: Yeah, our C, he's a laugh, bit of a poet.

Val: Oh right, top one, love a bit of poetry me, is he any good?

Adam: Not really, but he thinks he is.

Val: Is he all tha' hip-hop on himself?

Adam: That's it, very astute, wouldn't have you down as a poetry lover.

Val: Why?

Adam: Well, it's just…

Val: I'm a hooker?

Adam: Sorry, my bad, also what I'm doing here is trying to have a bit of fun with you.

Val: Warra I actually meant was wha' ye doin' in Manchester for a job, dick'ead.

Adam: Oh right, God, I am so super-slow tonight, accountancy.

Val: You an accountant?

Adam: That's what accountancy means.

Val: Brilliant, money, numbers 'n' tha'? *[Pause]*

Adam: *[Mimics Val's voice]* Yeah, money, numbers 'n' tha', I'm bang into money, numbers 'n' all tha', me…

Val: You alright?

Adam: *[Still mimicking]* Yeah, I'm alright me, a proper crack whore who'll bang anything me 'n' am still bang into money, numbers 'n' all tha'!

Val: *[Pause]* You takin' the piss mate?

Adam: No, but you fucking are, money, numbers 'n' tha'!

Val: Wha'?

Adam: You've been taking the piss all along, all night.

Val: No I haven't mate, serious!

Adam: All I wanted was blowing off and what did I get, just a quick crappy suck getting me hard that led nowhere, where I come from that's taking the fucking piss, I bought you drinks all night and that speed cost way too fucking much, that's taking the piss as well!

Val: I didn't force ye mate, y'said y'wanted some drugs, there was no sniff only tha', 'n' swear down that's the goin' rate, all I could get short notice, told ye I needed to get back 'n' what for.

Adam: Still taking the piss, isn't it slag!

Val: Wha' you onnabout, what's got into ye mate?

Adam: And you called me a daft cunt, a dickhead as well, 'chatting shit', if I remember rightly, piece of dog turd like you calling me a dickhead, you sick fucking bitch.

Val: *[Pushes him to the door]* Right mate, get the fuck out, get out of 'ere, y'freakin' me—

Adam: Get your fucking hands off me slag!

Val: Mate, mate, let's chill the fuck out 'ere, you're freakin' out 'n' so am I, so just leave—

Adam: Just leave? After all I've spent on you slag!

Val: Stop callin' me a fuckin' slag, will ye!

Adam: Why, that's what you are, isn't it, a fucking slag, a whore, a fucking crack whore.

Val: Mate, I was above board with ye, all the way, so wha' is it ye want, y'want me to blow y'big dick, I mean proper this time?

Adam: Fuck off slag!

Val: C'mon, y'liked it before…

Adam: That's before I knew you were a fucking low life crack whore.

Val: Come on now Adam, I told ye in Napoleon's, remember I said what I—

Adam: What did you just say?

Val: Don't know what y'mean…

Adam: What did you call me?

Val: Er, y'name, I called you Adam…

Adam: Who said you could?

Val: Wha'?

Adam: Call my name! Who gave a fucked-up piece of crap like you permission to call someone like me by their name?

Val: No one said I could, I just did—

Adam: Well, don't slag, you've no fucking right to use my name, piece of shit like you hasn't right to even look at me!

Val: Alright mate, let's just calm down eh—

Adam: I'm not your fucking mate and I said don't look at me bitch.

Val: I've gorra look at ye 'aven't I, to see y'massive big cock…

Adam: Fuck, you even talk like a slag.

Val: *[Sidles towards the door]* That's cos I am a slag mate, a big slag for you…

Adam: You rank fucking bitch!

Val: Yeah, your bitch mate, proper. *[Reaches for the door]*

Adam: What you doing, where you going? *[Grabs Val violently by the arm]* No bitch, you don't get out of here.

Val: Gerroff me will ye!

Adam: No, you fucking slag, I won't get off you!

Val: I'll call the police…

Adam: You are calling no one bitch and anyway, who'll hear you?

Val: Y'hurting me mate—

Adam: And for some unknown reason you're still looking at me, why are you looking at me when I said don't look at me?

Val: Let go of me then…

Adam: You're a mega-piece of shit ho, who hasn't earned the fucking right to look at me.

Val: Let go of me!

Adam: *[Punches Val to the ground]* When I say don't look at me slag, I mean it, don't fucking look at me!

Val: *[Looks away]* Please don't, don't hit me mate, don't hit me…

Adam: Don't speak!

Val: Wha—

Adam: *[Kicks her]* I said don't speak, didn't I, don't look at me and don't fucking speak… and I am not your fucking mate! God, you sound super-fucking thick, so stupid, you stupid fucking ho, you speak like a fucking crack whore bitch, a Mancunian fucking crack whore bitch, a stupid fucking slag. You want it don't you?

Val: Want wha'?

Adam: I said don't speak didn't I! Never think shit like you can actually speak to someone like me, you are beneath me bitch, beneath me!

Val: Sorry, sorry…

Adam: What did I say slag, I said don't fucking speak! You are so fucking thick aren't you, you thick fucking ho, so mega-fucking thick you can't even understand the Queen's English! *[Screams at Val]* What did I say? *[Val stays silent]* What did I say! What did I say bitch…

Val: Don't speak…

Adam: *[Kicks her again]* What you fucking speaking for then? If any cunt's a dickhead round here it's fucking you, calling me a dickhead when it's you all along, you stupid fucking slag! Dickhead, *me*? Won't forget that!

Val: I didn't mean it, honest —

Adam: Doing it again! I said don't speak and what do you do ho, you speak! Like all stupid slags, you want some of Adam's big cock don't you? *[Val stays silent]* Don't you! *[Val stays silent]* Answer me bitch, answer me, you want my big cock, don't you!

Val: *[Terrified]* Yes, yes, I want your big —

Adam: I said don't speak! How do I get it fucking through to your idiot skull, no fucking talking! That's it slag, you're mega-getting it. In every fuckin' dirty slag bitch hole you've got, you are so fucking getting it!

[Adam picks up a terrified, screaming, pleading Val and punches her to the bed. Blackout! As we hear Val scream for dear life for it to stop, there are slight flashes, a strobing of half-light, and in the briefest glimpses we witness Adam brutally rape Val. Vision and sound combine in a thudding, blood-dank, flesh-pounding surrealism to create a searingly disturbing body-beating über-pornographic soundscape as we hear what is happening to their bodies, minds and voices. The techno-like soundscape masculine-screeches to a pneumatically-enraged climax and suddenly stops. It is replaced with the furious panting of a sexually satisfied Adam and the heaving, breathless sobs of Val. Lights slowly come back up to show them pulling their clothes back on. Weeping uncontrollably, Val falls behind the bed.]

Adam: *[Fully dressed, reaches into his pocket]* There's a twenty, all I've got in cash. Not quite your fifty. What was it you said, "pony"?

Val: *[Face partially hidden behind the bed, still weeping]* What did y'do tha' for, wha' did you do tha' for, wha' did I do to make you wanna hurt me like tha'?

Adam: Don't know what you mean.

241

Val: Y'raped me, y'fuckin' raped me... wha' did y'rape me, hurt me for, wha' did I do, wha' did I say...

Adam: Hey, let's get this right bitch, no chatting shit. I didn't rape you, didn't rape anybody. First of all, you have to be somebody to get raped: you're nothing. I paid for a night out with a nobody, a slag, just drugs and sex. A bit rough like, but still sex. Old slags like it super-rough, desperate for anything younger between their legs. You did alright; got drugs, I got drugs, you certainly got a bit of younger and we mega-fucked. Come on now, we're probably both the oldest professions – think of it as historical accountancy, acting out a centuries-old tried and trusted financial transaction. Nothing new there.

Val: *[Still sobbing]* I thought you were nice, thought you understood...

Adam: Oh dear, looks like I'm not nice and don't understand.

Val: Don't come near me, don't come near me!

Adam: I'm not. Just picking up my shoe, slut!

Val: I don't want you anywhere near me, keep away, keep away!

Adam: Don't you worry about that, you won't be seeing me again.

Val: Warravya done to me, y'fuckin' monster, it's agony, I can't fuckin' move...

Adam: Yup. Monster. That's how fucking big it is.

Val: Me face, look at me face, look what you've done...

Adam: Didn't want to look your ugly mug before, why should I now?

Val: Can't believe this, look what you done to it.

Adam: No!

Val: I don't believe wha' you've done to me, me body, me face, you're not gonna be able to believe it either, look at it, after all the times you punched 'n' butted it, I mean you tries so hard to break it, fuckin' look will ye!

Adam: *[Turns to her]* What for?

Val: *[Still violently sobbing, hands on face]* No, really, really look, you punched seven kinds of shite out of it, repeatedly jabbed at it like a punch-bag 'n' look...

Adam: That's about right. I punched a bag, a mega-slag bag.

Val: Just look at wha' you've done to me...

Adam: How can I you stupid bitch, when I can't see your fucking face?

Val: Look wha' you've done, you cruel nasty bastard!

Adam: What you on about?

Val: *[Removes hands, still crying]* Look, not a scratch, not a bruise, no blood, nottin'.

Adam: *[Slowly realises something's wrong]* What, wait...

Val: It's like all that extreme effort you put into monstrously brutalisin' 'n' humiliatin' her, chokin' the life out, very nearly killin' her didn't work. Seriously dick'ead look, norra single mark...

Adam: What the fuck, you're right...

Val: *[Still crying]* I know I am, never been wrong, not since before the dawn of time mate, 'n' that's me goin' back a bit tha' is, way back. You left her for fuckin' dead 'n' not a mark anywhere on her face or body, nottin' at all to prove wha' a violent bastard'n rapin' cunt y'are. She liked the word 'bastard'n', she liked it a lot, one of her very favourite words. Have you got any favourite words, words you're historically fond of, linked to, y'know things tha' gently roll off y'tongue? Well, 'ave ye?

Adam: Wait a minute... *her*? What do you mean, *her*?

Val: Val. The prostitute you just brutally raped 'n' left for dead...

Adam: But you're Val...

Val: No, I'm not you fuckin' monster, no I'm not hun, babe, dude, sweetheart. God, it's all so confusin', monster, hun, dude, babe, sweetheart all sound practically redundant, meaningless. I don't know wha' to call ye now...

Adam: What's going on here? This is fucking weird!

Val: Oh yes it is Adam, seriously fuckin' weird, weirder than you'll ever know bitch – 'n' from now on in hun, I won't be able to help meself, it's gonna get a helluva fuckin' lot weirder. *[Stops crying and smiles]*

Adam: What the fuck's going—

Val: Freeze! *[Adam freezes]*

Adam: *[Panicked]* What, what's this, what the fuck's going on, I can't move, I can't move my body, what's happened, have you done this, have you, what have you done, wha—

Val: Shut it! *[Adam is silent]* Turn to me. *[Adam turns]* You've absolutely no right to speak to me, bitch. Close! *[Adam's eyes close]* And someone like you, a piece of shit like you, hasn't the right to even look at me. *[Val slowly circles him]* Stiff as a board. Nah, better than tha', stiff as your big fat rapin' cock. All a bit freaky inni bitch? All a bit horror movie, but real. Norra film though is it ho, norra a comic book, although strange as fuck, it's not *Doctor Strange* is it 'n' I should know. I know you're not gettin' any of this just yet, how could ye, all too much for y'brutal little noggin. Yup, I know your head's explodin' 'n' blood's pumpin' what's left of the life from y'heart. Hey, I bet it's bangin' away like two muscle-bound giants givin' double anal up a young Asian girl's, who looks younger than her years, arse, y'know like off Porn Hub. Bang, bang, bang, bang! *[Pause]* I fuckin' love this moment... the quiet. *Shhh*, just give it a little listen, give into it babe... Well, y'don't 'ave much choice do ye. *[Pause]* Don't y'just love quiet, Adam? I do. Delicate, pure, silence is my favourite bit of anything, after all the fury, 'n' don't get me wrong babe, love a bit of fury me, nowt wrong with rage. I generally negotiate a mad fucked-up proper bit of fury, it's my chaotic bag as it were. The peace of it afterwards though, man, it's palpable, almost edible, hmmm, yum yum, quiet. Eh, gerron this bitch, perhaps I do eat silence. Y'know, after all this time, 'n' it's certainly been time dude, I'd never thought of tha'. Seems the old sayin' is true after all, y'learn a little somethin' new every few millennia. I'm a silence eater, or better still, 'Val, The Eater of Silence'! Powerful dramatic epithet inni, bit Biblical 'n' tha', suitably mythical 'n' mysterious, in keepin' with the situation, the ingredients ghost stories are made from. Oh, 'n' if y'wonderin', that's wha' I am hun, the ingredients. Open! *[Adam's eyes open]* Now, I'm gonna let you speak for a bit babe, but you'll wanna babble 'n' scream, panic like the dick'ead I said you were before and, of course, the dick'ead you in all actuality are. Well, do y'self a favour 'n' don't, cos if y'do mega-babble 'n' super-scream, disturb the silence if you will, I'll just shut ye the fuck up again, quick as a flash, abracadabra 'n' all tha' crap. So, for your sake doll, hunny-buns, toodle-pips, for both our sakes, keep it calm 'n' quiet. Blink at me three times if y'get wha' I'm sayin' to ye. *[Adam blinks three times]* Oh, y'very good, d'ye like blinkin' Adam? Be an absolute hunny 'n' blink at me three times if y'like blinkin'. *[Adam doesn't blink]* Oh, so wait a minni 'ere, wha's goin' on, does you not blinkin' three times mean y'don't like blinkin'? Ooh, warra impossible quandary hun, tha' makes me think you may very well hate blinkin'. Well then, blink at me three times to tell me y'don't like, possibly even hate, blinkin'. Y'not blinkin' either way are ye mate, I must say Adam, y'makin' me job unnecessarily difficult. Ee-ar, let's get this right. At some point, 'n' in order for us to carry on, y'gonna have to fuckin' blink aren't ye! It's dead easy dick'ead. Child could do it, 'n' I should know, been many a kid, 'n' they fuckin' love it. Proper blink-'eads, kids. Right, let's start all over again shall we. Ooh, sound like y'nanny don't I. If y'like blinkin', blink three times. *[Adam blinks three times]* Fuckin' 'ell Adam, about time mate. Now I know y'like blinkin' we can press on, chop-chop as it were, 'n' I don't mean suey. Do us a really mega-big favour will ye Adam, and make the shape of a camp giraffe. *[Adam makes the shape of a camp giraffe]* Eh, y'make a good camp giraffe don't ye ho, who'd of fuckin' thought it eh? Tellin' you now for nowt, y'camp giraffe's well better than y'tender love-makin' kid. Now, how about a grievin' elephant? *[Adam makes the shape of a grieving elephant]* With a swingin' trunk. *[Adam swings his arm]* Fuckin' brilliant slag, that's by far the best grievin' elephant with a swingin' trunk I've seen in time, 'n' believe me ho, grievin' elephants 'n' me go back a long, long way. So long in fact, I can remember when they were grievin' mammoths. Tha' fuckin' ice age man, proper took its toll. Fuckin' 'ell warrami like me, camp giraffes 'n' grievin' elephants, y'can tell I've been 'angin' out with the gays can't ye! Wha' shape now? Oh I know, that's it, me fave... Make the shape of y'grandad double-fingerin' his arse. *[Adam obeys and Val laughs]* Never gets old tha' one, been around since before the dawn of time mate 'n' it still cracks me up! Crack, up, gerri? So 'ave y'really mega-gorri now babe, super-sorted are we, 'ave y'got tha' I control every single fuckin' inch of ye? You are now my very own bitch, my ho, you completely belong to me, savvy? If y'indeed do savvy, make the noise of y'grandad joyfully orgasmin' wi' double-fingers up his arse. *[Adam obeys]* Good t'see we're on the same page, even if it is *Razzle*. So, you are my ho 'n' I completely own your miserable shit-drippin' butt, gorri! Now like I said before, I'm gonna let you speak, 'n' because I own every square inch of y'quite fit arse actually, if y'get all panicky shite on yerself, I'll just shut ye up again. If you're gonna do wha' I say blink three times 'n' make the noise of y'grandad joyfully orgasmin', whilst simultaneously tryin' to un-stick the cum-stuck pages of *Razzle*, double-fingerin' his arse. *[Adam obeys]* Brilliant bitch, now y'can speak. *[Adam is silent]* What's the matter big boy, cat got y'tongue? Couldn't shut up before could ye – aren't I a stupid slag, ho, bitch anymore? Y'proper had loads t'say for y'self then, musta been the speed... worn off 'as it? Actually, I did rip you off, it was shit speed 'n' a pony's twenty-five quid not fifty, y'tool. Come on babe, let's 'ave a little chit-chat shall we? *[Silence]* Y'know wha' Adam, can't think what's happened to ye to bring this sulk on, y'seem right proper mithered, where's all y'too-intrusive incredibly stupid questions now eh? Y'feelin' poorly hun, has all the blood rushin' to tha' big massive dick of yours left y'feelin' a teensy-weensy bit fainty-wainty? That's how you say it in posh inti, a teensy-weensy bit fainty-wainty?

Adam: I don't know...

Val: Don't know wha' babe, y'seven times table, the capital of Uruguay, who played Sharon McCready in *The Champions*?

Adam: I don't know…

Val: Wha' now babe, how many beans make five, the intricacies of a threadworm's lifespan, if the moon's made of cheese or not and if it is, what kind, cream or halloumi?

Adam: What's happening, I don't know what's…

Val: I'll tell y'wha' y'don't know shit-'ead, you don't know what's fuckin' wha', do ye? Don't know what's just happened, why or how, y'so fuckin' scared right now, probably even forgotten where. More than anythin' though, more than any fuckin' thing in the whole wide fuckin' world, y'don't know who or wha' the flyin' fuck I am… do ye?

Adam: No, no I don't…

Val: Do y'wanna babe?

Adam: Want what?

Val: Know who or wha' the flyin' fuck I am?

Adam: I want to go home…

Val: Oh you ain't goin' anywhere… bitch!

Adam: Please, I'll do anything, I have got that ton, in cash, you can have it, more, we'll go the cashpoint, can get five hundred out, I can actually get five hundred out now, right now. Just please let me go…

Val: Let me just super-mega-think about tha' a minni dude… *[Pause]* Er, no!

Adam: Please, I'm begging you. I don't know what's going on, I don't know —

Val: Quiet! *[Adam is silent]* Disappointin' bitch, after all tha', wha' y'did before, didn't 'ave y'down as a crier, proper little whinge-bag aren't ye? Hate mitherers me Adam, been around too long, heard too much… borin'! Y'know, in my incredibly detailed experience people only cry when they know they've lost 'n' you've lost big time fellah. Can't believe y'didn't ask me wha' I am, love tha' B-movie bit me, the explainin'. Wait, wait, wait a cotton-pickin' minni 'ere, I wanna fuckin' explain, wanna hear me yap for a change. So, in a really camp queeny voice, 'n' I mean proper queeny Adam, pure seventies sit-com, the queeniest ever, after three I want you to say, "Ooh Val, I've come over all peculiar with an insatiable inquisitiveness 'n' am beyond merely desperate to know just who 'n' wha' you in all actuality are", got tha' bitch? One, two, three…

Adam: Ooh Val, I've come over all peculiar with an insatiable inquisitiveness 'n' am beyond merely desperate to know just who 'n' wha' you in all actuality are.

Val: Well, thank ye for askin', y'big stereotypical puff. Let me tell ye this for nowt, very soon babe, I'm gonna be, "surprise surprise, the unexpected hits you between the eyes, that's the surprise y'see, surprise surprise! Surprise surprise!" Love a lorra lorra Cilla me! Right Adam, in the same queeny voice as before, you say, after three, "Eh there's no way you're gonna surprise surprise me, not with those fuckin' roots 'n' tha' bastard'n scrunchie, 'n' anyway inni high time y'got those acrylics re-gemmed?" One, two three.

Adam: Eh there's no way you're gonna surprise surprise me, not with those fuckin' roots 'n' tha' bastard'n scrunchie, 'n' anyway inni high time y'got those acrylics re-gemmed?

Val: Now, cos I'm a sane, sorted supernatural ting 'n' ting, I'm gonna forget tha' nasty birra shade y'just flew at me about me roots 'n' scrunchie, never mind me acrylics, cheeky twat. Fuckin' love this scrunchie I do, three for a pound mate, Home 'n' Bargain. So, in answer to your first question, who 'n' wha' I am, well Adam, there's not really any point in answerin' tha' just yet, because very soon I'm gonna be someone else. Ooh, just when you thought it couldn't get spookier! I'm done with Val now, 'n' to be totally 'onest with ye mate, am fuckin' gutted about tha'. Where to fuckin' start eh! Ee-ar, y'know there's never any easy way of sayin' this… Right, every seven years I need to change bodies, find a new host as it were. *[Suddenly laughs]* A new host!

God, tha' sounded so fuckin' naff didn't it, feel ashamed, warra knob'ead, but that's exactly wha' it is, wha' I'm lookin' for, a new host. Sorry Adam, gimme a minni, in Val's body this supernatural Gothic shit don't 'alf sound funny. Fuckin' 'ell, find a new host, sounds proper mad dunni, off its 'ead 'n' all tha', feel like Vincent fuckin' Price on 'Thriller'. Don't ask me how babe, just wha' it's always been, wha' I am, 'n' been around so long even I've forgotten the fuck why. Eh, maybe that's because there isn't a why. Sorry hun, find a new host, fuckin' 'ell, find a new host, can't stop laughin', gonna need a minni, serious... Right, that's it, oh funny as fuck tha'. *[Pulls itself together]* Tryin' to find a better, easier way of explainin' it to ye. Now, how would a complete inconsequential tosser like you gerron somethin' as inhumanly deranged 'n' esoterically complex as this? See fooled ye didn't I, knew wha' esoteric meant all along. Ee-ar, gorri, I'm a bit like a vampire, not like film vampires, Bela Lugosi, Christopher Lee, *Draclear* vampires, no not all. It's not the cleavage-heavin' blood of virgins I need to feed on, no, more emotion, experience. I feast off who 'n' wha' you are, gone through, 'n' believe in, 'n' after seven years in ye body I need to evacuate the dancefloor so to speak, fuck off 'n' find some other cunt. Fuckin' 'ell, nearly said host then! Someone who won't be missed. I always know the 'won't be misseds', y'kinda glow a bit pink, a powdery neon pink. *You* certainly won't be missed, Pinky. After seven years of you gently fallin' off the radar, no cunt'll miss ye, or even remember ye. So, wha' am I? Good question Adam, even if I did kinda ask it meself. Wha' the actual fuck of all fuckin' fuckery am the fuck I... fuckin' 'ell that's a hard one. *[Pause]* I'm an eternal nottin', an invisible notion, somethin' always there but unseen. Eh, I don't even know wha' I am 'n' I'm me! But wha' I must *do* is carry on. There's a Shiver, Adam, ancient 'n' always been, 'n' in tha' Shiver there's any number of other things, 'n' I'm one of them other things, a shadow passin' ye window, unspeakable 'n' unthinkable desire, a sauna demon, the somethin' blind drunks can clearly see, the thing they laugh at or miss when punchin'. Y'see prick, somewhere between what's real 'n' imagined are all the things unreal 'n' unimagined. Think about it, makes a kinda sense. In between spaces there's space, 'n' in those spaces, wherever or whatever they are, *somethings*. That's wha' I am, the somethin' in between spaces. Perhaps it's where memories go to be forgotten, or where experience dies, one of the two, or both, or more. Who the fuck knows or cares. That's why I don't remember who I am, just tha' I am, 'n' that's wha' I am. *[Sings]* "I'm not what I am, I'm not my own special creation…" Y'with me? Speak.

Adam: No, I don't know what you mean, what this is…

Val: Fuckin' 'ell, just told ye didn't I. Did you go to university to be this bastard'n stupid? In a nutshell hun, I'm an ages-old supernatural bein' here to devour wha's left of y'tawdry, unlovin', beyond-miserable experiential soul energies! Piece of fuckin' piss mate!

Adam: It's too much, too much, I don't get it, don't understand…

Val: Man, you are turnin' my blood to dust.

Adam: I don't fucking understand!

Val: Shurrup dick'ead! *[Adam is silent]* Christ on a fuckin' bike you're thick! Val knew the score, gorri almost immediately; y'know, 'n' this is proper off its nut, in a funny peculiar way she weirdly kinda welcomed it, something in her eyes, like when you say *yes* to a kiss. Tell y'somethin' for nottin' though Adam, 'n' this is so unusual, 'n' I mean proper, for all the eternities I've drifted through, it's only happened a handful of times. I've really enjoyed bein' Val. When it came to experience, she was a fuckin' feast man, a smorgasbord of life. Faith even. Oh faith's delicious, she believed in so much, God as well, stupid bitch. Although I'm a formless nottin', body-hoppin' every seven years to survive, I'll tell y'now for nowt, there's no God mate. They invented tha' shite to keep you all in line, 'n' I should know, I were one of them. Name dropper! Where was I? Yeah that's it, I've been around for-fuckin'-ever right, 'n' there are very few bodies, lives, you actually remember or can be arsed rememberin'. Tellin' y'now, be a long time before I forget Val, if I ever do. Fuckin' 'ell, everything tha' could 'appen 'appened to tha' poor girl, never known anythin' like it, or her, 'n' I've known the Middle Ages. How she kept goin', beyond even me, a phenomenal human bein'. Born pissed, 'n' her first memory is bein' kicked around the room like a football, fuckin' bounced everywhere she was. Her mother was a drunken whore as well, all kinda dirty bastards 'angin' out of her. Val couldn't remember the first time she was fucked, her life were tha' relentless. D'ya know how she blocked it out? By punchin' herself in the face while they were doin' it to her. Wha' she remembers most is her twattin' herself in the gob. Wonder she had any face left. 'Ere's the fuckin' craziest thing with her right, off its fuckin' nut this, she still loved her ma, can y'believe it, devoted to her she was, 'n' tha' nasty bitch did nottin' but bring her untold pain. Val stayed by her right until the end, till she died, workin' the street to get her 'n' her ma smack, crack, whatever. Y'know Adam, sometimes I wish there were a God, cos then there'd have to be a Heaven, 'n' if there were a Heaven there'd have to be Hell, 'n' if there were a Hell Val's ma would be burnin' away down there right now that's for sure. Pure charcoal mate... nasty fuckin' bitch! Y'know wha' Adam, I thought I were proper amoral till I became Val. I feel like she's really tapped into something, mad. Wonder if I've been watchin' too much Jeremy Kyle. Poor bitch can't remember a time she wasn't a prossie, always on the game, always addicted to somethin' or other, put on the game when she was a kid by her fuckin' ma – 'n' please, don't get me started with her own kids; she had six, three died 'n' three taken off her, her whole life just one 'orrible thing after the other 'orrible thing, pure ugly madness. Rape, she's lost count mate! Bang, bang, bang! There are some lives where darkness is the only light, 'n' tha' was Val's. Through tha' dark, even more dark, 'n' yet still somehow managin' to get somethin' out of tha' completely fucked-up existence of hers. Tha' was the most delicious bit of her, her determination, her faith, 'n' above all, gerron this, her love for dancin'. That's where most of her faith was, how it manifested, in the disco. Man, she fuckin' adored a good bop, she was brilliant at it as well, top mover, could proper bust it. She wanted nottin' more out of life than to be pissed, pilled- or whatever'd-up on a dancefloor. Fuckin' loved the Gay Village, early days anyway, when it was proper gay before the downpour of hen parties. She used to joke "them hen-parties proper peck me head". She used to say to, well to anyone who'd listen really, the Village was only place she'd ever felt welcome. It were a kinda home for her, she loved the constant noise. And the Queers, she'd lay down her life for them! Fuckin' 'ell Adam, the fights she got into, afraid of no cunt, thin as a rake, norra pick on her, but man, raged-up she was fuckin' formidable. Any cunt, straight, gay, whoever or whatever, went for one of her mates she'd proper mow 'em down. She were like a skinny tank! For years she had this mate, gay lad, bit of a scally, always in The Number One they were... she worshipped him 'n' him her. She called him Bunnyscope cos he wouldn't shurrup about rabbits. Rabbit mad he were, lovin' 'n' hatin' them, tha' were his joke. Funny as fuck he was, proper witty, he was all about rabbits 'n' universal sound waves. He believed universal sound waves were spiritually embedded in music, in the speakers of clubs, 'n' instead of callin' himself a rave-'ead, a raver, he called himself a wave-'ead, a waver. They never once met up 'n' went out together, they'd just bump in, 'n' every time she clocked him, she just saw colours. She could see his face 'n' everythin', knew wha' he actually looked like, nice lookin' lad, but he was just colours to her, bright shinin' lights tha' lit her up like a revolvin' kaleidoscope... Bunnyscope. It was a dead-end down a one-way street for Bunnyscope 'n' she knew tha'. She was workin' the street parallel, but before they got to the end they promised each other the best time ever, 'n' they kept tha' promise. Then one mornin' Bunnyscope kicked it. Daft cunt, pilled-up, pissed, choked on his own sick. She knew it was on the cards; broke her heart 'n' mind like, big time, but she knew, knew one day sooner rather than later, she'd miss his colours. She didn't break her promise to him though. Every time she got off her 'ead she'd go down The Number One 'n' always dance for him. She kept their good time colourfully rockin' for ages after, just so fuckin' beautiful man. That was so goddamn ripe, so unbelievably juicy, I lived off that one bit of her for a year, a whole fuckin' year; unheard of! Tha' one memory alone was just so brilliantly clear, full of the most stunnin' vibrancy 'n' the purest kinda love. Although she'd rob a rattle out a baby's pram for a bag, or a baby come to tha', when she wasn't cluckin' she was the kindest, most generous soul. She'd hit the streets, whorin' or beggin' 'n' after any gear she needed. If there were enough she'd pop into Spar, dive on the yellow labels, pile round to whoever had a flat 'n' a stove with leccy 'n' cook a hot meal for everybody. God knows where she learned to cook, she didn't even know. When her 'n' her ma could afford or remember to eat it were the chippy, she was a pure chip barm-'ead. Seriously, no word of a lie 'ere Adam, in Val's house Pot Noodles were a treat. She was so funny, used to call Morrissey 'Mozzarella', cos it sounded a bit more middle-class. She'd say, "what's tha' Mozzarella kickin' off for now, what's he got to complain' about, tha' cunt's made a killin' outta suicidal teenagers", The Stoned Roses were 'The Stoned Posers', 'n' Oasis, 'Wasted', "are Wasted number fuckin' one again?" She wouldn't 'ave a mobile phone because of textin', "what's the fuckin' point in 'avin' a phone if all we're doin' is writin' letters to each other?" Thing about her was, behind it all, the addictions, the agonies, she knew there was somethin' else there conncoctin' away, diggin' deep inside her. In the spaces between her own particular nottin', she somehow knew there was somethin' 'n' someone she wanted to be. Her 'ead was so fucked, 'n' for so long. She never really worked it out, never had time, but I think – 'n' I'm good at pickin' up tha' kinda shit – she might've wanted to be a teacher or summat like tha'. She never went to school or owt, no school would 'ave her, she fuckin' stank 'n' forever gettin' expelled, but for some reason she could read a bit. She'd read things out to her mates, bits of comics, porn mag stories, poetry 'n' tha'. She really, really liked poetry. When she could make herself presentable, which wasn't very often, used to go to poetry things. Free gigs 'n' tha', where they'd do their stuff, fuckin' loved it, loved the mad generous vibe of it. Some of the poets were so freaky, made her feel normal. That's where she got her poetry from, off the poets given her their books for nottin'… Who knows eh, maybe she wanted to be a poet too, wouldn't put it past her. Maybe in another life, with other chances, she could have even taught poetry. I think she could anyway, she had a kinda poetry about her, somethin' pure man, she had a certain somethin' goin' on. There was a kind of natural authoritative energy about her; she could get people together to do stuff, like go to poetry gigs 'n' tha'. Not as easy as it sounds, 'ave you tried gettin' a group of alcoholic crack-'eads to a poetry gig? She was properly delicious, one of those where the levels of her never stopped; she was a profound thinker, survivors are, 'n' when she could, a real doer. Yeah, Val had a kind of clever about her tha' was completely about experience 'n' how she dealt with, 'n' how she felt 'n' lived, those experiences. She felt 'n' lived every-fuckin'-thing. One of the reasons she tasted so spirit-lickin' good. I've been many a genius me mate, dusty old duffers in even dustier rooms, coppin' a feel of students 'n' wankin'-off in between theories. Tellin' ye now for nottin' Adam, eatin' loneliness, sexual inadequacy 'n' marooned intellect is nowhere near as satisfyin' as gorgin' on full-lusted experience. If y'measured genius by every time you felt the back-hand of life, the kick of its hobnailed boot, Val would tower over any of those stupid professorial cunts. Yeah, that's it, that's wha' she was, a fuckin' genius. That's not even scratchin' the surface mate, the lives she lived man, off its fuckin' 'ead! Am I borin' y'Adam, yappin' on too much about some goin'-nowhere slag you just violently raped 'n' left for dead? Seriously, tell me if I am. Oh wait a minni, y'can't can ye! I control ye, you're the bitch slag ho now, 'n' y'all mine. Wha' to do with ye eh? Wha' the fuck am I gonna do with a violently ragin' rapin' mega-piece of super-shite like you? Ooh, looks like I'll 'ave to pop outta Val's body 'n' possess your dangerously dark miserable husk for the next seven years, dunt it? Doesn't bother me mate, won't be the first time, far from it, 'n' been a lot worse. I sent fifteen hundred kids to their deaths once... yum yum, 'n' tha' was just starters, shoulda seen the puddin'. *[Pause]* Wait a minute will ye, gimme a sec, need a birra quiet. One of those time things... *[Disorientated, holds onto her waist, as if something is leaving her body]* Alright now. Eh, bet there's all kinda tasty unresolved ragin' self-servin' garbage swirlin' inside a piece of human slurry like you. Yeah, I know, at this moment I look 'n' talk like a fifty year old smack-'ead Mancunian prossie, but believe me hun, I've been plenty a posh kid secretly plottin' to kill nanny because she took away y'tiffin. For all y'possessions, doilies, manners 'n' Rupert the Bear thank you notelettes, your kind get proper fucked-up, too I was once a General really into kids, no wonder y'ancestors didn't wanna give up the colonies. You must've gorri by now Adam, yeah, in about an hour's time, 'n' this supernatural shit's all about times 'n' signs – don't ask – I'm gonna have to leave Val's body 'n' transfer into yours. When I do, well, y'kinda instantly die really. There's no pain, sadly, y'just snuff it, gone. Then I plod on lookin' 'n' pretendin' to be you, livin' off the slowly ebbin' 'n' erodin' memories, the physical nuances of y'life's experiences. I know it's bonkers, but that's just wha' it is. Bit like bein' Rod Hull's arm jammed up Emu's arse. Mind you, he's snuffed it now... shame actually, wouldn't've minded bein' Rod Hull, he were fuckin' ragin'. Now I'm gonna let you speak again so listen, if y'panic babe, I'll just shut ye up, so there's absolutely no point whatsoever in freakin' out. Remember hun, this is gonna be y'last chance to speak to anyone before y'die. Y'gettin' all tha' sweetheart? If y'start screamin' blue murder that's it, shtum till y'dead, OK. Blink at me three times if y'get wha' I'm sayin' to ye 'n' if you'll indeed adhere to it. *[Adam blinks three times]* Thank fuck for tha'. Oh, 'n' do the *Razzle* grandad fingers thing again. *[Adam obeys]* Speak!

Adam: Look, I really don't know what's going on at all but I'm very frightened, very, very frightened, more than that Val, I'm—

Val: Eh, ee-ar, wait, wait, wait, before y'carry on, get y'fingers out y'arse 'n' let's get this right shall we. I'm not Val, never 'ave been.

Adam: Who, what are you then, what do I call you?

Val: Don't call me owt mate. I'm the spirit with no name, 'n' throughout all the millennia I've yet to meet a sprit with one. Told ye, I'm the imagined come alive, the reality of nottin', the air in smog…

Adam: What does that mean?

Val: I'm an ancient formless entity, dick'ead!

Adam: What?

Val: Like in ye comic books. Exactly like, 'n' I should know. I used to be Steve Ditko.

Adam: Steve Ditko?

Val: Yeah… I wouldn't touch Stan Lee with yours.

Adam: OK, oh I don't know, it's impossible, this is all impossible, what do I say to any of this, what does anybody say? Whatever you are I'm sorry, so, so sorry for what I did to you.

Val: Don't bother yerself luv, didn't hurt me or owt, can't be hurt, don't feel owt. Y'kinda just raped an animated human cadaver really, kept reasonably fresh by dark supernatural forces. Actually, wha' y'just raped 'n' left for dead were a corpse.

Adam: Please listen to me, please… I'm really very, very scared…

Val: I know luv.

Adam: I'll do anything, I mean anything, whatever you want, if you let me go…

Val: Hun, there's nowt y'can do. It's y'body I need to borrow, not a cup of sugar.

Adam: Look, please, listen, please, I'm just so scared right now, seriously terrified, I'll do anything, anything…

Val: Ey, if y'start panickin' again I'll just shut ye up, gorri? Now are y'gonna behave?

Adam: Yes.

Val: Good, can't stand it when they jibber-jabber, like talkin' to Su Pollard.

Adam: I'm sorry, really, really…

Val: Apologisin' ain't gonna get y'anywhere either Su, it's a done deal now. Your fate is sealed puny human.

Adam: What does that mean?

Val: I'm gonna devour ye.

Adam: I don't, this, whatever this is, no, it can't be happening!

Val: 'Fraid it is chuck.

Adam: I don't get it.

Val: Oh, you'll be gettin' it soon alright. In about three quarters of an hour y'gonna die bitch, 'n' I'm gonna live on in y'body.

Adam: Please, I don't want to die…

Val: Tough shit.

Adam: I really, really don't want to die, please Val or whatever you're called, please, I don't want to die…

Val: Eh, I told ye, y'kick off again it's Shtumsville Arizona.

Adam: *[Pause]* Can I ask you something?

Val: Ask away mate.

Adam: I'd like to move.

Val: Move?

Adam: Yes move, just move. If I'm going to die, I'd like to move one last time.

Val: Oh, is this like a last request or summat?

Adam: Something like that.

Val: Well, it's either a last request or it isn't, take y'pick!

Adam: Yes then, yes, yes, yes, yes, it is, it's a last request…

Val: Long as y'don't go crazy 'n' start panickin' 'n' yellin'. It'll do ye no good hun, there's no other cunts in the buildin'.

Adam: I won't, super-promise I won't. I just want to move.

Val: Alright then, but no funny business.

Adam: I mega-mega-promise.

Val: Wow, you're a piece of work aren't ye?

Adam: Sorry?

Val: Y'want me to accept the promise of a violent, possibly murderin' rapist?

Adam: I'm really really sorry.

Val: Eh luv, tell y'summat for nowt shall I, some things you can't apologise for.

Adam: I know, I know that now and you're right, there is no apology.

Val: Fuckin' 'ell, y'pathetic!

Adam: I'm sorry, so sorry, it's just I don't know what to say…

Val: Then don't.

Adam: OK.

Val: Oh, 'n' it were Alexandra Bastedo.

Adam: What was?

Val: Who played Sharon McCready in *The Champions*. Y'can move. *[Adam slowly starts to move his body]*

Adam: Thank you, thank you so much, like I say, I'm so super-sorry for what I did, I'm just so, so sorry…

Val: Don't waste what's left of y'breath thankin' me mate 'n' for fuck's sake stop apologisin'… doin' me nut in. *[Pause]* Bit quiet aren't ye?

Adam: I was just wondering…

Val: Wonderin' wha'?

Adam: Whether, erm, you'd like to, you know…

Val: I don't know. Wha' mate, wha' you on about?

Adam: Well, you said you liked it before…

Val: You gone mad?

Adam: [Rubs his crotch] You said you liked my big cock, maybe we could, you know…

Val: Wha', fuck?

Adam: Yeah, that's it exactly, maybe we could fuck, make love, I still mega-fancy you…

Val: You really are one sick fucked-up piece of shit, aren't ye... Hmmm, delicious.

Adam: [Panics and rushes to the door, but it will not open] Let me out, let me out, get me out of here, someone help, please help me, get me out, get me out…

Val: Fuckin' knew it…

Adam: Get me out, get me out, I can't open this door, I can't open this door, please somebody hear me, get me out of here, please, please help me, get me out… [Falls to the floor and sobs] I can't open the door…

Val: I've telekinetic abilities beyond y'ken 'n' Barbie y'daft twat, so there's really no point doin' owt like tha'.

Adam: Stay away from me, don't come near me…

Val: I'm not idiot… it's not time yet. Told ye, it's all about time.

Adam: You're evil, from somewhere else, evil…

Val: I'm from somewhere else, if that somewhere's nowhere, yeah, but not evil. Told ye before, I just am…

Adam: [Bolts to the Sacred Heart, removes the pink Rosary and points the crucifix part at Val] Stay away from me, keep back, don't come near me…

Val: Warra y'doin' y'daft cunt? Told ye, I'm not an actual vampire!

Adam: [Now hysterical] I don't know what you are, but you stay away from me, leave me alone, don't come anywhere near me, leave me alone, or I'll—

Val: Or you'll wha', point a plastic crucifix at me? Ooh, I've just shat meself I'm so frightened!

Adam: Just keep away from me, stay away…

Val: I knew y'd fuckin' flip… Freeze! *[Adam freezes]* Drop the stupid cross, take tha' ridiculous look off y'face 'n' come 'ere, y'gormless bastard'n knob'ead ye! *[Adam obeys]* Right, 'ere we go kid, now let's 'ave a look at what I'm gettin' into shall I? Look mate, I don't know if this'll hurt or not, sometimes does, sometimes doesn't, but I'm just gonna take a little tour around me new home, set up me kitchen so to speak, get me pots 'n' pans sorted, maybe even clean the fridge. First of all, let's tuck into tha' delicious unforgivin' 'n' unremittin' rage of yours shall we, 'n' the why 'n' how it is. *[Finger-feels Adam's head]* OK Adam, where the fuck is it? Should be screamin' out at me, usually does, maybe it's not y'dominant life trait. Eh, y'were so fuckin' savage a bit ago, automatically thought it would be. Mind you, been wrong before. Tha' means there must be summat else, yum yum, summat tastier. Let's just go for a general sweep shall we, see what thunders forward. D'ye like tha' Adam, 'thunders forward', suitably Gothic I think, bit like Toyah, kinda fits the moment. "Can you feel it breakin' through, can you feel it breakin' through, thunder 'n' lightnin', thunder in, thunder in, in the…" C'mon now, give it up kid, let's see wha' there is to properly chow down on. *[Pause]* Wha' the fuck's goin' on 'ere Adam, can't seem to find owt, just shitty, pithy little bits. You hidin' stuff from me? It happens sometimes tha', guilt, fear can get in the way, block things off. Some minds 'n' wills are stronger than others, but I wouldn't've put you in tha' category. Didn't feel it from you 'n' I usually do. Ah well, it's never stopped me before, I've been many a navvy, rich pickings them navvies. Hardly anybody misses a navvy, so it's just a case of diggin' deeper… Now this will hurt actually, not sorry about tha'. *[Val pauses feeling Adam's head]* Wha' the fuck's goin' on 'ere Adam, can't seem to get anythin'. *[Val starts feeling Adam's head again]* There's bits 'n' bats, but nowt proper, can't grab a moment, a time, a reason. Y'ead's full of shit man, I'm just gettin' numbers, loads of numbers, Xbox, porn 'n' bucket list, there's nowt else. There's a bit of attack 'n' rape, but it's all on the telly or video... is it on y'Xbox, yeah it is... oh y'beat up 'n' rape girls on y'Xbox. I'm not really sure wha' tha' means. I can get a tiny summat from it, but it's not concrete, where's tha' fuckin' rage man, warravya done with it? It's kinda like you haven't got any, 'n' y'should after wha' you just did. This really is gonna hurt Adam, proper, gorra get to the bottom of this. *[Val pauses feeling Adam's head]* Wow, this is makin' no sense, no sense at all. Y'don't 'ave any rage, in fact y'don't have anythin', just numbers really, numbers, receipts 'n' logic. So why did y'do wha' ye just did? Come 'ere a minni. *[Val starts feeling Adam's head again]* Bucket list, I'm getting bucket list again. Along with a ride in a hot air balloon, rapin' a prostitute was on y'bucket list; I really, really don't know wha' tha' means. There's no rage in there, just an irritatin' bleepin' noise, like summat from an office or hospital, 'n' even more receipts. Let's wind back to Val... Y'see her in a bar 'n' think she looks suitably feeble for you t'rape. Wha'? Well, y'got that wrong dick'ead! If she 'adn't've' been me, y'wouldn't've' stood a chance, she'd've' ripped y'fuckin' face off luv. What's really mad though is there's no rage. Y'just kinda did it cos y'could, 'n' decided it was summat y'wanted t'do before y'were thirty. You enjoyed it, yeah, gettin' tha', but not because it was a deep-down animal-like instinct, or hate or owt. Y'more enjoyed the fact y'engineered it 'n' pulled it logically off. It were a well-oiled operation, a job well done. I'm lookin' around 'ere Adam, 'n' there's fuck-all t'see, there's no rage, pain, y've had a really easy 'n' uneventful life. Wha's comin' through is what y'did before was kind of playactin', a disgustin' bit of playactin' – it were just summat y'were gonna tell y'mates. Fuckin' 'ell man, that's dark, but it's not *from* anywhere, just is wha' it is, just summat y'wanted t'do, to tick off. In fact, there's nowt in there, nottin at all. Y'don't believe in anythin', just an ever-colliding series of numbers, bleeps bangin' around in a blizzard of receipts, 'n' y'don't even believe in them, they're just wha' y'do. There's no soul, no recognition, no faith, no belief in anythin', 'n' the numbers are just there to pay y'wages. This fear you're feelin' now's a bit real, only real thing about ye, but that'd be gone in a week. There's fuck-all inside ye to feed on – y'empty! All there is in your mind is control 'n' numbers, control 'n' numbers, control 'n' numbers. It's like y'completely despirited 'n' dispirited or summat, wha' the fuck are ye? I can't be you mate, no fuckin' way, I wouldn't last three month in tha' body, nowt proper to feed off! [Pause] I can't be you, just can't, I've gotta find another host, there's just no way. Seriously man, wha' are ye? I've never come across anythin' like you before, wha' the flyin' fuck are ye?

[Val/The Entity hurries out of the bedsit leaving a still frozen and suddenly spot-lit Adam standing facing the audience. The whining, subterranean, inhuman soundscape starts again, slightly different from before, darker, earthier, bassier, more techno. After a short while, Adam snaps out of his frozen state, very calmly gets himself together, smooths and brushes down his suit, lifts his head and gently slys a half-smile direct to the audience. Blackout.]

The End?

Moment

They weigh tons,
held down, apple-bobbing and breathing,
mass in futiles of seconds.
That very big laugh, guffawed around,
individual as a lesser thumbed fingerprint.
Once you hear that laugh
you'll always hear that laugh.

Mountainous,
Purple dawn-stretch,
dense as the oldest rock,
shadow-peaks in cloud horizons.
That throw of arms.
Once held in that wrap
you'll always scent that wrap.

Bar-lit histories,
almost any tune,
tavern-red 'n' partly political,
thunder-chat and lightning roars,
where it wouldn't stop raining Supremes.
Once soaked in that kinship
we're drenched in that kinship.

It's like fifties fabric;
one perfect stitch,
gold,
sequin-shines,
completely woven,
glitteringly Diana
in snug-held covens of gin 'n' cardigan.

The True Grit Of Aunty Pearl
A eulogy for an adopted Mancunian

There's absolutely no doubt in anybody's mind, most importantly his, she always wanted and usually got the last word.

My overarching [perhaps just 'arch'] view of Paul De Lappe is one of sheer bloody-mindedness, mindlessness and mindfulness, a gravelling, hacking queeny beeyatch naturally possessing all three in gorgeous, gregarious, ginormous abundance.

There's a centuries-old Queer roar, lives in 'n' without the voices of our infectiously wise, it scrapes, shrieks for generously narcissistic attention and damn well makes sure it gets it. On the surface it's in possession 'n' possessed by an unholy godless tone, but underneath, that imperfectly pitched squall knows 'n' feels everything. Our Pearl was in sound possession of such a profoundly understanding, multi-tasking, ever-rasping, forever-echoing screech.

Whilst fecklessly pouring through arty postcards in the crumbling Cornerhouse cinema of auld, I could hear her squall skyward in our Gay Village local, Paddy's Goose. So powerful her aural cawing-card, was almost as if she was siren-like calling me to Paddy's for a Guinness or ten. Like his incomparable shriek, Paul was both incredibly piercing 'n' kind, and above all loved the company of friends. We spent so many boozy days/nights hollering out laughter, hysterically the abnorm with Aunty Pearl. After all, she was a prodigiously gifted comic with a finely tuned camp ear 'n' eye, a vivaciously ribald raconteur, a smouldering sexy pub chanteuse [her Marilyn doing the football results with Gilly had to be seen/heard to be believed], add to that a really, really good social media presence and caustically witty writer. "C'mon on, forty-seven, no bra, not bad eh!"

There was a real earthy understanding of life's ever-cascading, ever-absurd profundities in Paul. The good, bad, the ugly, most certainly the camp, but more importantly, far more, the augmented beautiful. Pearl liked things pretty, sparkly, to be surrounded by really nice stuff, liked things to be as shimmering as they could possibly be. She was defiantly magnanimous when it came to decoration, certainly loved more than just a li'l smidgen of anarcho-glitter. Anyone who witnessed the ever-growing, ever-glowing camposity of her Holiday village, 'Shady Pines', will know exactly what I mean. Thinking back, I'm pretty sure her ultra-luminescent tribute to *The Golden Girls'* retirement home was bigger than her living room, certainly bigger than Yuletide, but then so was she. Paul intuitively zoned into things like seasons, felt the turn of the Earth, holistically understood the tangible importance of Halloween, Bonfire Night and Christmas, loved the new 'n' ancient traditions of all our holidays. Always felt Pearl and I bonded over those depths of socialised esoteric feeling; we both hadn't stopped being big, daft, giggly, working-class queens.

Although an only child, there was most certainly something of the 'seventh son' about her, or spirited wicked stepdaughter, take ye pick. I deffo think that cranky auld witch had 'the sight'. He could certainly spot things others refused or wouldn't see and wasn't afraid to say why. Although occasionally vulnerable, he was at the same time both forthright and fearless. His undeniable courage something I'd later come to understand and holistically respect – that huge strength of character, the true grit in the pearl, would soon become something wholly defining him. Seriously, I've never been as privileged to witness such unequivocal bravery, never seen it so purposefully shaped and put into pragmatic everyday play. Move over Mother Courage, Aunty Pearl's about to steal your thunder, pinny, rollers, headscarf 'n' if y'not careful very probably ye fella!

* * *

Paul got ill with cancer, having to go to Christies to get it removed. It was incredibly shocking for us all as a group, but Paul, as always, constantly thinking of others, controlled and allayed our fears. Anyway, he's operated on, and seems it may have been successful. A little later, after another check-up, the cancer returned, but this time had spread. After feeling some initial celebratory relief, he was quickly told there would be no hope. A particularly cruel chain of events, stuff that could floor anybody, not Paul though, oh no, not our Pearl. He simply ripped down those curtains 'n' made her a Supremes sixties-inspired mini-dress and indefatigably carried on. "Stop in the name of Pearl!" She certainly wasn't gonna let cancer have the last word.

*　　*　　*

Paul, like me, absolutely adored Manchester, she loved every red-brick swaggering nuance of our adopted city, we'd pub jangle of it endlessly. He'd walk its streets for hours simply soaking up the quirky/dirty wit, attitudes 'n' atmospheres. Loved its people, particularly its women, history and architectural make up, loved it housed one of the most visible and forward-thinking gay communities in the world. She simply adored hysterical barmy queens and this city's full of them! There's a fair bit of Paul and Manchester's Queer legacies that are tied-in/tied-up together, making a lot of unifying/bonding sense. In her own inimitable way, Aunty Pearl was most certainly a Queer warrior, flying the rainbow flag for his peoples and their rights to be flamboyantly disco-free.

Paul was passionately opinionated and would certainly let you know exactly what he/she was thinking/feeling. We occasionally clashed [well, more than occasionally to be brutally frank] and I honestly loved it. I relish a fiery row, adore going hammering tongues with ye vile, caustic snatchy twisted sister. If you wanted or needed a *Coronation Street* Ena 'n' Elsie-like slangin' match, then Pearl was ye girl. There was more than a hint of the 'last word' Elsie/Ena/Betty/Hilda in how she attacked an argument, in how she attacked you... wunderbar! Paul could also lend a very sympathetic ear to almost anybody, but treated fools the way they

266

should be. Cobra-like whiplashings from a coiled-up venomous Pearl were hissing fuck-tongued, visceral joys to behold.

Paul was old 'n' new school when it came to almost everything, an ear in the past, an eye in the present and a six inch stillie firmly embedded in the weave of the future. She could run rings round time, so she could. A genius pop-culturist, knew so much about music and its Queer historical contexts. How could you not, when you were potty-trained to The Supremes? "Plop in the name of love, 'n' let me wipe your arse..." [true story].

Our raucous caucus coven of cackling queens really miss the presence she touched us almost daily with, dearly. Miss her right royally holding court with ribald tales of Carmen Rollers [a real person], her holiday romancings [ooh, she loved her cruises], her opinions on [let's face it] pretty much everything. He brought a blood-pumping heart 'n' soul into all that was said 'n' done, and no one said or done it quite like Pearl. I'll really miss the colourfully vivid noise of her. Loud, yes, very, but also all-encompassing, enveloping, covering us like a rowdy argumentative, very necessary, waspishly witty duvet. Paul knew he was in the room – more than that, relished being in the room and completely worked/owned it. Yet you could also have the quietest of times with him, be private, cocooned even, and know you were being very powerfully listened to. He had more sides to her than a dragged-up dodecahedron that one.

My thoughts go out to his mum and dad, who have lost their only child. I simply can't imagine how that must feel. Also, to his partner of many years, Johnny, who stood by him and helped at every turn. Johnny most definitely Paul's Romeo, and Pearl his loyal Juliet [and occasionally his acerbic, demonstrative, rolling pin in hand Peggy Mount... "Romeo, Romeo, where the fuck art thou Romeo, yer bastard'n dirty stop out ye!" – she could be a bit of a dragon queen!]. And Darryl 'n' Kieran, two gorge power-balladeering camp companions dutifully accompanying her on his last journeys, she adored them... share 'n' Cher alike.

*   *   *

Last time I saw Paul was in the Northern Quarter's Abel Heywood [a lovely communal hipstery bar], gently lit by a honey-mumbling ambience. Pearl had sent a round-robin and we all collectively descended, you could clearly see he was very moved by how many were there. It was a powerful, emotionally charged night, slightly intense, but as per, wonderfully and joyfully orchestrated by Paul: she was a class act and would never have let it fall into maudlin mawkishness. He made quite sure, with almost psychic precision, he/we had a damn good laugh.

At this point the growing tumour round his mouth had severely disabled his speech and was slurringly difficult to understand. Anyway, he comes over to me, slams herself down opposite and asks if I would write him his eulogy. Strangely, for all his muffled speech, in this loud bar [and I'm deaf in one ear], I could hear him; there seemed to be no slurring whatsoever, every word crystal clear as a diamond bell. All the way through this slightly hyper-real moment [we were both on his ora-morph] I thought him just so incredibly brave, confronting so much and able to freely ask such a thing. "Of course," I said, "it would be my honour." He quickly replied with, "The honour is all mine." See, that last word thing again. Well, of course, I let him have it, last word that is. Later on she Facebook PMs me, saying he's really pleased I agreed to write her 'curse' for him. I immediately messaged back it was my honour. Once again [the last word obsessed beeyatch] wrote the honour was all his and once again, I let him have it.

Thing is lurhdee [*Coronation Street* for lady], think on 'n' look sharp! Right now, I've got the last word/words and can quite categorically tell you, the gorgeous, fun-lovin', wise, raucous, partyin', drunken, dancin', howlin', cacklin', cracklin', gossipin', ABBAin', Diana Ross 'n' the Supremesin', Madonnain', Euro-visionin', campy, vampy, glorious Gaynorin', outrageous, contrary, serious, deliriously delicious honour... is most definitely all mine sister!

Outroduction

The Second Summer Of Love and
The Cocained Winter Of Discontent

or

Never Piss Off A Performance Poet
A cautionary tale of the betrayal of kinship

All the views set out in this essay are uniquely mine. The experiences,
although wholeheartedly wish they weren't, are also very sadly mine.
Any resemblances between the living, dead, the living dead or soulless
zombified undead, although deliberately pithy 'n' perhaps more than a
little bitchy, are completely unremarkable anecdotal accidents.

Part I
Ecstasy is the Socialism of Drugs

i

Now feels like a good time to start writing this, right time in
fact. After an extremely humid, oxygen-singeing hot spell, this
gloomy Sunday morning's suddenly blustery, raining and wintry-
unwelcoming.

This cautionary tale of the inexcusable betrayal of kinship is
also that.

Been putting this off for some time, not because still painful
[although some of it is], but I now wish to no longer live with,
or again remember, its bizarrely unloving protagonists: turgid
moribund creatures, who are long-bleached down the stinking
sink of my tower block kitchenette u-bend. One doesn't want to
spend any more valuable time dredging the swamp; as we all
know, swamp slime is notoriously, organically, ugly 'n' sticky, its
stench clinging to wall of skin, an obsequious body-rotten
scratch. This is an exercise in scraping away the last of that
pungent human mucus, therefore making the pond clearer for

future newer/fresher life. They, like their co-dependent social contagion, are now almost gone from my mind's-eye, but I simply can't write about my time in Manchester without detailing some, only *some* mind, of my absolute disgust at their lack of understanding, empathy and friendship. I would dearly love to truly name 'n' shame and tell a whole lot more [believe me, there's so much more to tell], but I'm nowhere near as sneakily shevil as they. So, to protect the guilty, I'll delete both locations and names. The emblematic environ for this dramatic/ poetic essay [piece of Scouse jangle] is still magically 'the eternal party', or what I *thought* the eternal party. If the ever-malleable genius of hedonistic Manchester taught me anything, it's the many-sided, altruistic über-joy of generous narcissism.

Their carefully de-augmented, 'protecting the guilty' names, are:

Why — *because why anybody could be his friend is beyond me.*
Diamond Hard — *Why's insignificant other and henchman.*
Sunflower — *a once supposed 'best' friend and most treacherous of this profoundly uncaring triumvirate of crap.*

ii

As you must well know by now, I was a second summer of love Rave Queer, most of that Queering molten-forged 'n' shaped in my beloved kiln of Manchester. Oh Manchester, you filled my heart with such fiery party; that burn, flame-scorching my soul, a sparking/sweating effervescing zhuzh which is always precious-cherished and lovingly clung to. There are moments of such startling reminiscence it's like recalling a multitude of strobing Heavens; flashing Paradises so out there 'n' in, they quickly became everywheres of everything. The rhythmic osmosis-like churn of smoke-machined club knowledge, beat-rapping bass and love into our ever-expanding heads 'n' hearts. After the iridescently freeing joyousness of The Everyman Youth Theatre, I thought I could never touch such clear improvisational hyperspace ever again, that glorious interstitial shit really did feel like a one-shot deal. WRONG! Manchester, you were a second silvering bullet, Emma Peel-placed in a diamante-studded golden gun. It was like being a glittery cowboying avenging teenager twice.

Taking Ecstasy [and the rest] within such carefree camaraderie allowed me an inroad to the humane spiritualism of Socialism, not just its communal vibe, but its multi-hallucinogenic anarchies. Rave is why I declare myself an anarcho-socialist. Like horse 'n' carriage, bread 'n' butter, The Krankies, it seems you can't have one without the other.

Early days, I was a bit of a ligger. Never had much money – still don't – and although professionally trained knew back then I didn't want professionally *in*. The crippling über-trauma of Brian's death, then two years later my mother's and very soon after that my brother Paul's, and increasing societal/class unease made 'the forging of career' mean little or nothing to me... continuing weights of grief meant I didn't see the point. I was an *out* ligger, clear and confident in my ligging, no shame, self-declared and if you didn't like it/me, fine, don't have me. At the risk of sounding cockily honest, people did like me, and they liked me [I think] because I gave loads back – y'see, I wasn't a selfish ligger. In fact, I felt it my earnest/sacred duty to entertain and that I definitely did. I'm something of a Scouse vaudevillian and easily able to hold a room 'n' dancefloor: I'm also a considerably-skilled disco-hoofer. I'm really quite funny, more than that, *witty*, fab at wordplay and can easily exude a fun-loving sense of community; it's what I'm socially good at. People wanted me around. I really liked people around me, too, so although something of a ligger, I was a ligger who very much cared and could choose where 'n' when to lig.

I'd long been lost-weekending in nineties Manchester with very good friends, Diamond Hard being one of them, and regulars at Flesh, Number One, Strangeways, Glory Hole and any cellar Rave club that would have us. Let's say by now, to save very necessary time, Diamond Hard had met Why and they'd become boyfriends. After clubbing we'd all giddily troll back to Why's to chill-out, and for a good long while it seemed fine, often really lovely. Off my bonce, with those people, those acid-engined quite crazy glittering moments were some of the best times of my life. Diamond Hard 'n' I were something of a comedic double-act, a hallucinogenically-enhanced Little 'n' Large [I was Sid]. Although at the time incredibly fond, I never wholly trusted Diamond Hard and was very aware of his obvious insecurities/paranoias. Always surface confident, there was something deeply unsettled about him, occasionally making him vocally volatile 'n' snappily mean-spirited. I was able to cut through that murky crap and for a long while we had superb communal comedic timing 'n' rapport. Diamond Hard had seriously wanted, but couldn't cut a theatrical career, ending up a very creative accountant. To his credit though, he was a gifted comic, mimic and improviser, so of course we gelled and I enjoyed our tripping, acrobatic theatrics immensely. Those chill-outs were completely of the time, quite hysterical and out of this world, with Diamond Hard 'n' I very often its entertaining molten core. I ridiculously thought I was building friends for life.

It was when I started bringing my new friend, Sunflower, to Manchester, letting her into my partying social circle and indeed life, that I first sensed something terribly wrong. After clubbing, I was taking her to Why's glorious chill-outs, thinking nothing of it and allowing her further 'n' further into my world. I'd known her from theatrical Liverpool and, although she knew some people there, she seemed a tad friendless, a little lost. I wanted to introduce her to my friends, to help build her confidence, hoping they'd party alongside 'n' bond. I genuinely thought that was indeed happening, until one particular chill-out when Diamond Hard hurriedly took me to one side. Could tell by the way he cantankerously manoeuvred me into the kitchen something was obviously irking him. I asked if everything alright and he said no. I asked what was up and he replied they didn't really want Sunflower around the house anymore. I was seriously staggered by this, as both he and Why were always incredibly friendly to her, welcoming even. I asked what's wrong with her being here and Diamond Hard laughed a slimy half-laugh suggesting I should somehow automatically know. I told him I didn't know and he smirkingly replied, "Well, c'mon bird [we called each other bird], she's a bit grubby, isn't she?" Astounded by this I said, "I don't think she is." He pointedly suggested I wasn't to bring her again. I said, "Fine, but if she's not welcome, I won't be coming around anymore either." Sometimes, when you're a ligger, people think they have automatic control over you. Take it from this ligger, *they don't!* Somewhat staggered, Diamond Hard then said, "Well, that's stupid. We don't want that, you're always welcome." I replied, "Well, I'm certainly not going to tell my close friend she's grubby and unwelcome, now am I?"

Needless to say, and after some intense bickering, I got Sunflower to stay, but what little trust I had in Diamond Hard was now on rocky ground.

That trust would be totally decimated at The Edinburgh Fringe.

iii

There was always a part of me feeling very sorry for Diamond Hard. I'm quite empathetic, can instinctively sense incompleteness in people, and there was a hole in his soul so wide you could punch a boxing-gloved fist through. So, I suggested he could direct a Chloe Poems show, which he generously did. Although certainly not good, he wasn't that awful a director. He'd unintellectually keep Chloe in a kind of Julie Walters/Mrs Overall bubble, something I creatively disliked and very soon rid her of. By this time, Sunflower and I were working creatively together and thought it an interesting idea to take Chloe on an Edinburgh Fringe adventure. Of course, Diamond Hard wants to come along and is sincerely welcomed by us both. The day before I was opening the show all three of us were in a bar drinking. I'm due to do an interview with some-such Fringe 'zine and casually say, to what I thought were my friends, something like: *As the artist what do you think I should blurb about the piece?* Immediately, I saw Diamond Hard's featureless visage shift from smiling open 'n' wine-glass-chatty to suddenly darkened and haughtily indignant. He viscously/viciously sneer-asked me what I just said and I repeated: *As the artist what do you think I should blurb about the piece.* Beetroot-skinned, he then went into this quietly raging tirade, actually accusing me of not being an artist. For some incomprehensibly bizarre reason [at the world's largest festival of art], he was incandescently furious at me using that word. He made it very clear I had no right whatsoever to the term 'artist' and wasn't backwards in coming forward with his quite disturbing vitriol as to why – his whole shtick being I was somehow undeservedly beneath the term.

Now, I'm a camp scally from Scottie Road, so his dreary/pithy middle-class rant concerning my artistic prowess didn't touch the sides, but I couldn't help thinking… *what an absolute cunt!* There's an ages-auld theatrical tradition where the director of a piece, certainly before a nerve-wracking first night, usually tries to imbue an upbeat confidence in both 'artist' and show. Oops, not this one it seems! If I'd been anybody else, his vulgar, amateurish attempt at character assassination might have worked, but I just looked at 'n' right through him [I'm rather good with looks, get it from my Grandma]. He immediately knew it didn't touch me and could see in increasingly boggling eyes both his anger and failure. His pointless desire to demean, devalue and diminish me, in a show he'd directed for fuck's sake, quickly became what it subconsciously was: a fruitless, idiotic act of unrealised self-sabotage.

After he flounced off [and it was some pub-shaking flounce, like a horny brontosaurus looking for its mate], a puzzled Sunflower and I automatically burst out laughing. I asked her why she thought he'd just made such an unholy show of himself. She replied, "Simple, he's jealous of you Gerry, always has been." I was completely surprised 'n' taken aback by that. I materially had nothing [still don't], not even a secure place to live. Diamond Hard was properly loaded, his own home, posh car, bloated gouty gut 'n' everything. Looking back, I get it more; he'd completely failed at his chosen vocation and there I was living, breathing, writing 'n' actually performing mine. The bitterly unfulfilled are darkly/snidely sad and it's a genuinely heart-breaking thing to witness, particularly if their social/artistic insufficiencies are directed at you. There are moments, though very few and far between mind, that I can almost conjure some semblance of pity for him.

iv

Now, his boyfriend Why and I got on famously. I powerfully adored that bloke, I felt we had a real creative/class-based bond and cerebral, humanly spiritual connection. In many ways, I saw him a kind of all-seeing teacher/mentor, he seemed in possession of a joyous kinda quiet I thought both gently stoic and inwardly/outwardly warm. At his exceptional best he exuded an almost Buddhist sense of honesty and calm. It always felt a great pleasure, an honour even, to be in the translucent aura of his company and within the party-palace of his home. He was the host of some seriously legendary do's and chill-outs, generous, kind, a great listener; I thought we'd be friends forever... Warra disappointment he would become!

I used to believe that, unlike his weirdo boyfriend, Why really got me. Here was a close friend who actually liked/admired my 'artistry', constantly telling me so and most certainly a huge Chloe fan [he particularly liked her poem 'The Effeminate']. I knew he found my Scouse anarchy and working-class irreverence both funny 'n' empowering, loved my dancing. We were, I thought, great 'n' forever comrades.

I clearly remember the night we properly bonded. It was a mutual friend's birthday party and Why had invited his incredibly 'dodgy' mate. Although large 'n' stoic in appearance, occasionally witty, this friend of Why's was something of an alpha bully. Completely out the blue, Why's mate, a gay man himself mind, suddenly starts to spout an incredibly insulting diatribe of disgustingly pointed homophobia. Really aggressively and in my face, demeaning camp and effeminacy, basically trumping [and I really mean trumping, stupid old fart] on about how gays like me were both societally ineffectual 'n' wrong. I could instantly see the embarrassing discomfort in Why's increasingly knotting body language [he looked like a just-squeezed sponge], never seen him so completely shame-faced. Of course, I wasn't standing for this punitive accusatory shit and promptly/expertly put Why's 'friend' in his dodgy place. I'm no bully, not by a long chalk, but I'm also no pushover. Whilst I'd do anything to keep a party laughing, active 'n' rocking, I don't think twice about flooring knob'eads! I left Why's mate head-hung beaten with bumbling/mumbling apology on his lips.

Sometime later, at one of his chill-outs, Why would tell me that night and my response to his 'friend' was a life-changing 'n' life-enhancing moment for him. Seriously taken aback, I asked why. He replied that he himself was having a crisis of confidence about his place in his own sense of sexuality; he'd lost any understanding that it personally or politically meant anything [no surprise, considering the company he kept]. He told me that my acerbically 'n' eloquently facing off to his 'pal' had given him a confidence he'd felt long gone, that I'd restored a pride in both himself, his sexual identity and in what being a gay man could powerfully mean. He thanked me and it was a brotherly moving/bonding moment. I'll never forget its touching, connecting, personally/politically Queer honesty.

Sadly, like his dodgy mate, he'd soon turn out to be a complete knob'ead, too.

v

I first became aware of Why's quite twisted knob'eadery at one of his chill-outs. I'm exceptionally fortunate in being someone who's taken all the drugs in the world twice, maybe three times, and never suffering the punishing mental indignities of a bad trip. Unfortunately, at this chill-out, Diamond Hard was. He'd really gone under and felt a very uneased paranoia at everything surrounding, including me 'n' Sunflower. I dutifully tried to ease him out of his deep unpleasantness, only to be met with a very caustic Diamond Hard classic, "I certainly don't need any of your positive affirmations." Vicious snatch! Sunflower and I stayed by him and were eventually joined by Why. Now to be honest, I'm not sure of the content of communication between Diamond Hard 'n' Why, but remember the tone being argumentatively fractious. I thought it somewhat insensitive for Why to be bickering with an obviously mentally disoriented Diamond Hard, but that would be nothing to what he'd say next, and I'll take this incredibly disturbing moment to my grave.

Out the blue and uncharacteristically nasty, he spat-spouted, "It should have been Gerry, not you. It was always Gerry!"

The room went that kind of silent rooms can only go when something so completely devastating is let loose. Given the state he was in, its effect on Diamond Hard must've been unthinkable. I quickly uttered something clumsily witty to diffuse the sitch, though even the wittiest thing ever could never have done that, and Why crankily left the room. It's all a bit blurry now, but we did that thing like absolutely nothing had happened, changing tone 'n' conversation to shoo the incredibly disturbing badness away. But something had happened and it was truly awful. More than that, I believe intentionally cruel.

It was far too much information to take in, leaving Sunflower and I unable to work it out. All groups have interactions, good, bad, but there are certain moments simply knocking you off your perch. Not saying I began to mistrust Why then, I certainly wasn't going to judge him, but things would never again be quite the same between us. I began to feel a kind of uncomfortable guilt if Diamond Hard saw us just chatting together, didn't want him too unnerved or upset by it. I would only go sparingly to Why's do's after that, birthdays and such, maybe the occasional chill-out. It would be me stepping slightly outside the group, giving a clearer insight of its increasingly odd 'n' cloying dynamic. I'm a rather confident outsider and looking outside in is so often the better view.

Before we leave Why, I have to mention that what happened hadn't stopped me being terribly fond of, or caring for him. C'mon, we sometimes hit it wrong... 'n' who am I to arrogantly sit in judgement? We all make mistakes, mistakes are human and perhaps that's just what it was, a silly drug-addled mistake. Although now more than a little wary, I still thought Why kind, generous, and would have done anything in my power to help him out.

One night, from a mutual friend, Sunflower and I got a disturbing phone call saying Why was having a lot of trouble at home. I rang Why and asked what. At that point he was living in a very rough area of Manchester and a violent gang of youths were physically threatening and verbally abusing him. There had already been a bloody violent incident leaving poor Why understandably panicked 'n' terrified. I told him I'd be around straight away and asked Sunflower for a lift. To her courageous credit, as I suggested she didn't have to, Sunflower came in with me. I'm not going to say much more, because this bit still really upsets me, but it's very important for me to explain. Ask anybody, I've got a big Scouse gob on me [ain't that fer sure], but I'm no fighter. I'm rubbish at physical violence, it frightens/disturbs me greatly. We stayed most of the night into the early morning with Why, and if those thugs had struck again, as they'd threatened, I would have stood shoulder to shoulder with him. I would have done my level best to help and protect. Where I come from that's what true friendship/kinship is about, protecting the people you love and care for. It's a class thing, an unwritten law. I thought I had that class thing with Why... I would soon be proven very, very wrong!

Don't know if you've ever seen the cinematic monochrome classic *All About Eve*, a brilliantly caustic Bette Davis film, the movie making her once again an 'above the title' star. In it she plays Margo Channing, an ageing stage actress at the top of her theatrical game. Although still wildly magnificent, she's also intellectually vulnerable and questioning. She meets up with stalker-like super-fan, Eve, whom she dutifully adopts and takes under her wing, generously bringing her into her close circle of friends. On the outside, Eve is the softest, kindest, sweetest thing, but inside, a sneaky, ambitious, social-climber like no other. Although merely a performance poet, I more than consider myself a sassy, well-versed entertainer; I've a rather confident manner and swarthy, swinging gait, not unlike a pithy/bitchy Margo Channing. My then supposed 'best friend' Sunflower, was and is quintessentially, Eve. When it comes to best friends, 'what a dump' Sunflower turned out to be. Up to a certain point I would have said the greatest inhumane disappointment in my life was Why... Sunflower would very soon eclipse even him. Fasten your seatbelts... it's gonna be a bumpy read!

I have now, and for some time, completely erased Sunflower from my life; I want nothing whatsoever to do with her. The thing is, she was once a very big part of my life, so for documentation's sake and only within this story, I sadly have to feature a semblance, a merest shade of her. The one thing I'll say is we made a lot of very important art together, wonderfully exciting counter-cultural work, properly reaching out and viscerally empowering so many others. There are lots of very successful artists working today who took part in what we did, who see it as the first steps in their creative journeys – a fact of which I'm very proud. Wish I could be as proud of Sunflower.

How can you rub out someone so important from your timeline, Gerry? I telepathically hear you trill.

By simply making it part of my timeline I physically hear me type.

This is *my* quirky, off-beat autobiography and these are my stories, and part of that story is now about erasing Sunflower from them. Believe me, it makes all kinds of autobiographical sense. Was going to list some of the stuff we did, but I can't have her tuneless blasé insignificance tonelessly banging about my head a second longer. "Out damn Sunflower... OUT!"

vii

So much of the above time was and still remains wildly nostalgically spectacular, certainly clubbing 'n' raving, even Why's festival-like parties 'n' chill-outs. Apart from the occasional darknesses [well, maybe not *that* occasional], it was a sparkling, gregariously uplifting, hysterically funny dancing time. Oh, the dancing... très magnifique! I could wax a lurid lyrical for many pages more about the collective purity of those days, the tumbling from place to place and the vibrating walls of sound 'n' rhythm. Anyone positively experiencing that time [not everybody did] will have memories, stories, sensations, just like mine. The main recurring theme being the gloriously supreme connectivity, the holistic understandings we were all human beings set equally free under the same roof, the same dramatic Manchester morning skies. It does make you wonder why some peoples, peoples you thought completely on-side, could go so deliberately out their way to discolour/discredit/ disavow it... and they have, soulless bastards! Although The Bourgeois Zeitgeist was skulking around back then, it wasn't yet garrotting the humanity out of everything, there was still a very anarchic *zhuzh* vibrating about it all. I believe the bonding of then was indelibly human – I still have lots of friends from those times, but let's be terribly honest here, it was also Ecstasy. Say what you will, E as a love-engine really drove the magic along. It wasn't The Second Summer of Love because the sun continually shone; it was the long hot 'Summer' it was because the drugs were far more than merely fabulous. But it's a sad and well-known fact... seasons must change...

Part II

Cocaine is the Capitalism of Drugs

i

It's no secret, dear reader, I, along with the next jiggling/juggling hedonist, love a line. If it's chopped out 'n' magically there, certainly won't be magically there long. Those little powders of light will sure soon find a cosy new nose-home. I have occasionally imbibed 'n' maybe bought the odd gramme, but cocaine has never really been my drug of choice. Not only is it far too expensive, the hit, although somewhat upbeat 'n' pleasurable, doesn't last that long. Now give me a good ol' fashioned dirty dab of cheap whizz, the sticky pasty stuff... and I'm a turbo-charged sassy wink of whirl-winding camposity!

When Ecstasy was leaving the building, cocaine seemed to ever so slyly take its place, also taking with it some of the overflowing joyousness of the time. Again, I'm not judging [I find judging and peoples who judge characterfully weak 'n' opaquely dreary], merely observing. People can and must do what they will, be who they want, but I do think certain drugs suit certain people more than other drugs. Back then, cocaine had a sleek, almost sociopathically confident sheen, largely in keeping with the well-paid 'young' professionals taking it. With that youthful, sexy, dark-clubbing swagger came a careerist, monied, 'city slicker' 'tude. Not necessarily because of the drug – it's just a dumb old powdery backstreet narcotic – but what one might pop-culturally 'imagine' the 'tude of the drug to be. My rapidly ageing gang most certainly weren't young or indeed sexy [far more Tudey Finnegan than y'actual tudey]; they didn't characterfully extend that kind of aggressively DJ-ing brio. Age had left us far too dishevelled, frightened, tattered 'n' torn for the then supposed 'character' of coke, but bless our cotton socks and handwoven nightcaps, it didn't stop us trying. I remember thinking everybody looked a bit like clowns dressed as sharks. I always felt with E that everything was more above board, visibly seen, physically vibrant. We didn't furtively rat-like hide in closed-off rooms 'n' locked toilets to individually snort our snort. We openly took our take in front of each other and very physically chorused.

ii

I've never made a child cry in my life, just not something I'd ever 'deliberately' do. I'm a very successful uncle to many, a great uncle [in fact, a great great uncle] and never once made any of them weep. I've a historical/hysterical legacy of drama 'n' youth theatre work second to none. Instead of punitively making young people discovering the all-encompassing joys of drama uncontrollably bawl, I very much made them laugh, helped 'n' encouraged them along. If this was social media and I was to ask if I'd empowered them, that update would be met with literally hundreds of glowing, positive responses.

I know that paragraph may seem a little out of the blue, but bear with me. It's incredibly important.

iii

Because of recurring difficulties with Diamond Hard, I really didn't want to go to that year's group Christmas dinner, but because invited and catered for, I idiotically did. Initially, everything was fine; there was certainly much to drink 'n' a flurry of fun stuffs to festively imbibe. The group collectively knew you didn't invite me to a party to be a blushing, retiring wallflower – quite the opposite. Generously filling me with booze 'n' coke will do what booze 'n' coke always does: make me camply gregarious, partying 'n' piquantly playful... also, *honest*.

There was a long, tedious moment when everyone started to coke-talk of things they wanted to buy. They were almost scenting the blood 'n' feed-frenzying over conservatries, kitchen utensils, bathroom suites, taps, houses, bits of cars, motorbikes, holidays, earrings, things of absolutely no interest to me. I loathe acquisitive talk, money language; nothing wants to make me change a topic of conversation more, especially if it's going on 'n' on. After a little while [I gave them some grace], I said something like: *Can we perhaps change the subject, it's meant to be a room full of radical revolutionary socialists isn't it, who the fuck's interested in monogrammed designer bog brushes?* It got a big laugh, but then big laughs were my job.

I thought everything was fine. It most certainly wasn't.

Then it came to the Secret Santa! I'm not big on ridiculous things like this, but they'd seen it on an episode of *Friends* and badly wanted to emulate. I think they felt themselves a Mancunian arm of that particular TV show [well, they had to get their characters from somewhere]. Part of this Secret Santa idiocy was a good/decent present and lots of daft/fun presents. There was one of the group's children round, a really great kid I knew 'n' was very fond of, and she me. We'd historically always chirruped a very playful banter and were true to form playfully bantering around the daft presents on display; we were simply having lots of Christmas chirrups.

I'd known that kid for some years and always had a fun-loving storytelling relationship with her. I clearly remember one party, so the parents could have a good old boogie, entertaining her and a gang of other kids for hours with little more than a just-used, be-stringed herbal teabag. I had about ten sugared-up children careering wildly around, hysterically laughing and joyous; how despicably, unquenchably evil of me! I still see some of those parents today and they remember that herbal teabag moment with great fondness, thinking it magical.

So, the Christmas dinner party carries on, there's a ton of chirpy cheery laughter, bits of daft dancing and it eventually, as all parties do 'n' should, ends. There's lots of friendly seasonal farewell hugs and tipsy be-lipped Merry Christmasses and off we go, on our even merrier ways.

Next party on the horizon is New Year's Eve. As with all previous New Year's Eve parties, I automatically think I'm invited, like I have been for the past ten years. I call Sunflower about it and she starts to stumble 'n' stutter. "What's the matter?" I worriedly ask, as she'd never responded to me like this before. It transpired Why didn't want me to go, in fact fiercely adamant I don't – *what the, why the, where the…?* It came as a complete shock to me, a bolt from the blue. I simply couldn't take it in or indeed work it out… what on Earth had I done? I immediately ring Why, got his answer machine and with very concerned politeness ask him to ring me back to chat about 'n' sort out the sitch, whatever the hell this sitch is. He doesn't return any of my calls. I ring Sunflower, again ask what's gone on and what terrible thing am I meant to have done. She sheepishly tells me Why doesn't want me there and that's all she knows. She also tells me that she and everybody think he's gone mad… her very words.

New Year's Eve: I'm having a wonderful time partying in Manchester's Gay Village, but can't quite shake the irksome dig of what's just been dug. It's really puzzling and bothering me. I bodily/physically know it's really puzzling and bothering me, as I'm obtusely dancing at elbow-sharpened right angles. *Fuck this for a game of blind-man's doctors 'n' nurses,* I think. *I'm gonna sort this stupid shit out once 'n' for all… and if I don't go now, I'll have some poor queen's eye out.*

From dancefloor to taxi, to out of taxi, off I power-mince to the party. I arrive and am semi-welcomed by some [must say, most were nice]. I have a little scour around, then, looking like a just-punched cushion, I spot Diamond Hard. I nod to him, stroll over 'n' ask what's going on. He just aimlessly blathers 'n' blurts at me, his featureless face baggier, more insipid than ever before. More like a too-apologetic Lollipop Man responsible for the death of a popular local pensioner than a super-sleek, sharp-witted, cocained raver. I again ask what's going on and nothing; he's just too ridiculous 'n' hopelessly sly looking/sounding to make anything even resembling sense.

It's all incredibly confusing; I'm apparently ostracised, I've come to non-violently but somewhat confrontationally find out why, and what were very recently my really good friends are behaving like frightened children. I'm stood thinking what on Earth could I ever have done to illicit all this!

A floor-sat, cross-legged Why is surrounded by a host of friends and I immediately sense they're harem-like protecting him. The whole thing is resonating/radiating a collectively paranoid, intense, dense, bad coke stench. I genuinely kindly try to say hello, hoping to make some kind of amends and he just slyly, sharp-smirks at me... seriously, hand on heart here, don't think I've seen anything quite so ugly. That sly, sharp-smirk was the first time I saw the true face of Why. That completely-failing-in-any-way-to-be cocky, far too queasy grin was his absolute real self. There was something of the too feather-boa'd deeply embittered drag queen about it. It looked like he'd somehow psychically generated an impregnable two millimetre forcefield around his entire body and filled it with fart, a kind of self-satisfied, petulantly smug, *I created this stinking smell*, farty forcefield. He was, I think, desperately trying to affect über-confident coke-face. It looked more like he'd just really enjoyed secretly shitting himself.

Why and his wide-eyed foot-soldiers are leaving 'n' I carefully gesture to him I'd like a word. Then he does something he's never done before, he tries to make a bitchy comment at me. Can't even remember what it was, for funny hysteric's sake genuinely wish I could. Buried in the scrum of his makeshift bodyguards, looking more like a rapidly deflating Danny La Rue than a once Buddha-like dear friend 'n' confidante, he stumble-stutter exits. Sunflower was dead right, he had gone a kind of mad.

iv

A couple of weeks on from that dreadful party and still none the wiser as to why I'm ostracised, I'm told somebody is saying terrible things about me. Trusting the source, I ask who 'n' what. Apparently, Why had been telling people I 'deliberately' – nay, 'brutally' – made a little girl cry on Christmas Day.

I'm not saying I didn't, if I did I was unaware of it, perhaps 'accidentally' it *could*'ve happened, surely we're all guilty of accident. But according to Why it was 'deliberately'. We do what we do 'n' see what we see, so I'll 'deliberately' say this: if you're someone who believes a drug can give you a kind of confidence, the confidence you think it may give you could be, shall we say, more than a little psychologically heightened. I've certainly come across lots of cocaine users who have not necessarily 'lied', but confidently 'exaggerated' what's gone on around them.

I've seen the little girl [now fully grown] I 'deliberately/brutally' made cry on Christmas Day quite a few times since. For somebody who deliberately/brutally made her cry, she always seems terribly pleased to see me, 'made up' as we say in Liverpool. On many occasions I've sat and drank, even disco-danced with her parents, good friends of mine who've expressed genuine friendship-based concern about Why 'n' me. They very much care for him. When I told them what he'd been telling people they looked more than a wee bit baffled. If I did deliberately/brutally make their child cry on Christmas Day [which they don't remember], it seems neither a big deal to them, nor indeed their child. Why oh why is it to Why? Seriously, when it comes to some of that group's 'extra-curricular' activities, daft, drunken moments on Christmas Day pale into all kinds of silly insignificance; so their malformed paranoid cunty judgments of me fall well 'n' truly flat! I'm of the sound mind none of us should become massively hypocritical judging cunts. It's certainly not, how we say in the gay world, 'a look'!

Thankfully I now no longer have to live within the puerile, often difficult hypocrisies dominating any of their lives. For too long, I was devastated by the emotionally barren, almost sociopathic barbarity of Why's actions. The last time I saw him was near where he lived. I was carelessly passing through, cheap yellow-label shopping, minding me own business 'n' spotted him. I stood still, a quite stoic non-aggressively yet semi-confrontational stillness… I think I looked kinda hot. I genuinely/finally thought we might have that conversation. Soon as he saw me he instantly panicked, froze, a rabbit-in-headlights kinda shock. Looking absolutely terrified, he cartoon-like juddered, dropping 'n' smashing his mobile phone. My last memory of him is knees on pavement, frantically picking up the bits 'n' pieces. He certainly didn't look like somebody steadfastly cocksure that I'd done something irreparably 'n' socially unforgivable. He looked like someone who'd done something disgustingly wrong. He had: he betrayed kinship 'n' class, broke an unwritten law, and had been well 'n' truly found out!

All we ever needed to do was chat, a little talk would have sorted everything. After all we'd been through as a group, the heart-breaking enormity of Brian's death being just one of those things, I deserved at least that. Even if after that talk I was no longer welcomed by Why, I would have been hurt, but would've understood, known and have moved on. That man is responsible for a lot of very unnecessary unpleasantness indeed.

v

Looking back, me having to leave that hotchpotch gaggle of 'friends' was always on the cards. I'd long been aware of The Bourgeois Zeitgeist and there was a faction within the group which was just so unmistakably that. So much of their conversation, increasingly dominated by plodding acquisitive avarice, meant we were quite simply/naturally, intellectually/politically distancing. I think the slimy execution of Why's elimination of me was more about me not fitting into the rapidly developing Bourgeois Zeitgeist narrative he and Diamond Hard were busily weaving. I was always poo-pooing talk of monied expensive shit, often laughing at it. I believe me sticking so rigidly/vocally to working-class anarcho-socialist credentials was the main reason I was so cowardly/viciously pushed. A friend once quizzed me and asked if I thought it was because Why secretly still carried a torch for me. I can't entertain the notion of Why somehow bitterly fancying me, fills my psyche with an actual physical revulsion, making me wanna shower. I think he did that "it should have been Gerry" thing in his kitchen to spiritually wound his obviously paranoid boyfriend.

Sad to say, they had definitely become a living breathing embodiment of The Bourgeois Zeitgeist, with soft sweet, 'only lovely' Sunflower, the most naturally bourgeois of them all.

vi

Until meeting 'n' dealing with King of Fools Why, don't think I'd ever been so completely fooled by anybody in my whole life. Wrong! Sunflower would soon greedily snatch his ever-twisting crown of thorns.

The very basis of Sunflower's and my relationship was a kind of mutual trust, profound kinship. We were slightly contrary outsiders, bonded by the love of both theatre 'n' art. Art, and making of, were what we successfully did best, benefiting many others along the way. For Sunflower to be responsible for me not making art is the greatest, most brutal betrayal of kinship, and a deliberately soulless betrayal of art itself. Think it safe to say she's broken all the unwritten laws!

vii

I'm not blowing my own trumpet here, just logically reading my life, but I am a natural empowerer of groups, situation 'n' people. The intensity, honesty and beauty of The Everyman Youth Theatre experience simply left me with those sets of social skills. Be it a rehearsal room or disco, I see it as a kind of personal duty to make people feel as cool about whatever, usually themselves, as they possibly can. I very much know who 'n' what I am, what I'm capable 'n' not capable of, and in quirky possession of those sparky improvisational qualities able to enhance experience. What I mean is, I can think really quickly on my disco-dancing/theatrical feet. Even Sunflower had spoken of how I'd given her confidence and stronger sense of self.

One day she came to me really quite troubled 'n' perplexed. She'd been with the group and they'd been talking of positive influences on each of/in their lives [probably saw it on *Friends*]. Very kindly, Sunflower had told them it was me, that I'd been the most influential/positive influence on her life thus far. Somebody had exclaimed: *Gerry? You serious? Don't be ridiculous, it can't be him!* Such was the damning/demeaning tone it left Sunflower really quite upset. I was also very understandably hurt to hear this, but didn't show it and replied, "C'mon Sunflower, this is coming from somebody thinking they can actually read auras, let's not let that bother us." It did bother me though; it felt bullying, punitive and sneeringly snide, qualities I never expected this particular person to possess. It seems Why was indeed doing an excellent job.

I'm not saying Sunflower owes me anything, I don't work that way, people captain their own ships, but I do think other folk can sometimes act as rudders. Some of those rudders are chaotic, wave-smashing turbulent, careering you off course 'n' crashing. Other rudders steer ripples of stiller waters, maybe not always becalmed, occasionally choppy, but somehow able to help you smoothly navigate the future. Sunflower was most certainly a rudder for me, but arguably I was a more influential/beneficial rudder for her.

When I first met Sunflower she was quite an isolated soul, thinking of leaving theatre altogether 'n' moving more into the field of conservation, numbering trees, counting corn, labelling pansies, that kinda thing. It was her direct involvement with me which gave her a national theatrical profile and professional visibility. Chloe Poems did an awful lot of fab country-wide stuff and was forever in the press. For some reason papers like *The Guardian* and certainly the then plentiful gay press really got Chloe. Her cabaret profile was vividly/vibrantly 'out there' – 'n' not just Chloe, there was a whole host of high-octane publicity-grabbing work going down, with both Sunflower and I greatly benefiting from the exposure. I was most certainly the rudder bringing her into the harbour of her current friendships and without my dogged determination 'n' 'loyalty' she simply wouldn't have them. As rudders go, I was ruddy useful [now you're getting the *All About Eve* connection].

My great sadness is I thought when it came to choppy waters we would always rudder each other through. No – the bourgeois element of Sunflower is so historically/familiarly powerful, like worms in the bowels of sand, squirmy, wriggling 'n' far too organically/biologically embedded. Having once suggested she may be of the counter-cultural underground, she's now very much reverted to class type.

I never ask anybody for anything, I'm either blessed or cursed with that kind of working-class moment. As artists go, I live a rather turbulent life, dangerous even, don't do it any other way but mine. I certainly don't want to be fiscally/professionally entwined in the manners, finance 'n' control of The Bourgeois Zeitgeist. I simply can't be a proactive agent of Inspirationalism 'n' Positivia, it would artistically destroy me. I've very definitely chosen this artistic path, this is my ship, the rickety junk I captain is precariously of my own make.

There was an awful time, not so long ago, when I thought that very little pocket of money would sink without trace. If it had sunk, it would have left me stranded on the rocks 'n' seriously shipwrecked, possibly leaving me homeless. I went to see Sunflower, who was by now running a theatre, and explained the potential calamity of my intensely distressing predicament. I said that I'm probably gonna need some kind of work really soon, and can she possibly sort something out, could she help. I was seriously panicked and desperately needed a little friendship/kinship ruddering. She was peculiarly distant, twitchy 'n' nervously nodding. To cut a tedious story short, it transpired she employs Diamond Hard, and I find out I can't make art in her building because of him, in case I upset him. If Diamond Hard had been Sunflower's rudder back in the day, the Diamond Hard she employs, the Diamond Hard claiming I had no right whatsoever to the word 'artist', the Diamond Hard who didn't want her around, wouldn't now be her friend and therefore have a job. If he'd steered the waters his way, he would gladly have never seen her again. As Margaret Thatcher once said when she was stabbed in the back by a nasty bunch of right whingers, *funny old world*.

I've left very strict instructions with true friends that if I'm to ever suddenly die [it's a familial trait], Sunflower is not allowed to attend or indeed send flowers to my funeral. I've even told certain friends that if I unexpectedly pop me clogs 'n' they ever happen to bump into Sunflower and she 'pretends' to offer the pantomime of condolence, to laugh – nay, heartily bray like bi-polar donkeys on the highest most manic high – right in her face. Being 'real' friends, they've dutifully promised they would. Although I'm happy as Larry now, we really were very close. Though for a little while, she broke my heart.

viii

I doubt they'll get to read this, but if any of them do, it'll be dear sweet, 'only lovely' Sunflower. If the other two get to peruse, they'd certainly be in denial of some of it, perhaps even calling me a liar, they've called me a lot worse. Sunflower will instinctively know I'm telling the whole truth and nothing but. She's certainly not without intuition and even half-aware Diamond Hard didn't necessarily like her back in the day... we used to really guffaw about it. I have no belief in supernatural thought/disposition, if did, I'd be joyfully relishing the decrepit karma-crash of all this. They deserve each other; they're very alike, even look alike, a kind of family – especially Why 'n' Sunflower, both employing the same manipulative emotional paths. How odd, out of the three it's Diamond Hard coming off best. He's certainly the most human of 'the triumvirate of crap'. Very like me, he doesn't and never has pretended to be 'only lovely'.

I will, however, thank the group for something. A poem – one meaning the absolute world to me. When I was so unceremoniously lashed [Scouse for 'fucked off'], I didn't understand it. I'd been successfully part of groups all my life – still am. Although maybe a little gobby, I'm really quite brilliant at them! When I lost those 'friends' it initially really hurt, so much that for a while I began to question where/what my community is/was. They'd been such an important part of my life for so long, naturally at first there was a group-shaped hole. To get through said hole, I wrote about who and what my actual community is/was, where it might be, where it's always been. I came up with *Planet Young*'s 'Drunks And The Ghosts'. It's one of my very favourite pieces and, when performing, I always give an abridged description the group's Machiavellian machinations. The amount of peoples identifying with it is remarkable, peoples who've gone through a very similar social darkness. The number who tell me that this tale and that poem have helped them negotiate the rat-infested sewers of their hellish experience is brilliantly manifold.

Thing is, dear reader, and this is an absolute unequivocal truth, I'd much rather have this story and that poem, than them. In so many ways, they've done me and many others an invaluable favour. Who'd have thought it, it seems that auld saying is so very true: *Behind every dark cloud of coked-up cunts… there is a silver line.*

The Absolute End…

P.S. Having earlier mentioned the startlingly brilliant Bette Davis as Margo Channing in *All About Eve*, I'd like to leave you with another of her most famous quotes, this time taken from the monochrome, hagsploititive genius that is *Whatever Happened to Baby Jane*…

On the searing, sandy heat of a Los Angeles beach, Baby Jane Hudson is precariously daddy-dancing to the ever-encroaching crowd around her. Melting ice cream in hand, looking like a decomposingly demonic Statue of Liberty, she is also weep-watching the life gothically ebb from her supposedly 'only lovely' yet secretly twisted sister, Blanche. Jane's a party-frocked, white-faced cracking, fucked-up pantomimical monstrosity, a hissin' blow-kissin' eye-wide gorgon; heart-hot incinerating and collapsing. Knee-falling to the sand and looking a clowny-childlike down, she silently wails at the already decayed, broken 'n' bruised body of her now 'dead' sister. Then with whatever's left inside, from deep down below, somewhere between a little girl squeal and universal howl, she cries a pathetically cloying throat-blistering half-cry… *"You mean all this time we coulda been friends?"*

The Nothings Never Said

Let them be wired,
waylaid on lines 'n' lanes of shopping,
buying what's left of top-shelf friendship
and fancy dress.
Let them whine, sip 'n' acid drop
each other's names and serial numbers.
They were always the no-marks
they feared they were,
the memories they never made.

They'll sit laughing at the nothings
they always did,
at the hurt they hurled,
at the balls thrown,
poison darts punctured,
hoops they crawled through and licked
to reach what wasn't there.

They curse the name of friendship,
give love the slurry of grief.